Poetry in a World of Things

Poetry in a World of Things

Aesthetics and Empiricism in Renaissance Ekphrasis

RACHEL EISENDRATH

The University of Chicago Press

CHICAGO AND LONDON

The University of Chicago Press, Chicago 60637
The University of Chicago Press, Ltd., London

Published 2018

27 26 25 24 23 22 21 20 19 2 3 4 5

ISBN-13: 978-0-226-51658-5 (cloth)
ISBN-13: 978-0-226-51661-5 (paper)
ISBN-13: 978-0-226-51675-2 (e-book)
DOI: 10.7208/chicago/9780226516752.001.0001

The University of Chicago Press gratefully acknowledges the generous support of Barnard College toward the publication of this book.

Library of Congress Cataloging-in-Publication Data

Names: Eisendrath, Rachel, author.
Title: Poetry in a world of things : aesthetics and empiricism in Renaissance ekphrasis / Rachel Eisendrath.
Description: Chicago ; London : The University of Chicago Press, 2018. | Includes bibliographical references and index.
Identifiers: LCCN 2017049043 | ISBN 9780226516585 (cloth : alk. paper) | ISBN 9780226516615 (pbk. : alk. paper) | ISBN 9780226516752 (e-book)
Subjects: LCSH: European poetry—Renaissance, 1450–1600—History and criticism. | Poetry, Modern—15th and 16th centuries—History and criticism. | Ekphrasis. | Spenser, Edmund, 1552?–1599. Faerie queene. Book 3. | Marlowe, Christopher, 1564–1593. Hero and Leander. | Shakespeare, William, 1564–1616. Rape of Lucrece. | Petrarca, Francesco, 1304–1374—Criticism and interpretation.
Classification: LCC PN1181 .E57 2018 | DDC 809.1/031—dc23
LC record available at https:// lccn.loc.gov/2017049043

Contents

Acknowledgments

What a delightful romp this life would be, writes Laurence Sterne, *if it were not for*— and the humor emerges when the subsequent list of vexations goes on and on, ranging from debts to melancholy to large jointures. Writing these acknowledgments in the closing days of 2016, I might reverse Sterne's formula: *What a wretched slog my life would be*, I might say, *if it were not for*— and provide the list below of people to whom I owe, in no small way, the very possibility of my mental life and certainly my happinesses.

Thank you, my teachers, mentors, and colleagues near and far. Thank you, Bradin Cormack, for your exceptional intellect, expansive imagination, and great generosity. Thank you, Michael Murrin, for your wistful and robust love of literary history. Thank you, Joshua Scodel, for your learning, allergy to pretension, and profound sense of decency. Thank you, Victoria Kahn, for your intellectual perspicuity, and thank you so very much for reading *everything*. Thank you, Laura Slatkin, for your delicacy of mind and heart. Thank you, Caryn O'Connell, generous fellow thinker, fellow reader, fellow writer. Thank you, Marc Fumaroli, for your scholarly vision. Thank you, Timea Széll, general of the good army, for your humane kindness, humor, and insight. Thank you, Christopher Baswell, for your erudition and for the delight of your company. Thank you, Peter Platt, for your steady guidance. Thank you, Lisa Gordis, caring and meticulously thoughtful superhero. Thank you, Achsah Guibbory, warm friend and discerning mentor. Thank you for your boundless support and kindness, Kim F. Hall, Anne Lake Prescott, Saskia Hamilton, Lydia Goehr, Ross Hamilton, Margaret Vandenburg, Mary Gordon, and Julie Crawford. Thank you, for reasons that I cannot articulate here, all my colleagues at Barnard and Columbia, especially Monica Miller, Jennie Kassanoff, James Basker, Pamela Cobrin, Patricia Denison, William Sharpe, Yvette Christiansë, Helene P. Foley, William B. Worthen, James Shapiro, and Jean Howard. With extra gratitude for your comments on chapter drafts, thank you, Nancy Worman, Alan Stewart, Molly Murray, and Kathy Eden. From the larger academic world, many scholars generously shared knowledge, provided encouragement, and, in many cases, read work in progress: thank you so very much, William Allan Oram, Froma I. Zeitlin, Heather James, Ayesha Ramachandran, Melissa E. Sanchez, Paul Kottman, Richard Meek, Lynn Enterline, Lauren Silberman, Jeff Dolven, Michael Witmore, Phillip Usher, Richard Strier, Maureen McLane, Robert W. Ulery Jr., Judith H. Anderson, Scott L. Newstok, Margreta de Grazia, and Heather Dubrow. From early in my life, thank you, Bruce Gagnier; thank you, Lisa Pence; thank you, Marty Dutcher.

Thank you, educational institutions, academic presses, libraries, and museums, which hold out for a more humane future. Thank you, Barnard College, especially Provost Linda Bell. Thank you, the University of Chicago. Thank you, St. John's College. Thank you, the New York Studio School. Thank you, Harvard and Radcliffe Colleges. Thank you, the American Philosophical Society, Folger Institute, Mellon Foundation, and the Schoff Fund of the Columbia University Seminars, all of which provided financial support for this project. Thank you, the archivists and curators at the Library of Congress, Huntington Library, Houghton Library, Folger Shakespeare Library, Marsh Library, British Library, Metropolitan Museum of Art, British Museum, Hampton Court Palace, and Morgan Library. Thank you, Alan G. Thomas and Randolph Petilos at the University of Chicago Press, none better. Thank you, Susan Karani and India Cooper, expert manuscript editor and copy editor. Thank you Thomas Hibbs, who worked on the index, and Andrew Miller, who skillfully helped check the proofs. And thank you, anonymous readers of this manuscript, for your erudition and sympathy, and thank you for understanding so well the underlying stakes of this book.

Thank you, the participants in numerous conferences and workshops both in the United States and abroad, especially the Sixteenth Century Society, Shakespeare Association of America, Columbia University Seminars, and the International Spenser Society, who listened to and remarked on parts of this project as it developed.

Thank you, my students at Barnard College, who aren't of course mine at all, especially the students of the Renaissance Colloquium, Shakespeare I, and the Words and Pictures Senior Seminar. Thank you, Mae Frances White, who has been reading and discussing ancient Roman history with me for so long that, really, at this point, you belong in the next paragraph.

Thank you, my friends. Thank you, very dear Hisham Matar, Charles Perkins, Valerie Cornell, Susan Tombel, John McGrath, Lucia Finotto, and Gael Mooney. Thank you, for more than I know how to reckon, O. H. K.

Thank you, my family. Thank you, Aaron and Arpoo Eisendrath, Idris and Tao Eisendrath, Craig Eisendrath, Roberta Spivek, Marvin Garfinkel. Thank you, the Gonzalez family. Thank you, the beloved memory of Marty Sternin, Betty and Stanley Kalish, and Lucy Eisendrath.

Thank you, my partner, Allyson Celeste Gonzalez, who walked with me over the Manhattan Bridge. To you, all.

Finally, thank you, my brilliant, defiant, and loving mother, Betsy Eisendrath, to whom I dedicate this book, in gratitude for a lifetime of talk and laughter.

* * *

Earlier versions of parts of chapters 3 and 5 are included in the following publications: *Spenser Studies*, volumes 27 (2012) and 30 (2015); *Ekphrastic Encounters: New Interdisciplinary Essays on Literature and the Visual Arts*, ed. David Kennedy and Richard Meek (Manchester: Manchester University Press, forthcoming); and *The Insistence of Art: Aesthetic Philosophy after Early Modernity*, ed. Paul Kottman (New York: Fordham University Press, 2017).

CHAPTER ONE

Introduction

"Art that is simply a thing is an oxymoron."

THEODOR W. ADORNO

The weather seems to be changing. In the first painting of Andrea Mantegna's 1484–92 series *The Triumphs of Caesar*, the sky gleams where the dark underpainting shows through, as though a storm were moving in, casting an ominous glow on the procession. In the collapsed frieze-like space, the soldiers appear both commandingly volumetric and almost ghostly. In the very act of asserting the power of their physical beings (and of imperialist force more generally), the men's bodies seem to be in the process of fading, vaporizing, sinking back into the clouds that swirl behind and above them. The left arm of the soldier in green has become semi-transparent, and his right arm is missing. Like Prospero's pageant in *The Tempest*, this procession threatens to dissolve "into air, into thin air" (4.1.150).

This ghostliness can be understood not only as an effect of time on paint[1] but also as a prompt for critical thinking about representation. Notice the paintings held aloft on the banners. Mantegna's early modern contemporaries were increasingly turning to the study of material objects to learn about the facts of the past, and Mantegna had conducted his own antiquarian research into Roman triumphs.[2] Scholars have long believed that Romans

1. On the history of these paintings, see Andrew Martindale, *"The Triumphs of Caesar" by Andrea Mantegna in the Collection of Her Majesty the Queen at Hampton Court* (London: Harvey Miller, 1979).

2. For example, the image of Cybele in the second painting of the Mantegna series is based on a second-century bust of Faustina which Mantegna owned and which is now displayed alongside the paintings at Hampton Court Palace. Furthermore, it is believed that Mantegna studied antiquarian histories like Roberto Valturio's *De re militari* and Flavio Biondo's *Roma triumphans*, which were both first printed in 1472. See Anthony Miller, *Roman Triumphs and Early Modern English*

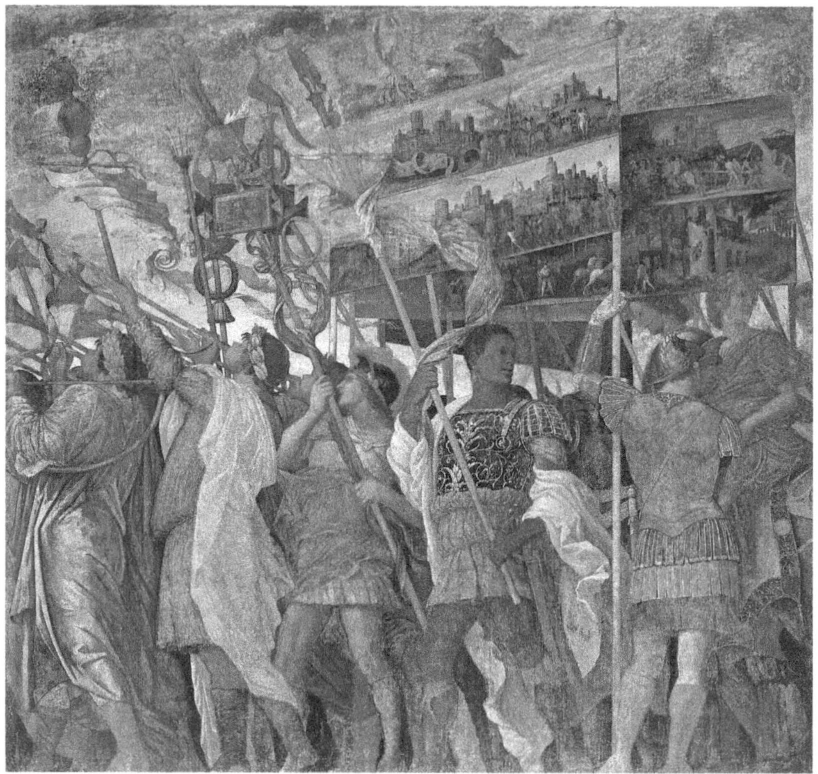

FIGURE 1. Andrea Mantegna, *The Triumphs of Caesar, I: The Picture-Bearers* (c. 1484–92). Hampton Court Palace. Royal Collection Trust © Her Majesty Queen Elizabeth II, 2016 / Bridgeman Images.

did indeed carry such paintings, which portrayed victorious battles as well as the suicides of conquered generals.[3] But while these ancient paintings may have offered for the ancient Romans a kind of second-order conquest and possession, Mantegna's painting does more than this, creating a space

Culture (Houndmills, Basingstoke, Hampshire, and New York: Palgrave, 2001), 122. Thanks to Yolanda Law, warder of Hampton Court Palace, for her guidance.

3. Ida Östenberg has recently argued that this widespread scholarly belief, apparently shared by Mantegna, is erroneous. Paintings depicting recent battles were produced only after triumphs, for display in public places. When, she says, paintings were carried in the procession, these were spoils taken from the conquered. Only sculptures and dramatic tableaux were made for the procession to commemorate the recent war. See her *Staging the World: Spoils, Captives, and Representations in the Roman Triumphal Procession* (Oxford: Oxford University Press, 2009), 190ff.

for viewers to reflect critically on this earlier aim. The soldiers he paints appear lost in a spectacle of objects. Some look forward at where they are going, others backward at what is behind them. None seems fully cognizant of what is actually going on. The motion of the pennants, whipped around by a wind, suggests relentless change. At one moment, the conqueror is perched at the pinnacle of worldly achievement; at the next, he will be flung to the ground by the downward turn of fortune's wheel. To put this point historically: parading now in glory in around 46 BCE, Julius Caesar will be assassinated less than two years later. Any sustained examination of this painting thus raises questions about the victory of men and empire that it is ostensibly celebrating.[4] Viewers soon find themselves staring past the putatively solid objects into the desire for possession that underlies them: the Romans' desire for power and the early modern antiquarians' desire for a history that is graspable, objective, literal, and contained.

This painting embodies a central issue for *Poetry in a World of Things*, namely, the complex relationship between aesthetic experience and the empirical objects of history. Even as antiquarianism and other empiricist methodologies began in the Renaissance to teach thinkers to bracket off their subjectivities in the hope of producing a more detached account of the objects of the world, art was becoming the complex repository of that partially renounced subjectivity. In consequence, the poets on whom I focus—Francesco Petrarch, Edmund Spenser, Christopher Marlowe, and William Shakespeare—actively and reactively developed a new, modern aesthetics in part by emphasizing the dynamic interplay of objective and subjective modes of thought. In tracing this historical reaction, my book also pushes back against the emphatic empiricism of a dominant trend in current literary-historical scholarship, which can tend to treat art as an artifact or *mere* thing. Drawing on the aesthetics of Theodor W. Adorno, I argue that this empiricist tendency undermines the complexity of aesthetic experience, by falsely conflating empiricist factuality and aesthetic experience, when what is crucial is the dialectical tension between them.

My exploration of these elusive issues focuses on one poetic and literary form, *ekphrasis*, which I understand, most simply, as an elaborate lit-

4. Purchased by Charles I in 1629, the paintings are currently displayed all in a line at Hampton Court Palace; since 2006, gilded columns have been positioned between them, as though the paintings themselves were part of a triumphal procession. This display almost actualizes Henry Peacham's 1615 prophecy to Henry Frederick, James I's grandson, that "in Hampton thou maist one day see" the "triumphs, trophees of thine ancestrie" (*Prince Henry Revived*). Miller, *Roman Triumphs and Early Modern English Culture*, 114, 122.

erary description of a thing. As I will discuss later, the term dates to the late-antique Greek rhetorical manuals known as the *progymnasmata*, which were subsequently translated into Latin and, importantly for this project, were widely used in Elizabethan classrooms.[5] According to these manuals, ekphrasis could be a vivid description of art objects as well as of other things; Aelius Theon's *Progymnasmata* in the first century CE lists as examples Homer's shield of Achilles, as well as descriptions of cities, meadows, and battles.[6] Indeed, Renaissance literature offers ekphrases of just about everything: of tapestries, boots, cities, helmets, belts, coins, fountains, forests, shields, cathedrals, paintings, sculptures, and ruins.

I select this form for attention because, as critics have long recognized, ekphrasis provides a model in miniature of aesthetic experience as such.[7] An ekphrasis is a literary showpiece where a poem, in describing an object in an emphatically aesthetic way, raises questions about the nature of art and artmaking. Generations of critics have thus situated this form in the tradition of Horace's famous phrase *ut pictura poesis* (as is painting, so is poetry). In so doing, they have narrated how poetry has defined itself by comparing itself to visual art. This tradition of defining poetry in relation to sculpture or painting is a story that has been well developed and well told.[8]

5. Elizabethan classrooms used Aphthonius's fourth-century CE *Progymnasmata* in Latin translation by Rudolph Agricola with commentary and additional examples by Reinhard Lorichius. See Lynn Enterline, *Shakespeare's Schoolroom: Rhetoric, Discipline, Emotion* (Philadelphia: University of Pennsylvania Press, 2012), 107ff. This manual includes ekphrasis as one of a sequence of fourteen exercises. See Peter Mack, *Elizabethan Rhetoric: Theory and Practice* (Cambridge: Cambridge University Press, 2002), 27; Donald Lemen Clark, "The Rise and Fall of Progymnasmata in Sixteenth and Seventeenth Century Grammar Schools," *Speech Monographs* 19, no. 4 (Nov. 1952): 259–63.

6. It was only after World War II that scholars began to think of ekphrasis exclusively as the description of art objects, as Ruth Webb has explored in *Ekphrasis, Imagination and Persuasion in Ancient Rhetorical Theory and Practice* (Farnham, England, and Burlington, VT: Ashgate, 2009). See also George A. Kennedy, trans., *Progymnasmata: Greek Textbooks of Prose Composition and Rhetoric* (Atlanta: Society of Biblical Literature, 2003).

7. I use the term *aesthetic* throughout this book even though the word does not originate until the eighteenth century (in Alexander Gottlieb Baumgarten's 1735 *Reflections on Poetry*). As Stephen Halliwell convincingly argues, the term may be relatively recent, but what we generally mean by it as a category of thought (having to do with the principles underlying the experience or production of fine art) already existed by the fifth century BCE. Halliwell shows how ancient writers, especially Plato and Aristotle, had a notion of fine art that linked together poetry, painting, sculpture, dance, and music through shared problems of mimetic representation. See Halliwell, *The Aesthetics of Mimesis: Ancient Texts and Modern Problems* (Princeton: Princeton University Press, 2002), especially 6–14.

8. See the foundational work of Leonard Barkan, Michael Baxandall, Lucy Gent, Jean H. Hagstrum, James Heffernan, Clark Hulse, Murray Krieger, W. J. T. Mitchell, and Rensselaer W. Lee, to

Rather than reiterating it, I want to emphasize in these pages how when an ekphrasis describes an object, the experience of that object is not reducible to its mere existence *as* object. My interest lies in the difference not between two kinds of art (poetry vs. visual art) but between a fully complex art object and any other kind of object. To take the example of the Roman triumph with which I began, there is an important difference between, on the one hand, Mantegna's own painting and, on the other hand, the paintings and other objects that he represents the Romans as carrying and that, to them, are yet more spoil. If a fully complex art object both is and is not an object like any other, then this book explores wherein the difference lies.

ALIENATED MODERN OBJECTS

In the early modern period, aesthetic experience came into conflict with a new worldview. In order to account accurately for things of the world, empiricists began to try to observe without subjective projections. "For God forbid," Francis Bacon writes, "that we should give out a dream of our own imagination for a pattern of the world."[9] In the prefatory materials (1620) of his *Great Instauration*, Bacon explains that the researcher must keep "the eye steadily fixed upon the facts of nature" in order to grasp the image of things "*simply as they are*."[10] By turning to the world for knowledge, and by relying on physical evidence, sensory perceptions, and experiments, Bacon aimed to provide an account of things without literary embellishment, an account of "things themselves,"[11] an expression that Joanna Picciotto calls "a signature phrase of experimentalist discourse."[12]

---

name a few. Discussion often turns on what poetry can do that visual art cannot, and vice versa. Sometimes this relationship with visual art is treated as analogous and sometimes competitive. Of these studies, I have turned most frequently to Leonard Barkan's work. I will refer several times to his *Mute Poetry, Speaking Pictures* (Princeton: Princeton University Press, 2013), which explores how painting wants the subtle signification of poetry; poetry, the sensual presence of painting. (This theme is also central to W. J. T. Mitchell's studies.) Although not about ekphrasis, Barkan's *Unearthing the Past: Archaeology and Aesthetics in the Making of Renaissance Culture* (New Haven: Yale University Press, 1999) will also be central. His intention in this book is to call the "bluff" of the poets by looking at the real sculptures being unearthed from the ground in the Renaissance. While both he and I are interested in the influence of material history on aesthetics, his work is part of the scholarly tradition centered on the conflict between different artistic media. He is focused on sculpture, in tension with a different kind of art (sculpture vs. poetry). In contrast, I am focused on poetry, in tension with empiricist objects (art vs. non-art).

9. *The Works of Francis Bacon*, vol. 4, ed. James Spedding (London: Longman, 1860), 32–33.

10. Ibid., 32. Italics mine.

11. Ibid., 19.

12. Joanna Picciotto, "Reforming the Garden: The Experimentalist Eden and *Paradise Lost*,"

Empiricist description was often opposed to literary or imaginative production. "Poetry is as a dream of learning," Bacon writes. "But now it is time for me to awake, and rising above the earth, to wing my way through the clear air of [natural] Philosophy and the Sciences."[13] What matters, Bacon explains, is to leave behind the "dream of our own imagination," and instead to take hold of things "simply as they are," that is, in their physical actuality apart from the cultural fantasies about them that we have inherited through textual authorities. To use rhetorical ornaments for literary effect and color in a scientific presentation is to hinder the clear view of an object of study or, in the words of Robert Boyle, "to paint the Eye-glasses of a Telescope."[14] Facts should be presented straightforwardly.[15] This idol-breaking reflected a Reformation sentiment, but also an empiricist one. In Italy, Galileo Galilei turned his gaze from books to his telescope, mocking any person who "thinks that [natural] philosophy is a sort of book like the *Aeneid* and *Odyssey*, and that truth is to be found not in the world or in nature but in the collation of texts."[16]

This push away from the literary and the textual *tout court* was, needless to say, neither complete nor fully coherent.[17] Recent scholarship has

---

ELH 72, no. 1 (Spring 2005): 23–78. Picciotto notes that Sir William Petty, Joseph Glanvill, Robert Hooke, John Locke, and Thomas Sprat all used this phrase (67n3). For the multiple meanings in Bacon's work of the expression, see William T. Lynch, "A Society of Baconians?: The Collective Development of Bacon's Method in the Royal Society of London," in *Francis Bacon and the Refiguring of Early Modern Thought: Essays to Commemorate "The Advancement of Learning" (1605–2005)*, ed. Julie Robin Solomon and Catherine Gimelli Martin (Burlington, VT: Ashgate, 2005), 173–202.

13. Bacon, *Works* 4:336. On Bacon's later reevaluation of the epistemology of detachment promoted by *Novum organum*, see Caryn O'Connell, "Bacon's Hints: The *Sylva Sylvarum*'s Intimate Science," *Studies in Philology* 113, no. 3 (Summer 2016): 634–67.

14. Robert Boyle, *Certain Physiological Essays and Other Tracts: Written at Distant Times, and on Several Occasions* (London: Printed for Henry Herringman, 1669), 12, quoted in Steven Shapin, *Never Pure: Historical Studies of Science as if It Was Produced by People with Bodies, Situated in Time, Space, Culture, and Society, and Struggling for Credibility and Authority* (Baltimore: Johns Hopkins University Press, 2010), 17, 102.

15. Needless to say, this apparently straightforward, authority-free, transparent presentation constitutes its own rhetorical strategy. Shapin describes Robert Boyle's disavowal of textual authorities as a key component of what is actually a scientific literary style, what Shapin calls a "literary technology of virtual witnessing" that was designed to "portray the author as a disinterested observer and his accounts as unclouded and undistorted mirrors of nature" (*Never Pure*, 97, 103).

16. Quoted in Anthony Grafton, "The New Science and the Traditions of Humanism," in *The Cambridge Companion to Renaissance Humanism*, ed. Jill Kraye (Cambridge: Cambridge University Press, 1996), 206.

17. In the eighteenth century, immersive experience and affect played a key role in empiricist thought, as Lisa Shapiro has explored. See her "Instrumental or Immersed Experience: Pleasure, Pain and Object Perception in Locke," in *The Body as Object and Instrument of Knowledge: Embodied*

emphasized the reciprocity of the arts and sciences in the Renaissance: how poets and painters of that time increasingly incorporated into their imaginary worlds factually based references to recent antiquarian and scientific discoveries. Many scientists had a background in the arts, or even practiced these two crafts simultaneously; recall, for example, Galileo's 1609 wash drawings of the moon's pocky surface in his *Sidereus nuncius*.[18] Scientists sometimes adopted into their discourses the strategies of poets; Bacon, for example, used metaphorical language to make arguments against literariness.[19] Yet, as I will emphasize, these areas of overlap were also becoming areas of tension between tendencies of thought that were increasingly understood as contradictory. Even Galileo and Bacon, whose lives and work can be seen as exemplifying the mutual imbrication of the arts and sciences, were the very same thinkers who also drew new lines in the sand, asserting that poetry was an imaginative (and subjective) dream but that the physical world was a real (and objective) thing. Fiction, they insisted, was not fact.[20]

Scholars from Jacob Burckhardt to Anthony Grafton have heralded this shift as the Renaissance "discovery" of the observable world. Objective descriptions of things were no longer preludes to philosophy as they had been in medieval scholasticism. Instead, in this newly emergent empiricism of the Renaissance, they were becoming the very keystones of knowledge.[21] To take one example, *observationes*, which had been readerly additions in the margins of canonical texts, evolved into a recognizable scholarly genre in fields like astronomy and medicine. The very word *observatio*, as Gianna Pomata has shown, straddles the shift from textual authorities to a direct encounter with physical evidence: the word is connected on the one hand to *observance* (conformity to authority), and on the other hand to *observa-*

Empiricism in Early Modern Science, ed. Charles T. Wolfe and Ofer Gal (Dordrecht, Netherlands, and New York: Springer, 2010), 265–85.

18. Eileen Reeves, *Painting the Heavens: Art and Science in the Age of Galileo* (Princeton: Princeton University Press, 1997).

19. Ronald Levao, "Francis Bacon and the Mobility of Science," *Representations* 40, Special Issue: Seeing Science (Autumn 1992): 1–32.

20. William Nelson, *Fact or Fiction: The Dilemma of the Renaissance Storyteller* (Cambridge, MA: Harvard University Press, 1973). Frédérique Aït-Touati explores how scientists wanted to shift a "poetics of wonder" into, she writes, "a poetics of the possible." See Aït-Touati, *Fictions of the Cosmos: Science and Literature in the Seventeenth Century*, trans. Susan Emanuel (Chicago: University of Chicago Press, 2011), 80. Earlier manifestations of this tension include Isidore of Seville's distinction in the *Etymologies* between *fabula* (fiction) and *historia* ("the narration of things that happened").

21. Gianna Pomata and Nancy G. Siraisi, eds., *Historia: Empiricism and Erudition in Early Modern Europe* (Cambridge, MA: MIT Press, 2005), 4ff.

tion (attention to individual phenomena in the physical world).[22] Alongside the humanists' bookshelves soon appeared their cabinets of curiosities, or *Wunderkammern*.[23] Similarly, ancient statues were being unearthed that, as Leonard Barkan has explored, evoked a new tension between the imaginary and the real, between fantasies of lost bygone worlds and the actuality of recovered material fragments.[24] In the domain of science, Bacon set out a plan for a vast compendium of descriptions of all perceptible things, to be divided into a list of 130 categories that descend from the heavenly (#1 "History of the Heavens; or Astronomy") to the earthly (#46 "History of the Excrements: Saliva, Urine, Sweat, Stools, Head-hair, Body-hair, Hang-nails, Nails and so-on").[25] Bacon refers to this planned compendium as a "warehouse or storage space" for descriptions of "the world as it is found to be."[26] The warehouse will hold uninterpreted and objective versions of things, versions stripped of "everything that makes for ornament of speech, and similes, and the whole repertoire of eloquence, and such vanities."[27] Accordingly, this warehouse is "not a place in which one is to stay or live with pleasure"; rather, "one enters only when necessary, when something has to be taken out for use in the work of the Interpreter which follows."[28] Through such complexly organized collections of knowledge, Bacon wanted to construct an empiricism that could mitigate the distortions of individual perceptions.[29]

A new empiricist "art of describing" started to become everywhere ap-

22. Gianna Pomata, "Observation Rising: Birth of an Epistemic Genre, 1500–1650," in *Histories of Scientific Observation*, ed. Lorraine Daston and Elizabeth Lunbeck (Chicago: University of Chicago Press, 2011), 47.

23. Paula Findlen places this interest in objects at the center of the humanist enterprise: "More than the claims of erudition or the revival of classical texts through philology, humanism was structured around the objects that served as a basis for most intellectual and cultural activities," she writes. Findlen, "The Museum: Its Classical Etymology and Renaissance Genealogy," in *Museum Studies: An Anthology of Contexts*, ed. Bettina Messias Carbonell (Malden, MA: Blackwell, 2012), 25.

24. Barkan, *Unearthing the Past*.

25. See the "Outline of a Natural and Experimental History" in Francis Bacon, *The New Organon*, ed. Lisa Jardine and Michael Silverthorne (Cambridge: Cambridge University Press, 2000).

26. Ibid., 226.

27. Ibid., 225.

28. Ibid., 226. "In other words," explains Peter N. Miller, "these 'histories' were presented by Bacon as a preliminary stage of work in which the raw facts were made available for subsequent elaboration." See Miller, "Description Terminable and Interminable: Looking at the Past, Nature, and Peoples in Peiresc's Archive," in Pomata and Siraisi, *Historia*, 359. For the tension between literature and the "things" of this catalogue, see Mary Baine Campbell, *Wonder and Science: Imagining Worlds in Early Modern Europe* (Ithaca: Cornell University Press, 1999), 78–85.

29. Shapin, *Never Pure*, 130. Subjectivity continued, of course, to affect the construction of pu-

parent: in early modern painting and science,[30] and in historiographical theory and practice.[31] Antiquarians of the Renaissance were increasingly examining and describing history's physical remains: the *things* of the historical record—coins, urns, fragments of statues, tombs, and ruins, what Bacon called "the spars" of "the shipwreck of time."[32] This emerging use of material evidence constitutes one of the fundamental changes in the Renaissance "sense of the past" and was a departure from an earlier mode of historiography that relied exclusively on ancient literary versions of history.[33] Peter Burke points out, for example, that the medieval English monk Bede lived near Hadrian's Wall but quoted a passage by Vegetius when he wanted to describe it.[34]

In sixteenth-century England, where the physical dissolution of the monasteries haunted many writers with a disturbing awareness of historical loss, antiquarian description gained extraordinary momentum.[35] By the end of the 1530s, John Leland was traveling through England and Wales to research his *Itinerary*, which was to be based on topographical and antiquarian descriptions.[36] Antiquarians like William Harrison, John Stow, and William Camden soon followed with highly descriptive accounts of the

---

tatively objective knowledge even in the realms of science. As Lorraine Daston and Peter Galison put it in *Objectivity* (New York: Zone Books, 2007), 197–98, "Subjectivity was the enemy within."

30. Svetlana Alpers famously characterizes seventeenth-century Dutch painting as "the art of describing," and Brian W. Ogilvie, playing off Alpers's title, calls Renaissance botany "the science of describing." See Alpers, *The Art of Describing: Dutch Art in the Seventeenth Century* (Chicago: University of Chicago Press, 1983), and Ogilvie, *The Science of Describing: Natural History in Renaissance Europe* (Chicago: University of Chicago Press, 2006). Also important is Alastair Fowler, *Renaissance Realism: Narrative Images in Literature and Art* (Oxford: Oxford University Press, 2003).

31. Miller writes that "much early modern historical scholarship takes the form of description" ("Description Terminable," 355). In one letter of April 2 or 3, 1605, preserved at the Huntington Library (EL 128), Bacon plays on the customary tag "painting is mute poetry, poetry a speaking picture," often associated with ekphrasis, but substitutes "history" for poetry: "For as statues and pictures are dumb histories, so histories are speaking pictures," he writes, thereby replacing poetical with historical description.

32. Bacon, *Works* 4:303.

33. Peter Burke, *The Renaissance Sense of the Past* (New York: St. Martin's Press, 1969). The break was never entirely complete, however. Even in many works of the sixteenth century, like Machiavelli's *Discorsi sopra la prima Deca di Tito Livio*, Roman history is still treated as essentially synonymous with Livy's account of Roman history.

34. Ibid., 7.

35. Margaret Aston, "English Ruins and English History: The Dissolution and the Sense of the Past," *Journal of the Warburg and Courtauld Institutes* 36 (1973): 231–55.

36. See Arthur B. Ferguson, *Clio Unbound: Perception of the Social and Cultural Past in Renaissance England* (Durham: Duke University Press, 1979), 78–125; F. J. Levy, *Tudor Historical Thought* (San Marino, CA: Huntington Library, 1967), 124–66.

material remains of English history. In some cases, this antiquarian work was imaginative.[37] In other cases, antiquarians attempted to produce something like Bacon's distinction between things in themselves and interpreted things. For example, Stow called his 1598 *Survey of London* the "outward view" of the city's historical sites, appending an anonymous Londoner's more obviously interpretive discourse, which Stow called the "insight."[38] In short, across a range of fields, description acquired status as a new form of objectivity.

In this context, elaborate descriptions of a kind familiar in poetry became a contested site. While poets on the one hand were using ekphrases to elicit complex aesthetic experiences, empiricists on the other were increasingly using factual descriptions not unlike ekphrases in temper to detail physical things. In this way, early modern ekphrasis marks the point at which the aesthetic starts to come into conflict with the empiricist.[39]

Partly because our own scholarly methods are based on the detachment that empiricists valued, we tend to celebrate it. But detachment is not simply innocent.[40] Bacon famously draws on the language of mastery to articulate his strategies; the history of the new science is deeply bound to the rise of merchant capitalism, as well as of colonialism. Consider, for example, Giovanni da Verrazzano's 1524 letter to François I. Commissioned by the French to look for a western route to China, the Florentine reached America near Cape Fear and eventually traveled up the Carolina coast. Verrazzano describes in great detail the native people, trees, and animals that he encountered. At one place thought to be near Virginia, he describes venturing on foot about two leagues inland accompanied by about twenty men. The natives flee in terror into the forests, but the Europeans eventually find a small group of women and children cowering in the grass. Verrazzano offers them food, which an old woman takes but which a young woman, about eighteen to twenty years old, throws angrily to the ground. In the same matter-of-fact style that he uses to describe the fruits and animals, the explorer narrates how he and his men proceed to kidnap one of the children and to try to kidnap the young woman:

37. For imaginative antiquarianism, see especially Angus Vine, *In Defiance of Time: Antiquarian Writing in Early Modern England* (Oxford: Oxford University Press, 2010).

38. Ferguson, *Clio Unbound*, 103.

39. Examining the multivolume encyclopedias of descriptions of the Enlightenment, Joanna Stalnaker has argued that description of that period was "the site of growing tensions between epistemology and poetics." Stalnaker, *The Unfinished Enlightenment: Description in the Age of the Encyclopedia* (Ithaca: Cornell University Press, 2010), 6.

40. Campbell writes in reference to Bacon of the "repressive energies of the emerging cultural formation" (*Wonder and Science*, 72ff.).

> We took the boy from the old woman to carry back to France, and we wanted to take the young woman, who was very beautiful and tall, but it was impossible to take her to the sea because of the loud cries she uttered. And as we were a long way from the ship and had to pass through several woods, we decided to leave her behind, and took only the boy.[41]

By her screaming the young woman avoided the horrors that, I assume, would have awaited her aboard the ship. As for Verrazzano, he makes no other comment about this woman, though he adds on the following page, in the margin: "we baptized [the coast] Arcadia on account of the beauty of the trees."[42] The Verrazano-Narrows Bridge, which connects Staten Island to Brooklyn, still bears the name of this explorer. What's most striking about this description is the way it conveys the natives' terror in the same tone as that in which it praises the material richness of the place. The narrator's detachment is typical among explorers' accounts, where subject-object distance has become a form of interpersonal disconnection in service of domination. Violence attends in such cases the production of objectivity. The European does violence both to the natives and to himself in that he ruptures any possibility of an empathetic connection with them.

At such junctures, the very idea of subjective experience can be displaced by the idea of detached observation. The history of the word *experience* reflects this legacy. The word comes from the Latin *experiri* (to put to the test), which in turn comes from the Greek *empeiria*, the basis of the English word *empirical*. Starting in the fourteenth century, the word *experience* could mean either the subjective awareness of events and conditions or the accumulation of facts and observations.[43] The lines of such a distinction blur in practice, but Michel de Montaigne's use of *experience* could be taken as an example of the former sense, in that he emphasizes the individual quirks entailed in reflecting on what happens to him and casts doubt on the reliability of raw sensation.[44] In contrast, a number of thinkers were

41. A transcription of this letter, with an English translation by Susan Tarrow, is available in Lawrence C. Wroth, *The Voyages of Giovanni da Verrazzano, 1524–1528* (New Haven: Yale University Press for the Pierpont Morgan Library, 1970), 133–43.

42. There are three manuscript copies of this letter, all written by scribes. The so-called Cèllere Codex at the Morgan Library is considered the most authoritative copy of the letter because of its marginal annotations, which are believed to be in Verrazzano's own hand. I am grateful to the Morgan Library for allowing me to examine this manuscript (MA 776).

43. *OED* and Martin Jay, *Songs of Experience: Modern American and European Variations on a Universal Theme* (Berkeley and Los Angeles: University of California Press, 2005), 10. For changing understandings of this term in the Renaissance, see also Peter Dear, *Revolutionizing the Sciences: European Knowledge and Its Ambitions, 1500–1700* (Princeton: Princeton University Press, 2009), 5ff., 127ff.

44. Jay, *Songs of Experience*, 28–29. Francis Bacon himself contrasts related uses of "expe-

promoting methodologies that would ostensibly be free of the personal idiosyncrasies central to the French essayist's reflections.[45] In their history of scientific objectivity, Lorraine Daston and Peter Galison locate its consolidation chiefly in the nineteenth century,[46] but even as early as the end of the sixteenth century, increased emphasis on fact and observation was evident in fields as disparate as botany, law, and history. Such developments were, of course, incomplete.[47] But that's also what makes the early modern period so valuable to study. The period confronts us with a moment of complexity before familiar binaries of object and subject have rigidified. Here are the rich beginnings of what would later become the ideal of knowledge of an object without a subject—what Thomas Nagel has called "the view from nowhere."[48]

If we track this complexity, what happens to subjective experience, in its fullness and messiness and even painfulness? This book argues that art became one repository for it. The early modern poetry I examine seems motivated over and over by a desire to rediscover the experience of violence entailed in producing objectivity.

THE RUPTURE OF THE MODERN MIND FROM ITSELF

Let me step back from my historical and theoretical argument to offer a literary view onto the problem I've been exploring. Consider John Milton's

rience"—a good kind that holds fast to experiment and a bad kind that is "blind and stupid" in "taking counsel only from things as they fall out." Bacon, *Novum organum*, in *Works* 4:70, quoted in Jay, *Songs of Experience*, 31, and Mary Poovey, *A History of the Modern Fact: Problems of Knowledge in the Sciences of Wealth and Society* (Chicago: University of Chicago Press, 1998), 346.

45. See Jay's development of the contrast between Montaigne and Bacon in *Songs of Experience*, 33–37.

46. Daston and Galison, *Objectivity*.

47. It can be argued that the emphasis on an object, existing independently out there in the world, correspondingly throws the subject into new relief. For example, René Descartes describes in his 1637 *Discourse on Method* a thought experiment that grounds the production of all knowledge in the mind's awareness of its own act of thinking. The first-person formulation of his famous "je pense, donc je suis" (or, in the later Latin version, "ego cogito, ergo sum") expresses how the basis of all knowledge is, for Descartes, based on a self-perception. Yet, in this supreme moment of the subject's importance for science, notice that Descartes excludes all objects of the world. In privileging the subject over the object, he still mirrors Bacon's aversion to the *commingling* of the two. Thus, the cogito reinforces the emerging separation of the subject from the object that I am tracing in this book.

48. Thomas Nagel, *The View from Nowhere* (Oxford: Oxford University Press, 1986). Andrew Bowie writes that "the crucial fact is, of course, that scientific method and bureaucratic rationalization actually attempt to *exclude* the individual in the name of 'objectivity'"; *Aesthetics and Subjectivity: From Kant to Nietzsche* (Manchester: Manchester University Press, 2003), 11.

Paradise Lost, a work often understood to mark the border between the English Renaissance and Enlightenment. As in accounts by explorers and conquerors such as Verrazzano, Satan first beholds the "foreign land" of Eden as a distant visual image or "prospect" (3.548).[49] In the tradition of epic heroes like Aeneas, Satan most of the time suppresses his subjective experience of this new world. However, in one ekphrastic scene, Satan glimpses what his distance from the world has cost him. When Satan approaches Eve in the garden just before the fall, Milton offers a lush ekphrasis of her among the flowers. In a profusion of sensuality, Milton describes Eve as "veiled in a cloud of fragrance" (9.425), a phrase that mixes together sights and smells, evoking Barkan's description of ekphrasis as a "synaesthetic utopia."[50] As she bends down to prop up the heads of drooping flowers, her tender gesture corresponds with the flowers themselves, which have also bent down. The effect of this vision, where objective limits blur, is to disarm Satan: "Her graceful innocence, her every air / Of gesture or least action overawed / His malice, and with rapine sweet bereaved / His fierceness of the fierce intent it brought" (9.459–62). Instead of Satan overcoming Eve, Eve (or her image) overcomes him. Object over subject. Distracted, he floats in a current that momentarily carries him away. As the scene unfolds, Satan seems to open toward that from which he has been cut off—whether that something is companionship or sex or love.[51] Adapting himself to the beautiful object, he becomes for a moment not exactly beautiful himself, but at least not evil: "That space the evil one abstracted stood / From his own evil, and for the time remained / Stupidly good" (9.463–65). But such a slack state must not last. Let there be no hanging out in this world. Only in breaking the aesthetic spell and reestablishing a subject-object divide can Satan resume his role as conqueror determined to dominate earth. It is no accident that in so doing he will draw on a very different kind of language, that of early modern empiricism. Satan refers to the forbidden tree, for example, as "Mother of science" (9.680), and he tempts Eve to act like a good scientist by advising her to taste for herself the apple and to "Wonder not" (9.532). It was only for a fleeting moment that Satan could experience

49. For the connection of this passage with explorers' accounts, see Stephen Greenblatt, *Marvelous Possessions: The Wonder of the New World* (Chicago: University of Chicago Press, 1991), 156. All citations of Milton from John Milton, *Paradise Lost*, ed. William Kerrigan, John Rumrich, and Stephen M. Fallon (New York: Random House, 2007).

50. Barkan, *Mute Poetry, Speaking Pictures*, 21.

51. Satan earlier described Adam and Eve as the couple "whom my thoughts pursue / with wonder, and could love" (4.362–63).

through aesthetic immersion an intimacy with the world that he otherwise does not allow himself.

Milton is a canny interpreter of changing times.[52] Satan's alienation points to a larger story that we continue to tell about modernization, wherein we find ourselves in a world that seems deprived of meaning. An image of such a world appears in Walter Benjamin's study of seventeenth-century *Trauerspiel*, for example, when he describes an early modern stage scattered with mute, dead things, emptied of their significance. Building on this image, we could say that art itself threatens to become such a thing—another fragment or ruin among the rest. In Benjamin's analysis, the problem is that human beings are infused with transcendental longings but have lost access to the divine. Without any religious source of authority, the player kings' "crowns of gilt paper"[53] and other props appear to lament their own loss of significance. But it is not the distance of the gods that is alone responsible for this situation. The empiricist point of view has also contributed, by emptying objects of the subjective life that people would otherwise project into them, thus leaving behind a stage of ruins.

Recent literary scholars and art historians who explore the limits of early modern empiricism have often positioned *religion* as the hidden "other" that has been repressed by the emergent empiricist worldview. Christopher Braider, for example, insightfully examines the unacknowledged debt of early modern realism to the late medieval focus on the bodily suffer-

52. For an alternative account of the core tension between science and art in *Paradise Lost*, see the final chapter of Angus Fletcher, *Time, Space, and Motion in the Age of Shakespeare* (Cambridge, MA: Harvard University Press, 2007). Fletcher focuses in this book on problems of motion that, he argues, lay at the core of both Renaissance poetry and science, which became united in a complex "cultural manifold" (7). While Fletcher emphasizes more than I do what science and art shared, he also scrutinizes the *tensions* that arose through this sharing. In the chapter on Milton, for example, Fletcher shows the importance of Galileo for Milton's conception of the universe. To my mind, he occasionally risks conflating these two thinkers' understandings of the universe (such as when he writes of "the Galilean and hence Miltonic universe," 144), and at these moments neglects to take account of the fact that Milton refers to Galileo to describe *Satan* and that Adam receives explicit warnings against pursuing too much knowledge. However, Fletcher repeatedly returns to develop an increasingly full account of what he calls the "affiliating differences between art and science" (156). He indicates how, for example, Milton suggests that science was one cause of our losing paradise (131), and most importantly, he concludes his book by arguing that as humanism began to lose ground, a world emerged where inner and outer realities were increasingly, rigorously, scientifically separated—until the final "divorce" that occurred with the development of positivism (155). He writes that "poetic language itself revealed the distress of the conflict" (150).

53. Walter Benjamin, *The Origin of German Tragic Drama*, trans. John Osborne (New York: Verso, 1998), 123; see also Victoria Kahn, *The Future of Illusion: Political Theology and Early Modern Texts* (Chicago: University of Chicago Press, 2014), 70.

ing of Christ. In a complex and wide-ranging discussion, he explores how an increasingly naturalistic vision of the world emerged from (but never extinguished) an unnamable, almost apophatic sense of reality, which he describes as "the sense of supplementary presences exceeding our power to comprehend them however sharply we focus our lenses."[54]

My argument has a different emphasis, secular in the sense not that it disavows the perception of "religious" presence but that it construes that perception as one expression of something possibly more fundamental. In my account, the ghostly presence that haunts early modern empiricism is not the medieval divinity per se but instead the subjective *experience* that lies at the heart of empirical reality fully perceived. Rather than focusing on the rupture of human beings from the divine, I draw attention to the rupture of human beings from themselves, and from their own subjective experiences of the things of the world. For me, art is "enchanted" not because it is magical or holy but because it preserves repressed aspects of experience in their complex and shifting relationship with the empiricist world. Instead of religion as the answer to the shortcomings of an empiricist worldview, aesthetic experience begins to offer a crucial third term.[55]

ADORNO IN THE RENAISSANCE

This book looks not only backward at Renaissance poetry but also forward at our currently vexed relationship with this poetry—and with aesthetic experience more broadly. In order to bring into awareness some of the problems inherent in our attempts to understand Renaissance poetry, this project draws on the thinking of Theodor W. Adorno.

Adorno writes that when it comes to *objective* and *subjective*, we have gotten the meanings backward. On the one hand, what we mistakenly call objective is, he says, "the non-controversial aspect of things, their unquestioned impression, the façade made up of classified data." However, these qualities are, in Adorno's view, actually subjective in that they indicate a refusal to engage with the specifics of the individual object. Rather than following the unfolding meanings of the object where they want to go, we immediately subordinate them to the pregiven categories of our own thought. On the other hand, what we mistakenly call subjective is "anything which

54. Christopher Braider, *Refiguring the Real: Picture and Modernity in Word and Image, 1400–1700* (Princeton: Princeton University Press, 1993), 11.

55. Kahn, *The Future of Illusion*, 3. Kahn similarly considers *poiesis* as a third term, but between religion and politics, whereas for me *poiesis* is the third term between religion and empiricism.

breaches that façade [of classified data], engages the specific experience of a matter, casts off all ready-made judgments and substitutes relatedness to the object for the majority consensus of those who do not even look at it, let alone think about it." Aesthetic experience has an important role to play in challenging any quick dismissal of such experience as "mere" subjective relativity:

> Just how vacuous the formal objection to subjective relativity is, can be seen in the particular field of the latter, that of aesthetic judgments. Anyone who, drawing on the strength of his precise reaction to a work of art, has ever subjected himself in earnest to its discipline, to its immanent formal law, the compulsion of its structure, will find that objections to the merely subjective quality of his experience vanish like a pitiful illusion.[56]

When we look carefully at a painting, or immerse ourselves in a literary text, we submit ourselves to the artwork's "immanent formal law," by which Adorno means the unfolding internal dynamics of the artwork's form. Through our immersion in the form, the artwork slowly reveals the ways in which it is not equivalent to its own objective aspects—creating the peculiar sensation that, as one critic says, "even in front of our eyes it is hard to locate the work precisely."[57] To access this aspect of aesthetic experience calls for subjective immersion. Even when our initial subjective impressions "miss the mark,"[58] as Adorno asserts elsewhere, they are still part of the process of attaining cognizance in the fullest sense. Adorno's account of aesthetic experience critiques a falsely standardized objectivity, which views objects only from outside according to their ready-made and "non-controversial aspect."[59]

What happens to aesthetic experience when the process of subjective immersion is in some way discouraged or forbidden? Adorno writes provocatively that the person who interprets a text in a rigorous and imaginative

56. Theodor W. Adorno, "Unfair Intimidation," in *Minima Moralia: Reflections from Damaged Life*, trans. E. F. N. Jephcott (London: Verso, 2005), 69–70.

57. Robert Hullot-Kentor, *Things Beyond Resemblance: Collected Essays on Theodor W. Adorno* (New York: Columbia University Press, 2006), 144.

58. Theodor W. Adorno, *Aesthetic Theory*, ed. Gretel Adorno and Rolf Tiedemann, trans. Robert Hullot-Kentor (Minneapolis: University of Minnesota Press, 1997), 175.

59. Adorno, *Minima Moralia*, 69. See also Theodor W. Adorno, "Bach Defended against His Devotees," in *Prisms*, trans. Samuel Weber and Shierry Weber (Cambridge: MIT Press, 1981), 143: "What calls for refutation, however, is that of which the purists are most proud—their 'objectivity.' The only objective representation of music is one which shows itself to be adequate to the essence of its object."

way is marked with a "yellow star" as someone who, "instead of accepting what is given and classifying it . . . , squanders his intelligence in impotent speculation."[60] By renouncing whatever might be accused of fantasy, thought is made to take up the job of actively policing and suppressing its own critical experience.[61] When that happens, the art object starts to look like any other kind of object—like an artifact, say, or a commodity—even though, despite all its inevitable embeddedness in the material world, something in art still "does not want to be an object, a thing among things."[62]

This argument is important today because, while we are well aware of the problems of an overly subjective account of art, we may have become insensitive to the problems of an overly objective treatment. Already in 1976, Donald R. Howard expressed concern over the increasing emphasis on objectivity in historical literary studies: advocating for a more dynamic model of objective-subjective intertwinement, such as is exemplified by the work of Erich Auerbach, Howard complained about critics who, in contrast, "go on talking about 'the text itself' and 'an objective examination of the text' as if they had moon rocks or a cadaver before them."[63] Objective criticism misfires in part because the Renaissance literature and art it analyzes were not intended to be objective. Rosemond Tuve made this point in 1947. The goal of Elizabethan imagery wasn't, she insisted, objectivity. If we in the twentieth (or twenty-first) century assume that the simplest purpose of an image is to translate a sensory impression, we need to remember that "not even the schoolboy of the sixteenth century is told to keep his eye on the object."[64] In the realm of the visual arts, even apparently mimetic images were painted from a culturally embedded point of view, an argument that David Summers makes by referring to the Renaissance commonplace that "every painter paints himself."[65] An aesthetic object thus depends on a range of complexities and cultural dynamics that require interpretation.

60. Theodor W. Adorno, "The Essay as Form," in *Notes to Literature*, vol. 1, ed. Rolf Tiedemann, trans. Shierry Weber Nicholsen (New York: Columbia University Press, 1991), 4.

61. Adorno begins one section of his 1951 *Minima Moralia* with the title "*Intellectus sacrificium intellectus*," torquing Ignatius of Loyola's call for "the sacrifice of reason to God" (*Dei sacrificium intellectus*) into a tautology in which the intellect sacrifices the intellect (122–23).

62. Adorno, *Aesthetic Theory*, 58.

63. Donald R. Howard, *The Idea of the Canterbury Tales* (Berkeley: University of California Press, 1976), 138.

64. Rosemond Tuve, *Elizabethan and Metaphysical Imagery: Renaissance Poetic and Twentieth-Century Critics* (Chicago: University of Chicago Press, 1947), 3.

65. David Summers, *The Judgment of Sense: Renaissance Naturalism and the Rise of Aesthetics* (Cambridge: Cambridge University Press, 1987), 111. The point is that a strictly objectivist mindset is going to misinterpret much or all Renaissance art. In his survey of Renaissance paintings

However, a tendency toward a strictly factual and anti-interpretive account of the art object is becoming ever more extreme. In some cases, the bias toward objective factuality is so strong that collecting data about books has replaced reading them. For example, Franco Moretti, the founder of the Stanford Literary Lab, promotes the use of computer-generated data for what he aptly calls "distant reading" in his 2013 book of that name. Moretti's aim is to produce a new kind of knowledge about books that offers insight into social and economic history by bypassing traditional methods of interpretation. In pursuit of this end, he uses computers to examine as many literary objects as possible throughout the world. On first glance this method appears objective—what could be more objective, after all, than no criteria of selection? And yet, if we keep in mind Adorno's criticism of nondialectical objectivity, Moretti's empiricist analysis may turn out to be unconsciously subjective. Rather than trying to follow the logic of a text as it unfolds, he immediately subordinates whatever the text might say by classifying it according to pregiven terms.[66] In his network analysis of *Hamlet*, for example, Moretti diagrams the connections among the characters: who talks with whom, and so on. Yet the borders he assumes in creating his units of analysis are precisely what this play is interrogating as it blurs the distinctions between past and present, or between the projected fantasies of one character and the realities of another. To call the ghost a "node" is to efface precisely his ghostliness. When, for example, Hamlet holds up pictures of the former and the current king and ekphrastically describes them, Shakespeare shows Hamlet's desire that these men's relative worth might be considered an objective matter. All his mother has to do, the prince insists, is to "look" and "see." "Look here upon this picture, and on this" (3.4.51), he says to her, as if the artwork were just a fact, representing an objective truth beyond interpretation. Yet when Gertrude finally responds to Hamlet, what she sees is an image of her inner self: "O Hamlet, speak no more. / Thou turn'st my very eyes into my soul" (3.4.86–87).[67] In making this

---

that show Jesus's penis, for instance, Leo Steinberg has illustrated how the apparent carnality of this art must be understood symbolically if it is not to be considered entirely blasphemous. Leo Steinberg, *The Sexuality of Christ in Renaissance Art and in Modern Oblivion* (Chicago: University of Chicago Press, 1996).

66. In language evoking Bacon's, Moretti writes that "the trouble is, we literary scholars are not good at that [asking questions]: we are trained to listen, not to ask questions, and asking questions is the *opposite* of listening: it turns criticism on its head, and transforms it into an experiment of sorts: 'questions put to nature' is how experiments are often described, and what I'm imagining here are questions—put to culture"; *Distant Reading* (London: Verso, 2013), 165.

67. William Shakespeare, *Hamlet*, ed. Ann Thompson and Neil Taylor, Arden Shakespeare, 3rd ser. (London: Thomson Learning, 2006).

statement, she models the problems of interpretation that confront viewers of Shakespeare's play. Shakespeare wanted to provoke his audiences to try to reconstruct imaginatively what was not actually depicted, and to explore the problems of doing so. Trained in classical traditions of forensic rhetoric, Renaissance playwrights of the late sixteenth and seventeenth centuries developed characters who, confronted with limited physical evidence, engage in complex processes of interpretation and judgment, as Lorna Hutson has richly explored.[68]

When the gap between empirical factuality and the process of interpreting that factuality is eliminated, the space the play constructs for critical thought may also disappear. For example, scholarly studies that emphasize the role of economic interests in the construction of art objects may, despite their claim to be Marxist, actually end up "developing an ethical and political commitment to *things*" and, by downplaying other forms of experience, "chime[ ] perfectly with market ideology," in the words of David Hawkes.[69] In the *Dialectic of Enlightenment*, Adorno and Max Horkheimer argue that attempts to demystify our situation easily turn out themselves to be unconscious forms of mystification. To use their terms, enlightenment can readily transform into myth, without our even realizing it. Simon Jarvis notes, "It is not that capitalism invents mystification but that in capitalism mystification presents itself, to an unprecedented extent, *as demystification*."[70] Within this system, the claim of transparent meaning becomes a ubiquitous fantasy that is hard to perceive as such. "The more rapidly and brutally thought cuts itself free from illusion, the more it is entangled," writes Jarvis.[71] Scholarship that might have aimed to support the political left ends up aligning with consumerist interests on the right.[72] Critics who position themselves as radical unconsciously align with the status quo.

68. Lorna Hutson, *The Invention of Suspicion: Law and Mimesis in Shakespeare and Renaissance Drama* (Oxford: Oxford University Press, 2007), and *Circumstantial Shakespeare* (Oxford: Oxford University Press, 2015). See also Katharine Eisaman Maus, *Inwardness and Theatre in the English Renaissance* (Chicago: University of Chicago Press, 1995), 32.

69. Jane Bennett, for example, quotes a 7-Up soda advertisement, "You Like It. It Likes You," as the epigraph to her "The Force of Things: Steps toward an Ecology of Matter," *Political Theory* 32, no. 3 (June 2004): 347–72. See David Hawkes, "Materialism and Reification in Renaissance Studies" (review article), *Journal for Early Modern Cultural Studies* 4, no. 2 (Fall/Winter 2004): 115.

70. Simon Jarvis, "Adorno, Marx, Materialism," in *The Cambridge Companion to Adorno*, ed. Tom Huhn (Cambridge: Cambridge University Press, 2004), 93–94.

71. Ibid., 80.

72. Current materialism constitutes sometimes a strange reversal of Marx's original historical materialism. Marx's intention was, arguably, never to undermine the importance of ideas or subjective experience—rather, it was to reveal how experience has been rendered unfree by be-

One reason to use a modern thinker like Adorno in a study of past literature is that we are modern, and he helps us to become aware of and to critique the unconscious assumptions that shape our thinking. Many of his criticisms of modern thought, unlike Benjamin's, have not been absorbed into scholarly practice and seem to catch us at the very points where we are least self-aware. For example, many early modern literary scholars working today would agree with the problem that Benjamin raises about philosophies of art: "in the arrogance of its philosophical knowledgeability," Benjamin writes, such criticism often ignores the actual artworks themselves, "spar[ing] itself any profound study" of them.[73] Adorno would concur, but would challenge us by including positivist empiricism among such systems of thought that, paradoxically, can end up disregarding their objects by regulating or even effectively banning our immersive aesthetic involvement with them.

Hugh Grady helps show the importance of Adorno's aesthetic philosophy for understanding art in early modernity. Whether one thinks of the emergence of the commodity, the new science, the Protestant Reformation, or the discovery of the New World, the seeds were sown in the Renaissance, he says, for the "permanent crisis of meaning" that would undergird modernity.[74] Focusing especially on Shakespeare, he argues that Renaissance poets struggled presciently with issues such as commodification and reification that have been commonly identified with modernity. In *Timon of Athens*, for example, Shakespeare relentlessly interrogates the relation of art and commodities and must be understood as, in Grady's words, a "proto-theorist of the aesthetic."[75]

But it's not just that early modernity anticipated Adorno. It's also that Adorno pondered early modernity. What has gone largely undiscussed is that, at various moments throughout his corpus, Adorno refers to Francis Bacon as the "progenitor" of modernity. The *Dialectic of Enlightenment* begins with a substantial discussion of Bacon; and, in his *Lectures on Negative Dialectics*, Adorno refers to Bacon as "the founding father of empiricism" and suggests that the "exuberant" phase of empiricism may have begun

ing entrapped within oppressive systems of economic production. See Hawkes, "Materialism and Reification in Renaissance Studies," 115. See also his "Against Materialism in Literary Theory," in *The Return of Theory in Early Modern English Studies: Tarrying with the Subjunctive*, ed. Paul Cefalu and Bryan Reynolds (London: Palgrave Macmillan, 2011), 237–57.

73. Benjamin, *The Origin of German Tragic Drama*, 136.

74. Hugh Grady, *Shakespeare's Universal Wolf: Studies in Early Modern Reification* (Oxford: Oxford University Press, 1996), 56; Grady, *Shakespeare and Impure Aesthetics* (Cambridge: Cambridge University Press, 2009), 17.

75. Grady, *Shakespeare and Impure Aesthetics*, 41.

with this thinker.[76] Although most of Adorno's examples of literature and visual art are modernist (largely explaining the almost complete neglect of the Renaissance in Adorno studies), the problems of modern rationality derive for him largely from positivist empiricism. "Since my earliest youth," he wrote in May 1960, "I knew that everything that I stood for found itself in a hopeless struggle with what I perceived as the anti-spirit incarnate—the spirit of Anglo-Saxon natural-scientific positivism."[77]

PROBLEMATIZING THE TRIUMPH OF OBJECTS

This book tells a story about how early modern artworks push back against empiricist objecthood. If the historical process of objectifying the past has brought into being a modern landscape scattered with artifacts and other mute dead things (as Benjamin describes), or a triumphal procession of spoils or commodities (as Mantegna's painting suggests), there has also been an aesthetic tradition that critiques this very transformation of experience into things.

I begin my exploration into this tradition by looking at the Renaissance antiquarianism that was an early outgrowth of the emerging emphasis on observable objects in studies of history. For background, I explore Petrarch's accounts of Roman ruins (chapter 2) in passages that initially appear to be factual but turn out to be highly subjective. I then proceed to late sixteenth-century England, my primary focus. Each of the three chapters that follow centers on a different problem inherent in objectivity by examining how the problem appears in the ekphrases of one poet. Each of these facets of objectivity is different and, because of that, requires thinking in a new way about the emptying out of experience entailed in the emerging empiricist worldview. In Spenser's *The Faerie Queene* (chapter 3), I focus in particular on the problem of detachment; in Marlowe's *Hero and Leander* (chapter 4), on reification; and in Shakespeare's *The Rape of Lucrece* (chapter 5), on fragmentation. In each case, I locate my analysis of the relation of aesthetics and objectivity in the poetic descriptions of things, and in the working out of these passages' tensions with the factual world. These chapters, which open and close with images of ancient ruins, show the varied ways in which

76. Theodor W. Adorno, *Lectures on Negative Dialectics*, ed. Rolf Tiedemann, trans. Rodney Livingstone (Malden, MA: Polity Press, 2008), 31, 83.

77. In *Frankfurter Adorno Blätter VIII*, ed. Rolf Tiedemann (Munich: Edition Text + Kritik, 2003), 14. Quoted in Roger Foster, *Adorno: The Recovery of Experience* (Albany: State University of New York Press, 2007), 89.

early modern poetry was haunted by the kind of subjectivity that empiricists were beginning to renounce. My further argument is that a new and complex sense of modernity gradually emerged at the precise points where these poems sought this subjectivity within the images of alienated objects that were themselves becoming emblematic of a different (and narrower) modernity.

The book ends with a coda (chapter 6) that loops back to the beginning of the ekphrastic tradition, focusing on ekphrases in Homer and Virgil, and also looks forward to some seventeenth-century writers, including John Webster and Miguel de Cervantes. In this final section I explore a quality of ghostly animation that arises from their characters' own troubled contemplation of themselves as reified constructions of a future history. In looking at this ancient and early modern material, my book explores the very roots of art's problematic relation with its own objecthood.

A note about terminology may be in order. When a scholar uses words like *objectivity* and *subjectivity*, words with philosophical purchase, the demand is often that she should define her terms. The hope is that by defining her terms the writer will render her thinking more precise. But is this always the case? "It is a bias," writes Leo Spitzer, "to believe that understanding must always wait on definition. To define even the word *table* is more difficult than to use the word correctly."[78] Spitzer goes so far as to suggest that some definitions, if conceived of too narrowly, can even hinder thought. The problem is that definitions may fortify the hygienic systemization of thought, creating what I might call a kind of "precision effect" by emphasizing the intellectual system's clarity and internal consistency—all the while keeping the messiness of intertwined reality at bay. Adorno articulates the problem this way: "In order to be able to operate with the clean, clear concepts it brags about, science establishes such concepts and makes its judgments without regard for the fact that the life of the subject matter for which the concept is intended does not exhaust itself in conceptual specification."[79] In the case of the specific words *objectivity* and *subjectivity*, it may be more useful to think of these words as having a *history* rather than a stable *definition*, and it is this problematic history that my book explores. For good or bad, the omission of such definitions is not an accident, but a choice that is bound up in my larger thinking in this book about illusory forms of objectivity.

78. Leo Spitzer, "Geistesgeschichte vs. History of Ideas as Applied to Hitlerism," *Journal of the History of Ideas* 5, no. 2 (April 1944): 193.

79. Theodor W. Adorno, *Hegel: Three Studies*, trans. Shierry Weber Nicholsen (Cambridge, MA: MIT Press, 1993), 69.

* * *

Poetry in a World of Things critiques the conflation of aesthetic experience with empiricist objecthood that has become so prevalent today as to be ever more difficult to see. Take one brief recent example: Jeff Koons's massive metallic balloon dogs, one of which recently sold for a record $58.4 million. Such work asserts its objecthood by emphasizing its surface sheen and declaring its alliance with the realm of commodities. In a recent article in the *New Yorker* called "Selling Points" (July 7, 2014), Peter Schjeldahl celebrates Koons's work: "If you don't like that," Schjeldahl writes, "take it up with the world." In other words, the artwork has become identical with the world in its most objectified aspects, closing down the space for critical reflection. The object is the object. It is hard even to begin to register this attitude's aggressiveness toward critical thought. Not unlike the elephants paraded in a Roman triumph, Koons's massive balloon dogs participate in the procession of things, bringing up the rear in this era of advanced capitalism, rather than offering any critique of the procession.

The early modern artworks I examine did something more complex.

This book is an attempt to resist the collapse of art into empirical objecthood—which is not to deny that artworks are also objects, with all that condition implies. In a world where art that "breaks the rules" can be found in corporate lobbies throughout America (Adorno made a related point almost fifty years ago), I retrieve a lost history in order to argue for the importance of critically immersive aesthetic experience. No longer is there anything inherently radical about emphasizing the empirical objecthood of art. What is radical now, at least potentially, is to enter fully into a complex artwork that questions from within the way things are. If the nonempirical qualities of art are elusive and difficult to describe, that may be precisely because they do not fit in with the modes of thought that currently dominate our world—and yet, even in not fitting in, they remain part of our world.

CHAPTER TWO

Subjectivity and the Antiquarian Object: Petrarch among the Ruins of Rome

SURVEYING THE RUINS

Others had been there before. If the traveler's greatest pleasure is discovery, what was left for him to discover among the ruins of Rome in 1867? Traveling to Europe and the Holy Land aboard the *Quaker City,* Mark Twain complained that no sight remained in the Eternal City that others had not already seen, no intellectual pebble still existed that some other "brain-plow" had not already turned up. At the top of St. Peter's dome, he noted the graffiti testifying to the "millions" of other people who had already made that same climb, and he described the view in such a way that his ekphrasis echoes a much-repeated literary trope—and is itself a recognizable intellectual pebble. Scanning the terrain, he described the prospect of broken bridges and buildings and aqueducts and roads, associating them with the key scenes from Roman history that had occurred at those places. He mentioned, for example, "the ruins of temples, columns, and triumphal arches that knew the Caesars, and the noonday of Roman splendor," as well as the Appian Way, "looking much as it did, perhaps, when the triumphal procession of the Emperors moved over it in other days bringing fettered princes from the confines of the earth . . . [and] the long array of chariots and mail-clad men laden with the spoils of conquest." Twain proceeded then to describe the remnants of Christian Rome, and, noting the great difference between the brutal ignorance of pagans and the merciful kindness of Christians, his eyes rested on the building of the "pleasant Inquisition," which did all it could to persuade the barbarians to love and honor the merciful Christ, "first by twisting their thumbs out of joint with a screw." Marveling, Twain noted how very soothing and persuasive was the good Mother Church, who "always convinced those barbarians."[1]

Twain is parodying a letter of Petrarch's in which the fourteenth-century poet reports his own visit to Rome, when he too surveyed the ruins, starting with pagan sites and ending with Christian ones. That Twain may have known the letter directly is not out of the question; his interest in Petrarch was thorough enough that he reportedly examined Petrarch's copy of Virgil during this same tour, and meditated on the poet's tragic affair with Laura—although his sympathies went, he remarked, not to the poet, who at least was recompensed for his sufferings with fame, nor to Laura, but to the one who derived nothing from the semi-imaginary relationship, that is, Laura's anonymous husband, whom Twain calls "poor Mr. Laura."[2]

Even if Petrarch's letter from Rome has dropped out of the public imagination, it is hard to overestimate its importance to intellectual history, especially to the history of antiquarianism. Long before Twain's parody, the letter set a new precedent for those interested in Roman ruins. Shortly after Petrarch died in 1374, Giovanni Dondi repeated the letter's central conceit by describing the ruins in his own letter about Rome. Pier Paolo Vergerio the Elder followed with another such letter in 1398. Poggio Bracciolini introduced his c. 1448 *On the Inconstancy of Fortune* by telling how his text, like Petrarch's letter, was occasioned by a walk through the ancient city in the company of a friend. Just as Petrarch and his friend Giovanni Colonna ascended the Baths of Diocletian to view the city and reflect, so Poggio and his friend Antonio Loschi climb the Capitoline Hill to look out over the crumbling vestiges of ancient glory and discuss there the decline of the Eternal City.[3] Poggio does not miss Petrarch's references to Virgil's description of the pre-Roman Capitol in the *Aeneid* book 8, but plays on the lines describing the site's prehistorical state.[4] Flavio Biondo begins his guide to

1. Mark Twain, *The Innocents Abroad; or, The New Pilgrims' Progress; Being Some Account of the Steamship Quaker City's Pleasure Excursion to Europe and the Holy Land; With Descriptions of Countries, Nations, Incidents and Adventures, as They Appeared to the Author* (Hartford, CT: American Publishing, 1869), 266–75.

2. Ibid., 183–84.

3. One ancient literary ancestor of this image may be Virgil's description of Aeneas on the roof, looking out on his falling city, *Aeneid* 2.302–12.

4. Poggio writes of Rome: "Her primaeval state, such as she might appear in a remote age, when Evander entertained the stranger of Troy, has been delineated by the fancy of Virgil. This Tarpeian rock was then a savage and solitary thicket: in the time of the poet, it was crowned with the golden roofs of a temple; the temple is overthrown, the gold has been pillaged, the wheel of fortune has accomplished her revolution, and the sacred ground is again disfigured with thorns and brambles. The hill of the Capitol, on which we sit, was formerly the head of the Roman

the ruins, *Roma instaurata*, composed 1444-46, which remained the authoritative account until the sack of Rome in 1527 (after which it was replaced by Giovanni Bartolomeo Marliani's 1544 handbook), by echoing language from Petrarch's letter regarding the deplorable state of knowledge about the ancient city. Most famously, Edward Gibbon reports that he conceived of his magnum opus *The History of the Decline and Fall of the Roman Empire* when, on the fifteenth of October 1764, he "sat musing in the Church of the Zoccolanti or Franciscan friars, while they were singing Vespers in the Temple of Jupiter on the ruins of the Capitol."[5]

In twentieth-century scholarship on the Renaissance, this 1341 letter of Petrarch's is often treated as what initiated the turn to a more evidential form of scholarship, one based on the examination of physical remains. Angelo Mazzocco calls the letter "the first antiquarian document of humanism."[6] Seminal studies of antiquarianism like Roberto Weiss's 1969 *The Renaissance Discovery of Classical Antiquity* give Petrarch's ekphrasis of Rome pride of place near the beginning of their histories. Yet such histories, which of course do not focus on Petrarch, are more like *Bildungsromane* in which this early modern scholarly practice is the hero.[7] In such a context, Petrarch's letter can appear to be an immature version of what antiquarianism would later become.[8] Scholars note, for example, Petrarch's various "mistakes"—such as his failure to differentiate between republican and imperial walls—not infrequently adopting a tone of condescension toward this poet who,

---

empire, the citadel of the earth, the terror of kings; illustrated by the footsteps of so many triumphs, enriched with the spoils and tributes of so many nations. The spectacle of the world, how is it fallen! how changed! how defaced! the path of victory is obliterated by vines, and the benches of the senators are concealed by a dunghill." Edward Gibbon uses this same passage to begin the last chapter of *The History of the Decline and Fall of the Roman Empire*, vol. 3, ed. David Womersley (London: Penguin, 1994), 1062–63. See Catharine Edwards, *Writing Rome: Textual Approaches to the City* (Cambridge: Cambridge University Press, 1996), 69, 74.

5. Edward Gibbon, *Memoirs of My Life*, ed. Betty Radice (London: Penguin, 1984), 143.

6. See Angelo Mazzocco, "Petrarca, Poggio, and Biondo: Humanism's Foremost Interpreters of Roman Ruins," in *Francis Petrarch, Six Centuries Later: A Symposium*, ed. Aldo Scaglione (Chapel Hill: Department of Romance Languages, University of North Carolina, 1975), 355.

7. By the last page of Weiss's 207-page study, Renaissance antiquarianism is well established in the world. Major collections of antiquities can be found in Florence, Rome, Genoa, Ferrara, Venice, and Padua. "The testimony which could be extracted from ancient ruins, from statues and mosaics, but particularly from coins and inscriptions, was now fully appreciated, and any serious historian who dispensed with it, obviously did so at his personal risk," he writes. See Roberto Weiss, *The Renaissance Discovery of Classical Antiquity* (Oxford: Blackwell, 1969), 206.

8. In the nine pages of *The Renaissance Discovery of Classical Antiquity* that cover Petrarch's nascent antiquarianism, Weiss acknowledges in passing that Petrarch was not trying to be antiquarian. Weiss concedes that "Petrarch's letter is not a guide to old Rome, nor does it set out to be one" and that in this letter Petrarch "does not try to describe the monuments" (33).

after all, lived only in the Trecento. "As an antiquarian," Weiss remarks, "Petrarch was not above accepting some puerile traditions."[9]

As important as is the story of the shift to a new mode of history—one that relies on physical evidence—the question arises of whether Petrarch's aims, if understood on their own terms, can properly be considered antiquarian. In contrast with Petrarch's emphasis on the role of the writer in conjuring up the ghosts of the past, antiquarianism promises the solid knowledge of things themselves. In the Renaissance, as in the ancient world, antiquarianism served as an antidote to skepticism; according to Arnaldo Momigliano, antiquarianism prevailed when skepticism was especially strong, developing as a reaction against the unsettling questions of interpretive relativism that threatened to cast the objectivity of all historical writing into doubt.[10] "It is a known fact," the antiquarian Bernard de Montfaucon wrote in the eighteenth century, "that marbles and bronzes instruct us much more reliably on funeral ceremonies than the ancient authors; and that the knowledge that we glean from monuments is much more reliable than that which we learn from books."[11] Antiquarians desired that meaning inhere in things, which, seemingly immune to the problems of literary interpretation and historical relativism, would provide a bulwark against hermeneutic slipperiness. Most antiquarians reacted to scholarly disagreements by shoring up facts, by collecting and cataloguing and describing "evidence of undisputed authenticity—coins, statues, buildings, inscriptions."[12] The Comte de Caylus wrote about what could be "demonstrated by the monuments

9. Ibid., 31. Such an approach is also not uncommon in more recent scholarship: Mazzocco writes, "Petrarca's less than brilliant accomplishment in the field of archeology is due, it seems, to a lack of confidence in archeological remains vis-à-vis literary sources as means of historical evidence"; Philip Jacks writes, "His reliance on such wives' tales notwithstanding, Petrarch's letter also shows the efforts of considerable historical research"; and Anthony Grafton writes, Petrarch "had delightful antiquarian colloquies in the Baths of Diocletian," but "still accepted and passed on, unscrutinized, many popular beliefs that a close look at the stones in question could have refuted" and repeatedly made "jarring errors and anachronisms" (88). Mazzocco, "Petrarca, Poggio, and Biondo," 356; Philip Jacks, *The Antiquarian and the Myth of Antiquity: The Origins of Rome in Renaissance Thought* (Cambridge: Cambridge University Press, 1993), 38; Anthony Grafton, "The Ancient City Restored: Archaeology, Ecclesiastical History, and Egyptology," in *Rome Reborn: The Vatican Library and Renaissance Culture*, ed. Anthony Grafton (Washington, DC: Library of Congress, 1993), 88.

10. Arnaldo Momigliano, "Ancient History and the Antiquarian," *Journal of the Warburg and Courtauld Institutes* 13, nos. 3/4 (1950): 285–315, and *The Classical Foundations of Modern Historiography* (Berkeley: University of California Press, 1990), 54–79.

11. Quoted in Françoise Choay, *The Invention of the Historic Monument*, trans. Lauren M. O'Connell (Cambridge: Cambridge University Press, 2001), 41–42.

12. Momigliano, *The Classical Foundations of Modern Historiography*, 72.

themselves."[13] Such assertions represent an almost full reversal of Horace's claim that (his) poetry will prove more reliable than monuments (*Odes* 3.30).

Even among some very early humanists like Dondi, one finds something of this antiquarian attitude: not so much in an emphasis on evidence per se but on the permanence and solidity of things and on the sense that they could somehow, as eternal, tangible mementos, contain and preserve within themselves Roman *virtù*. Shortly after Petrarch's death, Dondi wrote of "the statues . . . of bronze or marble preserved to this day and the many scattered fragments of broken sculptures, the grandiose triumphal arches and the columns that show sculptured into them the histories of great deeds." Dondi then added: "as I remember reading about [the monuments], not without some remarkable excitement, wishing you also might see them some day, similarly strolling and stopping a little somewhere and perhaps saying to yourself: These are indeed the testimonies of great men."[14] For Dondi, words may still seem more real than things, but he manifests nonetheless the underlying antiquarian impulse to complete the experience, as Leonard Barkan says,[15] and to close the interpretive gap. To subsume Petrarch's ekphrasis of Rome into the story of antiquarianism may have helped to explain and authorize the humanists' study of the historical artifact but has failed to grasp what is special about Petrarch's work. As much as Petrarch may have invented humanism, humanists may also have invented Petrarch.

So how, then, are we to make sense of Petrarch's interest in ruins? Is he an objectivist poet who develops a new proto-antiquarianism, or is he a subjectivist poet who, according to one critical tradition, "finds in the consciousness of his individuality, severed from all external ties, accidental preoccupations and concerns, his *pure self*"?[16]

Instead of flattening our understanding of Petrarch's relation to ruins into one side or the other of this dichotomy, I will explore how, for Petrarch,

13. Anne Claude de Caylus, *Recueil d'antiquités* (Paris, 1752–67), 3:52, cited in Choay, *The Invention of the Historic Monument*, 51.

14. From a letter to Fra Guglielmo Centueri quoted in Richard Krautheimer and Trude Krautheimer-Hess, *Lorenzo Ghiberti* (Princeton: Princeton University Press, 1956), 295. For the complete letter, with translation and commentary, see Neal W. Gilbert, "A Letter of Giovanni Dondi dall'Orologio to Fra' Guglielmo Centueri: A Fourteenth-Century Episode in the Quarrel of the Ancients and Moderns," *Viator* 8 (1977): 299–346.

15. Leonard Barkan, *Unearthing the Past: Archaeology and Aesthetics in the Making of Renaissance Culture* (New Haven: Yale University Press, 1999), 7. See also Barkan's discussion of Dondi, 47–49.

16. Giuseppe Mazzotta, *The Worlds of Petrarch* (Durham: Duke University Press, 1993), 3. My italics. Note that Mazzotta's own interpretation in this book is much more dialectical; I will return to his insights later in this chapter.

it's the tension itself that's important. In his work, a new kind of modern subjectivity emerges through his encounter with material historical things, as a result of an often uneasy, frictional meeting of inner and outer realities. Ekphrases of ruins provide an ideal place to explore such issues because ekphrases portray the poet's encounter with the objective things of history.

To explore this tension, I will focus on two of Petrarch's ekphrases, both of which represent the ruins of Rome. In part 1, I will start by exploring in detail the much-discussed letter to which I have been referring, which is in the sixth volume of Petrarch's *Rerum familiarum libri*. In part 2, I will then proceed to a closely related ekphrasis that has received less attention, which is in Petrarch's epic *Africa*. In this latter case, Petrarch repurposes the ekphrasis of Rome to show its ruins from a very different perspective, that of defeated Carthaginians who are being given a tour of the ancient city during the Second Punic War. This passage in *Africa* casts a new light on the letter—by showing how historical things (such as ruins) may be the only traces left of subjectivities that have been vanquished.

PART 1

Things Become as Fluid as Thought for the Poet in His 1341 Letter from Rome

Petrarch sets up his reader to think that he is going to describe what he and his friend, the cardinal Giovanni Colonna, saw during their walk around Rome. Petrarch introduces the ekphrasis by saying that "at each step" the friends found "present what would excite [their] tongue and mind."[17] He then provides a long list of deictic statements[18] that seem to point at the physical world he and his friend are passing through on their walk. The ekphrasis, which is about two pages in most editions, is so consistent in how it presents the scene that a quotation of the first dozen lines or so will convey a sense of the whole:

> Here the palace of Evander, here the temple of Carmenta, here the cave of Cacus, here the wolf-nurse and the fig tree of Rumina with the truer name "Of

17. 6.2.5: "aderatque per singulos passus quod linguam atque animum excitaret." All Latin citations of this letter from Petrarch, *Lettres familières, IV–VII. Rerum familiarum, IV–VII*, ed. and trans. Ugo Dotti, Christophe Carraud, Frank La Brasca, and André Longpré (Paris: Les Belles Lettres, 2002). Translations of Petrarch mine, unless otherwise noted, with abundant thanks to Robert Ulery and Lucia Finotto for their kind suggestions and corrections.

18. For a recent discussion of early modern deictics, see Heather Dubrow, *Deixis in the Early Modern English Lyric: Unsettling Spatial Anchors like "Here," "This," "Come"* (Houndmills, Basingstoke, Hampshire, and New York: Palgrave Macmillan, 2015).

> Romulus," here the passage of Remus, here the circus games and the rape of the Sabines, here the marsh of Capri and Romulus, who is disappearing, here the discussion between Numa and Egeria, here the battle-array of the triplets [the Horatii and Curiatii]. Here Tullus Hostilius, the victor conquered by a thunderbolt of the enemy and the master of warfare, here the king and builder Ancus Martius, here Priscus Tarquinius the divider of the ranks lived; here Servius's head burned, here fierce Tullia sitting in the carriage passed and made the street infamous with her crime. This, moreover, is the Via Sacra, these the hills of the Esquiline, this the Viminal, this the Quirinal, this the Celius, this the Campus Martius and the poppies struck off by the hands of Superbus. Here pitiable Lucretia lying on her sword.[19]

Petrarch recounts a journey that is ordered not by space but by time. He moves through the temporal sequence of Rome's history. Starting in the period before the city's foundation, the tour proceeds to Romulus, goes past the rape of the Sabines, and progresses through the early kings until the birth of the Republic that was initiated, so the myth goes, by Lucretia's rape and suicide. The tour is through book knowledge. The lines quoted above bring us through the major events, in order, of book 1 of Livy's *Ab urbe condita*.[20] The ekphrasis eventually ends by listing, in a similar mode, the major sites of Christian history, and thereby connects pagan and Christian Rome, as Jennifer Summit has emphasized.[21]

By repeating variants of the deictic *hic* (here or this) over seventy-five times in this ekphrasis, Petrarch insists on the connection between his knowledge of Roman history and the place where he is walking with his friend. But the fact that Petrarch doesn't actually describe the ruins at all in the ekphrasis, and mentions them only once later in the letter,[22] renders this relationship between past and present Rome especially elusive. The

19. 6.2.5–7: "Hic Evandri regia, hic Carmentis edes, hic Caci spelunca, hic lupa nutrix et ruminalis ficus, veriori cognomine romularis, hic Remi transitus, hic ludi circenses et Sabinarum raptus, hic Capree palus et Romulus evanescens, hic Nume cum Egeria colloquium, hic tergeminorum acies. Hic fulmine victus victor hostium artifexque militie Tullus Hostilius, hic rex architector Ancus Martius, hic discretor ordinum Priscus Tarquinius habitavit; hic Servio caput arsit, hic carpento insidens atrox Tullia transivit et scelere suo vicum fecit infamem. Hec autem Sacra Via est, he sunt Esquilie, hic Viminalis, hic Quirinalis collis, hic Celius, hic Martius Campus et Superbi manibus decussa papavera. Hic miserabilis Lucretia ferro incumbens."

20. Thomas M. Greene writes that "the letter exhibits the imaginative projection onto a landscape of a historical coherence which that landscape could only begin to suggest"; *The Light in Troy: Imitation and Discovery in Renaissance Poetry* (New Haven: Yale University Press, 1982), 88.

21. Jennifer Summit, "Topography as Historiography: Petrarch, Chaucer, and the Making of Medieval Rome," *Journal of Medieval and Early Modern Studies* 30, no. 2 (Spring 2000): 211–46.

22. Petrarch says that he and his friend climbed to the top of the Baths of Diocletian. 6.2.15:

letter is, as the Krautheimers have said, "almost emphatically nonvisual."[23] Something's present, but what's present belongs to the past: buildings that have vanished and events that have long ago transpired.

Why does Petrarch point at things that are now absent? Because, as we will see, he wants to foreground the *problem of the poet's subjective relation to material Rome.*

By Petrarch's time, a long tradition of literary ekphrases of Rome had already cleared Rome of its materiality; the Eternal City had become a place for the play of various kinds of longings.[24] Virgil, most importantly for Petrarch, had played extensively with the temporality of Rome. By setting the *Aeneid* in pre-Roman times, Virgil was able to evoke places and events that lay in the future for the characters in his epic but that had already occurred for him and his Roman readers. For example, in book 8, Evander gives Aeneas, newly arrived in Pallanteum, a tour of what Virgil's readers would recognize as their own Rome. This Rome—which, as the future home of Aeneas's people, is the object of his desire, the goal of his quest—flits like a phantom around the rustic pastoral landscape where Aeneas treads. Virgil makes this play of temporalities explicit in his poem by referring to what didn't yet exist; he mentions Romulus and, most famously, the Capitol "golden now, then bristling with brambles of the forests."[25] Virgil's Roman readers would know well that Romulus and the Capitol lie several hundred years in the future of the era in which the epic is said to occur. In a similar vein, Ovid and Lucan also describe an insubstantial Rome.[26] The reader

---

"Both traversing the walls of the broken city and sitting there, the fragments of the ruins were under our eyes."

23. Krautheimer and Krautheimer-Hess, *Lorenzo Ghiberti,* 294.

24. In his discussion of the letter (*Unearthing the Past,* 20–25), Barkan describes how Rome had, almost from its beginning, seen itself as "a symbol whose reality is in the past": in early ancient history, Rome's reality seemed to belong to the vanquished Greeks; in the later empire, when power had started to spread from Rome to various external administrative sites and then to the East, Rome's temples and hills transformed themselves from being real sites of rule into symbolic imperial showpieces for tourists; in Petrarch's fourteenth century, during which the papacy evacuated Rome for Avignon, it was the center of a unified Italy that could have been but was not. Barkan goes on to explore how this age-old symbolism was put to the test when real sculptures began to be unearthed.

25. Virgil, *Aeneid* 8.348.

26. Abounding with deictic references that evoke an absent city, Ovid's account in book 3 of the *Tristia* is probably the closest in form to Petrarch's ekphrasis. Ovid presents Rome not as a material place but as a place of dreams: it is where the exiled narrator longs to be. The ekphrasis of Rome in Lucan's *Bellum civile* is just as insubstantial. In book 9 of this epic, Caesar visits a Troy that, for reasons elaborated by Andreola Rossi, is recognizable as a stand-in for Rome; "Remapping the Past: Caesar's Tale of Troy (Lucan *BC* 9.964–99)," *Phoenix* 55, nos. 3/4 (Autumn/Winter

finds in all these ekphrases that the solidity of the city has dissolved; she is staring past the city into desires and fantasies that play over and through one another across literary history.

In the Middle Ages, such evocations resonated with medieval Christian eschatology. In histories like Otto of Freising's twelfth-century *The Two Cities*,[27] the emphasis came to be on dissolving the solidity of things by (in contrast to what we will find in Petrarch) adopting a point of view outside of time. From the perspective of God's eternity, things on earth hardly seem to matter. Everything passes away like a shadow, the wake of a ship, or the flight of a bird, leaving no trace. Benedetto Croce draws attention to the radical de-emphasis of concrete particular things in such medieval histories. Their perspective, says Croce, easily slides into a kind of asceticism "in the name of which the whole actual history of mankind is covered with contempt, with horror, and with lamentation."[28]

In the realm of medieval literature, such a feeling found perhaps its most concise expression in the *ubi-sunt* (where are . . . ?) motif.[29] It is worth not-

2001): 313–26. Through this ekphrasis of a city so destroyed that even its ruins are unidentifiable, Lucan tacitly warns of a possible Rome of the future utterly laid to waste by war. Although Lucan writes that "no stone is without a name" (9.973), it is not at all clear how such significance really adheres to the things in this wrecked landscape. Caesar unknowingly crosses the river Xanthus (9.974–75), now just a trickling stream, once the site of so many heroic struggles in the *Iliad*. And the guide must tell him that the grass is the remains of Hector (9.978).

27. In the last book of *The Two Cities,* Otto reflects on the emptiness of the vast panorama he has crafted, which relates all of world history from Adam and Eve to the current era: "Let us, viewing the whole series of emperors or kings of that city [the city of this earth], say with Wisdom in the name of them all, 'What did our arrogancy profit us? or what good have riches and vaunting brought us? These things all passed away as a shadow, and as a message that runneth by—and as a ship passing through the billowy water, whereof, when it is gone by, there is no trace to be found, neither pathway of its keel in the billows; or as when a bird flieth through the air, no token of her passage is found' [Wisd. of Sol. 5:8–11]." We seem to enter into a kind of void. See *The Two Cities: A Chronicle of Universal History to the Year 1146 A.D.*, trans. Charles Christopher Mierow (New York: Columbia University Press, 2002), 483–84.

28. Benedetto Croce, *History: Its Theory and Practice,* trans. Douglas Ainslie (New York: Harcourt, Brace, 1921), 210–11.

29. On the *ubi-sunt* formula, see Claudia Di Sciacca, *Finding the Right Words: Isidore's "Synonyma" in Anglo-Saxon England* (Toronto: University of Toronto Press, 2008), 105–48; Lionel J. Friedman, "The Ubi Sunt, the Regrets, and Effictio," *Modern Language Notes* 72, no. 7 (Nov. 1957): 499–505; Étienne Gilson, *Les idées et les lettres* (Paris: J. Vrin, 1932): 9–38; Johan Huizinga, *The Autumn of the Middle Ages*, trans. Rodney J. Payton and Ulrich Mammitzsch (Chicago: University of Chicago Press, 1996), 156–59. The *ubi-sunt* motif was so popular in the Middle Ages that a reader can almost wind her way through the medieval canon by tracing it. In the *Consolation of Philosophy,* Boethius asks, "Where now remain the bones of faithful Fabricius?" (2.7.15). And Dante finds a gentle humor in asking the question in Purgatory, where it gains in that context an unexpected practicality, like a visitor's request for directions: "Tell me where is our ancient Terence, Cecilius and Plautus and Varius" (22.97–8). Petrarch himself employs the trope in several works, such as in his *Remedies for Fortune Fair and Foul,* where Reason laments the impermanence of great build-

ing that when Pier Paolo Vergerio, who edited Petrarch's *Africa,* continued Petrarch's 1341 letter from Rome with his own letter in 1398, he used this *ubi-sunt* formula.[30] This formula was one of the major motifs through which the medieval period expressed the feeling that the world was not entirely real or solid or lasting; that the world, set beside the eternity of God, was a kind of "shadow" or "dream." As Isidore of Seville (d. 636) put it: "Tell me, where are [ubi sunt] the kings? Where (are) the princes? Where (are) the emperors? Where (are) the rich in possessions? Where (are) the powerful of this world? They passed away as if they were a shadow, they vanished like a dream."[31] Although in the classical world the motif could have other meanings,[32] in the Middle Ages, it was, with few exceptions, an existential lament, a refrain of mourning, "a soft elegiac sigh," in Johan Huizinga's words.[33] Consider, for example, the Blickling homily of the tenth century:

> But where have the riches, and the adornments, or the vain pleasures gone? or where have the great throngs that went with them and surrounded them gone? And where are those who praised them, and spoke to them flattering words? And where have the adorning of their houses gone, and the collection of pre-

ings: "Where is now that proud Ilium Troy? Where is Byrsa, the citadel of Carthage? Where are the tower and walls of Babylon, which is now a dwelling place of wild beasts and snakes?" and etc. In this dialogue, Hope is on the defensive and stutters stupidly: "I hope for glory from my buildings"; "I earn glory by building"; "I seek glory by building." Petrarch, *Remedies for Fortune Fair and Foul,* trans. Conrad H. Rawski (Bloomington: Indiana University Press, 1991), 314–16 (1.118). For a listing of ancient and medieval appearances of this motif, see Gilson, *Les idées et les lettres,* 31–38.

30. Petrarch's and Vergerio's letters were closely linked in the minds of humanists: Barkan (*Unearthing the Past,* 33) notes that the letters were bound together in some early manuscript copies but does not develop the *ubi-sunt* motif as a context for understanding Petrarch's 1341 letter.

31. *Synonyma* 2.91, quoted and translated in Di Sciacca, *Finding the Right Words,* 106.

32. For example, Cicero uses the formula in two orations to impress upon his audience the idea that the current times are bad, but he seems unconcerned with making any metaphysical claim about the perishability of all things mortal. In "Pro Cnaeo Plancio," he complains that his opponent has no tolerance for his client's truly Roman liberty of expression: "What has become of the tradition of old? And the equity of our legal system, where is it? Where is the freedom of ancient days?" See Cicero, *Orations: Pro archia. Post reditum in senatu. Post reditum ad quirites. De domo sua. De haruspicum responsis. Pro Plancio,* trans. N. H. Watts (Cambridge, MA: Loeb Classical Library, 1923), 13.33. Valerius Maximus uses the same *ubi-sunt* formula not to lament the inevitable oblivion of human things but to celebrate the deeds of the Scipios and to assert the lasting memorability of their virtue. In the context of glorifying various examples of Roman heroism, he writes: "Where are the lofty walls of proud Carthage? Where the maritime glory of her famed harbor? Where her fleet, a terror to all shores? Where so many armies? Where her numerous cavalry? Where her ambition, not satisfied with the immense expanse of Africa? All this did Fortune divide among the two Scipios." And he goes on to argue that even the glory of Carthaginian heroes will last, "not extinguished even by the destruction of their country" (5.6, ext. 4). See Valerius Maximus, *Memorable Doings and Sayings,* books 1–5, trans. D. R. Shackleton Bailey (Cambridge, MA: Loeb Classical Library, 2000), 523–25.

33. Huizinga, *The Autumn of the Middle Ages,* 157.

> cious gems, or the vast acquisition of gold and silver, or all the wealth which they amassed daily, more and more, and knew not nor took heed of the time when they should leave all? Or where have their wisdom and their ingenious skill gone? And (where is) he who gave false judgments? And where is the splendour of their beds and their couches, or the manifold dissembling of their friends, and the great multitude of their servants, and the fretwork of their lamps which burned before them, and all the great crowds that went with and thronged about them? All those are now gone from their eyes.[34]

The material world's ephemerality is both lamented and morally upheld as a Christian lesson in human vanity. With each repetition of the question, the material world seems to disappear, "more and more," with all its beds and lamps and friends and houses, and the listener can say nothing. Part of the power of this question as an existential lament derives from the fact that it is a rhetorical question. Expecting no answer, it constructs a rhetorical vacuum that is not unrelated to the sense of nothingness it expresses (i.e., the expected silence of the respondent prefigures the eventual void of the world). Karl Löwith's description of medieval universal history, that it "takes one's breath away,"[35] could be used to describe the sense of nothingness that the *ubi-sunt* question evokes through its content, as well as the silence that it produces through its rhetorical form. The unspeakable answer to the *ubi-sunt* question, to François Villon's "Mais où sont les neiges d'antan?" (But where are the snows of yesterday?), is, of course, "nowhere"—but this "nowhere" is *so* nowhere it cannot even be said. Solidity loses all confidence in itself. The question opens an abyss that absorbs into its silent nowhere all things, including both speaker and listener.

In this context, the things in Petrarch's 1341 letter start to come into sharper focus. Against the traditional question, "Where are . . . ?," which expects no answer, stands Petrarch's repeated deictic declaration, "Here is. . . ." Petrarch is playing on this tradition I have been discussing (of Rome's and the world's flickering material existence) by transforming it, as the letter proceeds, into an image of human thought.

In the letter, Petrarch considers the question of the world's impermanence not from the divine position of the *nunc-stans*[36] but from his own

34. Quoted and translated in Di Sciacca, *Finding the Right Words*, 123–24.

35. Karl Löwith, *Meaning in History* (Chicago: University of Chicago Press, 1949), 4.

36. The *nunc-stans* describes the relation of God to eternity, outside the realm of human temporality. J. G. A. Pocock explains it as the "standpoint in eternity from which God saw every movement in time as simultaneously created and present; but whether the individual affirmed the

experiential position as a man in time—himself on a certain day, taking a walk with his friend through the city. This time is personal as well as historical. Although Petrarch only dates the letter with the month and day, he positions it in a collection scattered with references to contemporary political events. Within the letter itself, he also coordinates the day it describes with the larger political situation by mentioning the city's emptiness (a reference to the pope's absence[37]). If, from the position of the *nunc-stans*, the world and thinker are subsumed by and swallowed up into the eternal, in Petrarch's ekphrasis the world's flickering appears reflective of the mind's flickering: the world's insubstantiality is inextricable from Petrarch's own consciousness. A new sense of subjectivity starts to emerge as a peculiar effect of his insistent pointing at the problem of the objective world's absence-presence.

After listing the events of Roman history for approximately two pages, in such a way as to raise but not resolve the problem of the relation of this knowledge to his current world, Petrarch abruptly interrupts himself: "But where do I go? Can I really describe Rome to you in this short letter?"[38] We are made to hear in this line the present breaking in: at first this present ("Where do I go?") seems to refer to the moment of Petrarch's physical/intellectual wandering through Rome, but then the moment is revealed to be even closer—the actual moment in which Petrarch is writing the letter ("Can I really describe Rome to you in this short letter?"). Petrarch is no longer just wandering through Rome, but rather wandering through his own mind as he writes.

From this new perspective, the things of Roman history no longer appear simply out there, freestanding and objective; rather, their context is in here, within the province of one individual's thought in the temporal medium of the present. Petrarch's letter stages a series of transpositions, where what he's writing about eludes him and loops back on itself to become none other than a depiction of the passage of his own thought through time: "Just as this pen moves, so do I," Petrarch writes in another letter.[39]

The rest of the letter powerfully shifts the location of historical knowledge

---

nunc-stans as an act of intellect or faith, it was evident that he could not share it"; *The Machiavellian Moment: Florentine Political Thought and the Atlantic Republican Tradition* (Princeton: Princeton University Press, 1975), 7.

37. As Summit discusses, this was the era of the so-called Babylonian Captivity (1309–77), during which the pope was based in Avignon instead of Rome—much to Petrarch's regret.

38. 6.2.14: "Sed quo pergo? possum ne tibi in hac parva papiro Romam designare?"

39. Petrarch, *Letters on Familiar Matters, Rerum familiarum libri*, vol. 3, *Books XVII–XXIV*, trans. Aldo S. Bernardo (New York: Italica Press, 2005), 312 (24.1).

from the realm of material objectivity into the shifting circuit of interpersonal human relationships. Petrarch describes looking with his friend at the ruins from the top of the Baths of Diocletian. It seems that his friend had asked him about the origin of various kinds of knowledge (the liberal arts and mechanical arts) and now wants him to enclose in this letter whatever it was that he said then. But Petrarch finds himself unable to repeat the words that were exchanged on that day in this more fixed form of a letter: "You ask now that what I said that day, I repeat and commit to a letter. I said many things, I confess, that if I desired to say with unchanged words, I could not. Return to me that place, that leisure, that day, that attention of yours, that natural bent of my talent: I will be able to do what I once could do. But all things are changed: the place is absent; the day is gone; the leisure is lost; instead of your face, I look at a silent letter; hindering my talent is the din of matters left behind, which still now thunders in my ears."[40] A unique sense of historical knowledge starts to emerge in this letter. Knowledge of Roman history is not a constant objective commodity, not something that Petrarch can merely repeat, as the reader might have initially thought from the recitation of Roman history with which the letter began. Rather, knowledge, like intimacy, exists within human relationships and is reflective of—and vulnerable to—conditions that come and go, conditions that depend on unique contingencies. This might be what Petrarch meant when, in an earlier letter, he talked about "the *intimate* mystery of truth."[41]

The sense of loss that underlies the *ubi-sunt* lament can still be heard, but echoing now in a deeply interiorized tone. When Petrarch writes that "the place is absent; the day is gone; the leisure is lost; instead of your face, I look at a silent letter," it is as though one person's subjective experience of personal loss has absorbed the *ubi-sunt*'s original world loss. Paradoxically, it is this subjective experience of loss that actually provides the ground for Petrarchan self-knowledge. He realizes that he is that which passes.

The solidity of things momentarily gives way to the fluidity of an individual's thought in time. Giuseppe Mazzotta writes perceptively about the "poetics of objects" in this letter. He explores how the ruins evoke the poet's memories, and in so doing speak to the permeability of the boundary

40. 6.2.18: "Queris nunc ut quod illo die dixi, repetam ac literis mandem. Multa, fateor, dixi que si non mutatis verbis dicere cupiam, non possim. Redde michi illum locum, illud otium, illam diem, illam attentionem tuam, illam ingenii mei venam: potero quod unquam potui. Sed mutata sunt omnia; locus abest, dies abiit, otium periit, pro facie tua mutas literas aspicio, ingenio meo relictarum a tergo rerum fragor officit, qui adhuc in auribus meis tonat."

41. 1.9.10: "ad intimum veritatis archanum."

between his inner and outer worlds. Petrarch finds, Mazzotta writes, that "the canon of knowledge, like the plot of history, is not a sacrosanct, untouchable concept but a historical construction liable to change and subject to manipulations."[42] Petrarch achieves this new understanding in part by discovering Roman history from the standpoint of a single human being positioned within the ever-unfolding temporal world.

It is the poet's own life, for all its vicissitudes and varying stages, that is the only medium within which Roman history can be known. As Petrarch's thoughts about the ruins shift and take different forms, human history appears as restless as human beings themselves. But Petrarch's analysis of Roman ruins, and of the relation of human subjectivity and historical objects, does not end there. If the letter showed how historical things can give rise to a new subjectivity, *Africa* shows how subjectivity can be rendered into historical things.

PART 2

Subjectivity Solidifies into Thingliness in Africa

Many current American scholars of the Renaissance seem already to know that Petrarch's *Africa* is bad—*already* because they often hold this opinion without having read the work. The history of how this received idea began, and how it was transmitted, is hardly to the point here.[43] What's regrettable

42. Mazzotta, *The Worlds of Petrarch*, 23.

43. Although a passage from *Africa* (Mago's death speech in book 6) that circulated during Petrarch's life received some criticism, the epic's immediate reception both during Petrarch's life and shortly after his death was mostly positive. Many of Petrarch's contemporaries anxiously awaited the epic and welcomed it with overflowing admiration when it first arrived. Barbato da Sulmona, in a letter to Petrarch, quoted Scripture to beg him to release the work for the good of humanity. When the Paduan humanists who had taken charge of the manuscript after Petrarch's death finally released it, Coluccio Salutati read *Africa* in three nights, and wrote to Francescuolo on January 28, 1377, to say that he "had never read any work more serious, more fully developed, nor, finally, more appealing than this." See Aldo S. Bernardo, *Petrarch, Scipio and the "Africa": The Birth of Humanism's Dream* (Baltimore: Johns Hopkins Press, 1962), 175. It should be noted, however, that Salutati's response was not without ambivalence; see Revilo P. Oliver on this point, "Salutati's Criticism of Petrarch," *Italica* 16, no. 2 (June 1939): 49–57. Furthermore, in the fifteenth century, the epic's status dropped drastically, as James Hankins has shown; "Petrarch and the Canon of Neo-Latin Literature," 2004, available online at http://nrs.harvard.edu/urn-3:HUL.InstRepos:3342975. After the turn of the century, reactions among the next generation of Italian humanists were measured, disdainful, ironic. The depiction of Petrarch in the *Dialogi ad Petrum Histrum* (c. 1405) by Leonardo Bruni suggests attitudes current in the early fifteenth century; see *The Three Crowns of Florence: Humanist Assessments of Dante, Petrarca and Boccaccio*, ed. and trans. David

is the relative neglect of this epic[44]—not the criticism of it. *Africa* is a text that constantly calls itself into question, as several scholars have shown.[45] Indeed, Petrarch is a poet who in general may be more compelled by problems than by solutions. In this epic that he struggled over for thirty-five years, problems rise to the surface and become part of the poem's self-questioning dynamic whereby it interrogates history and—most importantly for us—interrogates the relationship between subjectivity and historical things.

The epic, which is set near the end of the Second Punic War (218–201 BCE), tells the story of Scipio the Elder's defeat of Hannibal, and the subsequent fall of Carthage. Although this Roman victory marked an important step in the progress of empire,[46] Petrarch constantly colors his story with ambivalence. Even as readers witness Scipio's triumph, they know that Car-

---

Thompson and Alan F. Nagel (New York: Harper & Row, 1972). In the first part of the dialogue, Niccolò Niccoli describes the great buildup of expectation for *Africa* while Petrarch was working on it, and then the great letdown when it was finally released, referring to Horace's saying about the mouse born after the labor of mountains. Although in book 2 Niccoli retracts this depiction by claiming he only gave it to elicit a eulogy of Petrarch from Salutati, at whose house the dialogue is set, he goes on to praise Petrarch in a manner that is shot through with irony. He says, "I prefer an oration of Petrarca's to all the epistles of Virgil, and the poems of Petrarca to all the poems of Cicero" (51). As the dialogue's humanist audience would have known, Virgil's epistles were medieval forgeries, and disparagement of Cicero's poetry went back to the ancient world. Hankins has shown that what is at issue in this harsh treatment of Petrarch's *Africa,* as well as of his Latin works generally, is the purity or impurity of classical style in the humanist Quattrocento. See also David Quint, "Humanism and Modernity: A Reconsideration of Bruni's *Dialogues,*" *Renaissance Quarterly* 38, no. 3 (Autumn 1985): 423–45.

44. Although a new translation of the epic has now been commissioned by the I Tatti series of Harvard University Press, no current complete scholarly English translation of this important work is available. The most recent translation, which is not literal, is forty years old: *Petrarch's "Africa,"* trans. Thomas G. Bergin and Alice S. Wilson (New Haven: Yale University Press, 1977). There is a good prose translation of books 1–4 by Erik Z. D. Ellis (written as an MA thesis at Baylor University, 2007), which is available online: https://hdl.handle.net/2104/5144.

45. Ugo Dotti, for example, insightfully describes the epic in terms of its "doubts and contradictions"; *Vita di Petrarca* (Rome: Laterza, 1987), 99. Similarly, John Kevin Newman cogently analyzes the epic's proem in order to show how the epic marks itself from the beginning with what Newman calls the poem's "unrealized dilemma"'; *The Classical Epic Tradition* (Madison: University of Wisconsin Press, 1986), 282–92. For a contrasting approach, see Simone Marchesi's account of *Africa* as a poem that supports what he calls "the reasons of epic" (122). He suggests, for example, that "the irresolute author of the *Rerum vulgarium fragmenta* has been replaced by a poet with programmatic ethical resolution" (117). See Marchesi, "Petrarch's Philological Epic (*Africa*)," in *Petrarch: A Critical Guide to the Complete Works,* ed. Victoria Kirkham and Armando Maggi (Chicago: University of Chicago Press, 2009), 113–30.

46. According to Polybius, the war was "the most essential step towards universal empire." Up until that time, Polybius says, history was "a series of disconnected transactions," separated by geography. The effect of the Roman victory over the Carthaginians was that history became "a connected whole." Rather than thinking of themselves as the masters of only a part of the world, the Romans began after this war "to stretch out their hands upon the rest" and to seek their "final

thage will rise again, and that Scipio himself will soon be banished and die in exile, inscribing his tomb with a message of bitter remorse.[47] In *Africa*, as in most Renaissance epics, the underlying pattern of the *Aeneid* shows through in many places: in the abundant prophecies of future Roman history; in the visit with the dead father; in the Dido-like story of the defeated Numidian queen Sophonisba; in the lavish epic similes; and, most importantly for us, in the many ekphrases. This is an epic with little plot, one that arguably doesn't begin to move forward until book 6. A great proportion of *Africa* is devoted to ekphrastic tableaux, such as the one that describes artworks in Syphax's elaborately wrought palace, the ones about the landscapes in and around Italy, and the one—which will be my focus—about the sites of Rome. It is in this ekphrasis that Petrarch's exploration of ruins gains a new dimension: he suggests here how a historical object may be the only trace left of a subjectivity that has been violently eradicated.

By book 8, when this ekphrasis occurs, it is no longer a good time to be from Carthage. Scipio has just decisively defeated the Phoenician army, and its general Hannibal has skulked away, dejected and ashamed. Weeping and prostrate, the Carthaginian ambassadors have come to Rome to beg the Senate for mercy. After promising their city's capitulation, these envoys are given a tour of Rome.

The Rome of *Africa* is in many ways like the Rome of the letter, relying largely on Livy. In both ekphrases, Petrarch mixes the Romes of different times. Although scholars are surely right that Petrarch makes mistakes in his picture of third-century-BCE Rome (for example, by introducing the Pantheon—the original version of which was really built by Marcus Agrippa only after the Battle of Actium in 31 BCE), the reader may also wonder whether the story that these scholars tell of the development of antiquarianism makes them miss the intentionally synchronic poetic effect of Petrarch's mixing of the ages of Rome.[48]

---

success in grasping universal empire and dominion." Polybius, *Histories*, vol. 1, trans. Evelyn S. Shuckburgh (London and New York: Macmillan, 1889), 1.3.

47. At 2.549, Petrarch refers to Scipio's tomb, which, according to Livy (38.50–54) and Valerius Maximus (5.3.2), was inscribed with words berating his "ungrateful country." Petrarch, *L'Afrique: 1338–1374*, trans. Rebecca Lenoir (Grenoble: Éditions Jérôme Millon, 2002), 470. All Latin quotations of *Africa* from her edition.

48. Rebecca Lenoir explains: "The itinerary of the Carthaginians is precise and corresponds to a real route that can be reconstructed. But it is hardly Petrarch's habit to confine himself to this kind of topographical mode. It is evident that he distances himself from the historic truth as much as he wants, here as in the letters, to offer a sample of his erudition and perhaps to introduce

At first *Africa*'s ekphrasis of Rome seems relatively unproblematic. If in the letter Petrarch longed for the resurrection of Rome, here ancient Rome exists all around the envoys in its concrete reality. Even the stories from the earlier founding of the city seem closer and the vision of long-dead heroes less spectral:

> The Appian Way received the men first on its marble threshold;
> Soon they see the Palatine walls forming a great circle,
> On the mountain where was built the royal palace of Evander,
> The first and celebrated location of the new city;
> Here, as they know, were signs of letters impressed,
> Here the guide himself related the divine inspiration
> Of the propitious Arcadian, and the most important prodigies of history,
> And the discovered books, work of the Prophetess Carmenta.[49]

The envoys' experience begins as one of pleasure and almost aesthetic absorption. Entering by the Appian Gate (the Gate of San Sebastian), they first behold the ancient walls built around the Palatine. They then are led through the city, where they hear the stories behind the famous names of the Aventine Hill and the Sublician Bridge. The story about Hercules bathing the oxen in the stream is a "pleasing discourse" (placido sermone), and Petrarch notes that the envoys "admire" (mirantur) the Temple of the Sun.[50] As will soon become clear, however, the narrow divide that separates the present from the past suddenly breaks down when the envoys reach the Temple of Jupiter, where, among all the attractive booty on display, they suddenly recognize their people's own things. At this point, history rushes forward into the present to claim these living men, who until now seem to have been thinking they were only taking in innocuous stories about the days of yore.

Just before the Carthaginians reach the temple, their admiration becomes tinged with a semi-religious dread of the signs of Roman power. Petrarch writes that they ascend "quaking" (paventes) to the height of the

himself into this journey. . . . Undoubtedly, Petrarch commits some errors, and he still remains the product of his century's beliefs as conveyed by the *Mirabilia*, but perhaps less than certain commentators suggest" (547). Translation from the French mine.

49. 8.862–69: "Appia marmoreo suscepit limine porta / Prima viros; magno mox obvia menia giro / Pallantea vident, quo structa est regia monte / Evandri primusque nove locus inclitus urbis; / Hic elementa notis impressa, hic Archados alme / Divinum ingenium et miracula maxima rerum / Monstrator docet ipse vie librosque repertos / Fatidice Carmentis opus."

50. 8.874, 8.879.

Capitoline, where they think they touch the sky itself.[51] Disturbing suggestions begin to appear that these Carthaginian envoys already belong to the Roman history that is being recited to them: Petrarch writes that when the envoys hear the story of the human head (signifying Rome's future world-dominance) that was found at the first construction on the Capitoline, they lament as they remember that it was an ox head (signifying their own future servitude) that was discovered at the founding of their own city.[52]

Soon they reach the Temple of Jupiter:

> Here they saw the sanctuary of Jove, which was richer
> Than any other, and the tax set back under the high cliff,
> And the thresholds already trampled then by innumerable triumphs
> And the snowy-white chariots and the arms seized from enemies,
> And also the golden diadems of great kings
> And the scepters and bracelets and necklaces stripped from their necks
> And the bejeweled reins and ivory thrones set in order.
> Here the shields and broken boats and Punic signs
> And breastplates that they know are theirs; and a silent grief went
> Through them all recalling the vestiges of the old war.[53]

Everything at first gleams with a seductive, incantatory power, as the envoys admire the shiny chariots and golden diadems and arms and scepters and bracelets and necklaces and gem-studded reins and ivory thrones. The reader hardly notices the occasional flashes of violence glinting off these objects (the "necklaces stripped from their necks").[54] All is "in order" (ex ordine). One thing follows another like the linear pattern of history itself.[55]

51. 8.880–81. This quaking has Virgilian origins. During the tour of the future site of Rome in the *Aeneid* 8.349–50, Virgil notes that "even then the ominous sanctity of the place terrified the quaking country people."

52. It is hard to say whether Petrarch intends for his readers to notice that the Carthaginian story is being subtly falsified to suit the victors' version of history. It was relatively well known from Justin that the Carthaginians chose to dig in a more auspicious location after coming upon the ox head; they then unearthed a horse head, as Virgil mentions in the *Aeneid* 1.443. It is as if the Carthaginians' own version of the story must be destroyed, or modified, to conform to the victors' story.

53. 8.886–95: "Hic cellam videre Iovis, qua ditior usquam / Nulla fuit, censumque alta sub rupe repostum, / Liminaque innumeris iam tunc calcata triumphis / Et niveos currus et rapta ex hostibus arma, / Aurea magnorum nec non diademata regum / Sceptraque et armillas et dempta monilia collo / Gemmatosque frenos sellasque ex ordine eburnas. / Hic clipeos fractasque rates ac Punica signa / Et phaleras novere suas; tacitusque per omnes / Luctus iit veteris referens vestigia belli."

54. This line recalls an earlier moment when Hannibal, speaking to his troops, evoked golden rings that were hacked from bloody fingers (7.882).

55. A related order is found in the *Aeneid* on the shield of Aeneas, where Augustus watches the

The shock comes in the last three lines: the reader suddenly encounters the Punic signs. Since Petrarch has constructed this description to convey the Carthaginians' subjective experience, they recognize at the same time as the reader does that *they* are the defeated from whom this booty was plundered. What they see is none other than "the shields and broken boats and Punic signs and breastplates that *they know are theirs*."[56] They realize that what had at first appeared to them as attractive, glittering riches are in fact their people's own desecrated spoils of war.

At this moment the Carthaginians find themselves frozen in a medium of history that is no longer fluid, that no longer moves in the supple manner of thought, but that has become hard and resin-like. Instead of being history's agents, they are becoming history's objects: "a silent grief went through them all recalling the vestiges of the old war." It is worth noting their silence (tacitus), which is emphasized again at the end of the tour:

> Returning at last from the summit of the Capitol,
> They slowed their weary step, then suddenly a great
> Stupor strikes them thinking over the sights again. After that, sitting,
> Stunned, for a long time they were silent.[57]

Deprived of agency, the envoys slow; they stop. A great "stupor" overtakes them. They sit down, astonished. The reader is made to witness the men's metamorphosis into things from the perspective of the men themselves, who feel this great weariness overcome them and must sit. Simone Weil, writing about the *Iliad* in the first year of World War II, describes war as the "power of converting a man into a thing." She describes those who are

---

triumphal procession that files by in a long line (longo ordine), a phrase that several scholars, most notably David Quint, have understood as providing an image of the linear form of historical narrative. See his *Epic and Empire: Politics and Generic Form from Virgil to Milton* (Princeton: Princeton University Press, 1993), 32.

56. The Temple of Jupiter indeed served as a repository for artworks and other precious things—gifts, dedicatory offerings, trophies, and spoils. By the second century BCE, this temple was so crowded that, as part of a public works project, shields and standards were removed because they obstructed the view (Livy 40.51). It is generally agreed that the Carthaginians' recognition of their shields in the Capitol derives from passages in Livy and Pliny. These writers tell of a battle in Spain where the Romans slaughtered as many as thirty-seven thousand men and captured much booty, including a 138-pound shield. Pliny (*Naturalis historia* 35.4.14) says that this shield bore on its surface an image of its owner, Hasdrubal, and thus provided "a copious inspiration of valour" when it was suspended over the gate of the Temple of Jupiter on the Capitoline Hill. See also Livy 25.39. Noted in Lenoir, *L'Afrique: 1338–1374*, 550.

57. 8.952–55: "Ut Capitolino redeuntes vertice tandem / Defessum tenuere gradum, tum protinus ingens / Visa revolventes stupor arripit. Inde sedentes / Attoniti siluere diu."

enslaved as "a compromise between a man and a corpse." If a corpse is the ultimate object-fate of a person, there is a kind of horror that arises when a living person identifies with an object: "The idea of a person's being a thing is a logical contradiction. Yet what is impossible in logic becomes true in life," Weil writes.[58] Frantz Fanon describes his experience of dehumanizing racist colonial oppression in similar terms: "I am an object among other objects."[59] As in these twentieth-century accounts, Petrarch's emphasis on the severely determinate material power of history positions the reader very far from the semi-mystical vision of human freedom later expounded by some Quattrocento humanists like Giovanni Pico della Mirandola, for whom man is, famously, "constrained by no limits."[60]

The transformation of people into things continues in the ensuing lines, where the envoys then are made to witness the long files of the trembling captives, their countrymen:

> The troops, trembling and despondent, were standing in long lines,
> And their pale cheeks were swollen,
> And their tangled hair, for a long time uncared for,
> Fell on their naked backs, and their visage
> Was covered with dirt, and bore a wretched odor.
> Iron chains constrained
> Their slowly dragged march,
> And heavy manacles denied them the joy
> Of embracing those dear to them.
> Then the men exchange sweet words with them,
> But the shaken chains clang in the air,
> And tears flow over their cheeks
> With great feeling. They ask what is the fate,
> What is the condition of their ancestral city,
> What deities look after the vanquished.[61]

58. "The *Iliad* or The Poem of Force," in *Simone Weil: An Anthology*, ed. Siân Miles (New York: Grove Press, 1986), 184, 168.

59. Frantz Fanon, *Black Skin, White Masks*, trans. Richard Philcox (New York: Grove Press, 2008), 89.

60. Pico della Mirandola, "Oration on the Dignity of Man," trans. Elizabeth Livermore Forbes, in *The Renaissance Philosophy of Man*, ed. Ernst Cassirer et al. (Chicago: University of Chicago Press, 1948), 225.

61. 8.956–68: "Stabant horrentia longo / Agmina mesta situ pallentiaque ora tumebant / Nudaque perplexis onerabat terga capillis / Cesaries incompta diu squalorque tegebat / Luridus effigiem tristemque ferebat odorem. / Ferrea vincla gradum lento suspendere tractu / Cogebant, maniceque graves complexibus illos / Carorum vetuere frui. Tum verba vicissim / Dulcia permis-

It is the captives' physical bodies that are emphasized: their stench and filthy hair and swollen cheeks and naked backs. This procession is like those that occur in epic journeys to the underworld, such as in the *Odyssey*, the *Aeneid*, and the *Inferno*, where the dead throng around the newcomer and ask for news of loved ones (an analogy that Petrarch makes explicit in lines 8.968–79). The reader has now reached the final stage of the envoys' metamorphosis into things: they have become like the dead.

A new dimension begins to open on Petrarch's understanding of ruins: the things of history are not simply innocent but are, potentially, the traces of lost subjectivities. We learn in this epic that, for the defeated, the realization of the "now-time" of history is no longer experienced as fluid subjectivity but as reification. History strips the defeated of their agency and claims them as its objects. The natural flow of mental life that Petrarch evoked so beautifully in the letter has come to an abrupt halt. Instead of thought springing forth from things, thought congeals into things. When that happens, it means that some kind of violence has occurred. Historical objects are in this case the traces left behind of annihilated subjectivities.

Petrarch's interest in ruins as testaments to the eternal glory of great deeds is well known. Scipio's father, for example, talks about the eternal record of the "remembering sepulcher" (2.549, memorique inscribe sepulcro).[62] Less familiar is Petrarch's analysis in *Africa* of the violence that can be involved in the making of these monuments. Speaking in the narrator's voice, Petrarch evokes the arbitrariness of human affairs—and the role of conquest in the construction of history and historical artifacts.

> For if by chance destiny had favored in the end the Punic side,
> Who would doubt that impious Carthage dominating throughout the immense globe
> Would hold the reins of everything,
> And the name of the Romans would convey nothing to these times?[63]

---

cent, sed perstrepit ere cathenis / Redditus excussis stridor lacrimeque per ora / Egregia pietate fluunt. Que fata, quis urbis / Sit status inquirunt patrie, que numina victos / Respiciant."

62. See also Petrarch's "Coronation Oration," wherein he quotes Cicero's *Laws* 2.2 as an explanation for his own coming to Rome: "Our emotions are somehow stirred in those places in which the feet of those whom we love and admire have trodden. Wherefore even Athens delights us not so much through its magnificent buildings and its exquisite works of ancient art as through the memory of its great men: 'twas here they dwelt, 'twas here they sat, 'twas here they engaged in their philosophical discussions. And with reverence I contemplate their tombs." See Ernest H. Wilkins, "Petrarch's Coronation Oration," *PMLA* 68, no. 5 (Dec. 1953): 1241–50.

63. 7.1036–39: "Favisset si forte etenim sors ultima Peno, / Quis dubitet quin immensum

The memory of all mortal things is dependent on the outcome of violent battles. Heroic names may be remembered, but, as Hannibal suggests in trying to rouse his troops before battle, only those of the winning side (7.909–12). Such an idea stands in evident contrast to the belief expressed by heroes like Aeneas, who in a famous ekphrastic scene in the *Aeneid* book 1, expresses the hope that meaning can inhere in things, even for the war's losers. Examining the scenes of the Trojan War depicted on the walls of the Temple of Juno in Carthage, Aeneas seems to feel reassured that such scenes will even here "touch the mind" (1.462).

In *Africa,* historical objects tend to be less reliable. From the poet's Christian perspective, part of the problem is the ephemerality of all mortal things: Scipio's father, for example, explains that all things fall to dust, and that eventually even names on marble are effaced, whatever their promises of permanence.[64] But the problem is also, more specifically, the violence associated with Roman imperial glory:

> Nothing remains at all in mortal affairs; how
> Can a man or a people truly hope for what bountiful
> Rome cannot? The centuries easily slip away:
> The times disperse; to death you hasten; a shadow,
> A shadow you are and light dust, or scant smoke in the air
> Which the wind blows. By what bloodshed was glory obtained?[65]

As Enrico Fenzi has argued, Petrarch undermines an imperial edifice of epic *Romanitas,* even as he builds it.[66] At the beginning of book 8, after the victorious Romans have taken possession of the Carthaginian gold, Petrarch

dominata per orbem / Impia Carthago rerum tenuisset habenas, / Romanumque nichil foret hec in tempora nomen?"

64. "But if false glory seduces (your) wavering mind, / Behold what you would desire: the times will pass, this body / Will fall apart, and your limbs will give place to an unworthy tomb; / Soon even the funeral pyre will fall to ruin, and the inscription carved in marble / Will be effaced: hence you will suffer a second death, son." "Quod si falsa vagam delectat gloria mentem, / Aspice quid cupias: transibunt tempora, corpus / Hoc cadet et cedent indigno membra sepulcro; / Mox ruet et bustum, titulusque in marmore sectus / Occidet: hinc mortem patieris, nate, secundam" (2.429–33). Petrarch constructs the lines to enact this process of falling apart, as the enjambed lines seem to fall into the following lines.

65. 2.346–52: "Nec manet in rebus quicquam mortalibus; unde / Vir etenim sperare potest populusve quod alma / Roma nequit? Facili labuntur secula passu: / Tempora diffugiunt; ad mortem curritis; umbra, / Umbra estis pulvisque levis vel in ethere fumus / Exiguus, quem ventus agat. Quo sanguine parta / Gloria?"

66. Writing about Petrarch's work in general, Fenzi says that "the edifice remains majestic, even as his words attack it from behind" (57). Enrico Fenzi, *Pétrarque,* trans. Gérard Marino (Paris: Les Belles Lettres, 2015).

reflects that "Africa now regurgitates all this mixed with blood. What could be the value of so much rapine? The robber despoils the robber."[67] Although Petrarch presents his observation of reciprocal thievery as though it applied only to the Carthaginians, who had taken their gold from the Libyans, Sardinians, Ethiopians, Numidians, and Moors, its applicability to the Romans in this context is implicit. This idea that the history of *translatio imperii* is really the story of one thief stealing from another recalls Augustine's idea that without justice, kingdoms are nothing but "gangs of criminals on a large scale."[68] Literary history reflects on this violence associated with the attempt to render names permanent by inscribing them in marble, to accumulate imperial riches, as well as more generally to make history. What James Simpson says about Petrarch's *Trionfi* applies to *Africa*: "Literary history takes shape here as the witness to recurrent subjections to an imperial, triumphal power."[69]

CONCLUSION

For Petrarch, the purpose of any kind of knowledge is ethical. Throughout both his vernacular and his Latin works, Petrarch repeatedly raises the question of whether a field of study will make us morally better or happier, and in so doing he opposes what Fenzi has called "the pseudo-scientific notions of his time."[70] The limitations of knowledge are an Augustinian theme, inspired by the Bible (Eccl. 1:18: "In much wisdom is much grief").[71] They are also a literary theme, drawing on Ovid.[72]

A version of this tension between the claims of technical knowledge and of ethics is the crux of the debate in *On His Own Ignorance*, where Petrarch

67. 8.27–29: "Id totum sanguine mixtum / Africa nunc revomit. Quid tot valuere rapine? / Raptor raptorem spoliat."

68. Augustine, *City of God*, trans. Henry Bettenson (London: Penguin, 1984), 139 (4.4).

69. James Simpson, "Subjects of Triumph and Literary History: Dido and Petrarch in Petrarch's *Africa* and *Trionfi*," *Journal of Medieval and Early Modern Studies* 35, no. 3 (Fall 2005): 490.

70. Fenzi, *Pétrarque*, 11.

71. Fenzi writes: "Petrarch deliberately eliminates from his discourse all speculative technicality and places himself at a completely different horizon, where it is not the accumulated materials of knowledge which are the decisive factor, but rather the particular configuration of each person's moral experience" (ibid., 91–92). My translation.

72. The impotence of knowledge is the problem of Ovid's Medea, for example, who says that "I see and approve what is better; I follow what is worse" (*Metamorphoses* 7.20–21, video meliora proboque, / deteriora sequor). And she, in turn, is following the path of Euripides's Phaedra, who says that "we know and perceive what is good; we do not do it" (*Hippolytus* 380–81, τὰ χρήστ᾽ ἐπιστάμεσθα καὶ γιγνώσκομεν, / οὐκ ἐκπονοῦμεν δ᾽).

describes being berated by a group of neo-Aristotelian pedants. Petrarch defends himself against them by challenging not whether the knowledge they profess is correct, but rather whether it has the power to make him better. He describes having learned Aristotle's meticulous and painstaking delineations of the various properties of vice and virtue but evokes a sensation of emptiness, of futility in this hard-won knowledge. "Having learned this, I know slightly more than I did before. But my mind is the same as it was; my will is the same; and I am the same."[73] The knowledge has not changed him. As though revising Medea's line about knowing what is better but following what is worse, he concludes that it is better to will the good than to know the truth.[74] For Petrarch, knowledge is only valuable to the extent that it can become moral knowledge that makes us improve, by promoting what Gur Zak calls Petrach's care of the self.[75]

The importance for the later Renaissance of the debate concerning the role of knowledge cannot be overestimated. Writing broadly about the period, Anthony Grafton describes an "interpretive schizophrenia" between the attempt, on the one hand, to make sense of a text by situating it in its time and place and, on the other hand, to make it meaningful in the present.[76] For Margaret W. Ferguson, it was this latter mode of interpretation that dominated the period: "Renaissance authors pay little attention to protecting the intentionality of individuals or texts from the dangers of subjective interpretation. The reader is not only allowed but encouraged to master any secular (literary) authority in order to serve his true 'self interest.'"[77] The goal of these readers was, she argues, to interpret the books they read in light of the needs of their own souls.

It is easy to see how this line of reasoning can become an argument for literature over other forms of discourse and knowledge. Poetry will emerge in the Renaissance as one answer to this problem of the possible impotence of knowledge (no matter how objective this knowledge may be). Drawing on ancient rhetorical theory, which aimed not only to teach people but also, as Cicero put it, to move them, poets like Sir Philip Sidney will explicitly

73. Petrarch, *Invectives*, trans. David Marsh (Cambridge, MA: I Tatti Renaissance Library, Harvard University Press, 2003), 315.

74. Ibid., 319.

75. Gur Zak, *Petrarch's Humanism and the Care of the Self* (Cambridge: Cambridge University Press, 2010). Mazzotta also emphasizes this point (*The Worlds of Petrarch*, 117ff.).

76. Anthony Grafton, "Renaissance Readers and Ancient Texts: Comments on Some Commentaries," *Renaissance Quarterly* 38, no. 4 (Winter 1985): 637.

77. Margaret W. Ferguson, *Trials of Desire: Renaissance Defenses of Poetry* (New Haven: Yale University Press, 1983), 158.

position poetry as what can not only teach people to *know* the good but also uniquely to *move* them to want to do the good. Poets, Sidney will say, "imitate both to delight and teach: and delight to move men to take that goodness in hand, which without delight they would fly as from a stranger."[78] Poetry prevails over philosophy, which aims too high for people to understand, and also over history, which aims too low to elevate them.

For Petrarch, as for Sidney and many other Renaissance poets, the study of historical objects should eventually transform the subject. If it does not, the study simply serves no purpose.

78. Philip Sidney, *An Apology for Poetry (or The Defence of Poesy)*, ed. Geoffrey Shepherd; revised and expanded for 3rd ed. by R. W. Maslen (Manchester: Manchester University Press, 2002), 87. Julius Caesar Scaliger makes a closely related case in his *Poetices* (1561).

CHAPTER THREE

Here Comes Objectivity: Spenser's 1590 *The Faerie Queene*, Book 3

For Francis Bacon, the imagination is a wayward tendency. Like original sin, it must be controlled—not by grace but by the application of technique and method. The problem with the imagination is that it creates grotesque mental amalgams by "mingling" people's internal nature with the external things they observe in the world.[1] In his 1605 *The Advancement of Learning*, Bacon compares credulous and superstitious people to the mythic Ixion, who brought forth the race of centaurs and other chimeras by accidentally copulating with a cloud: "So whosoever shall entertain high and vaporous imaginations, instead of a laborious and sober inquiry of truth, shall beget hopes and beliefs of strange and impossible shapes."[2] Bacon's highly imaginative prose may billow into its own surprising metaphors and elaborate conceits;[3] however, despite such complexities, his overt message in this early work[4] is that a new kind of learning is needed that will no longer

1. *The Works of Francis Bacon*, vol. 4, ed. James Spedding (London: Longman, 1860), 54.

2. Francis Bacon, *The Advancement of Learning*, ed. William Aldis Wright (Oxford: Clarendon Press, 1869), 123.

3. Ronald Levao cites this passage in his exploration of central paradoxes of Bacon's approach to science, such as his "polymorphous curiosity about the world and ways of knowing it that turns repeatedly into the fields it has declared off limits" (3). See Levao, "Francis Bacon and the Mobility of Science," *Representations* 40, Special Issue: Seeing Science (Autumn 1992): 1–32.

4. Caryn O'Connell argues that Bacon later reevaluated his early epistemology of detachment; see her "Bacon's Hints: The *Sylva Sylvarum*'s Intimate Science," *Studies in Philology* 113, no. 3 (Summer 2016): 634–67. On not entirely dissimilar lines, Guido Giglioni offers a reading of Bacon's late and posthumously published *Sylva Sylvarum* that emphasizes the connections between the so-called "appetites" of matter and of human beings. His reading thus shows the interconnections of subject and object, even as he acknowledges that this aspect of Bacon's late work was

entail entering into the experience of the object, but rather holding oneself apart from it. In this and other early texts, he paradoxically constructs verbally elaborate arguments against the elaborate use of words. The method he advocates is to study "*things themselves*,"[5] without any admixture of the investigator's imagination.

This emphasis on the factuality of things was of course not unprecedented, whether one thinks of nominalism in theology or the passages of realistic observation in Chaucer or some of the passages I have just been examining in Petrarch. One can trace the roots of such attention to things-as-things even further back. Take a relatively unfamiliar example: monastics at St. Victor in Paris were, in the twelfth century, already emphasizing the literal level of physical descriptions in scripture, setting under way what Beryl Smalley describes as "a scientific movement."[6] In regard to Ezekiel's temple vision, for instance, Hugh of St. Victor advised his followers not to despise the literal meaning of scripture because "what the letter tells you was done physically and visibly," and the oft-cited principle that "the letter killeth" can become, he warned, a mere "excuse for preferring our own ideas to the divine authors'."[7] Through emphasizing the literal aspects of elaborate descriptions, he wanted, Mary Carruthers writes, "to objectify and de-trope the ekphrasis, understanding it less as an instance of rhetorical *allegoria* and more as the linguistically 'transparent' description of an object."[8]

The emergence of objectivity is simply too large-scale a change to happen in a tidy linear way. The drops fall here and there, the sun still seems bright, more drops fall, and then at some unspecifiable point: it's raining. The wonky concatenation that is intellectual history proceeds, if it proceeds at all, lurchingly.

And yet, somehow, a paradigm shift was coalescing. By the sixteenth century, an emphasis on objectivity was becoming evident throughout Eu-

largely disregarded by most of those Royal Society members who claimed to be his followers. These "post-Baconian experimental philosophers reinforced the idea of the human being as the sole subject capable of knowing and desiring while demoting nature to the status of a lifeless object of dispassionate study" (150). See his "Mastering the Appetites of Matter: Francis Bacon's *Sylva Sylvarum*," in *The Body as Object and Instrument of Knowledge: Embodied Empiricism in Early Modern Science*, ed. Charles T. Wolfe and Ofer Gal (Dordrecht, Netherlands; New York: Springer, 2010), 149–67.

5. Bacon, *Works* 4:19. My italics.

6. Beryl Smalley, *The Study of the Bible in the Middle Ages* (Notre Dame: University of Notre Dame Press, 1964), 97.

7. *De Scripturis* 5.13–15; *Didascalicon* 6.4.804, quoted in Smalley, 93–94.

8. Mary Carruthers, *The Craft of Thought: Meditation, Rhetoric, and the Making of Images, 400–1200* (Cambridge: Cambridge University Press, 1998), 184.

rope in a wide variety of fields. Not just botanists and doctors but also scholars of the humanities were focusing on the *things* of the world. What was new was not, of course, an interest in the material world but, rather, a heightened concentration on things as objects of evidence. Historians began to describe the past in new ways by examining ruins, coins, fragments of old documents—what Bacon would call "the spars" of time's shipwreck.[9] In Spenser's sixteenth-century English context, the dissolution of the monasteries contributed to this interest in historical reconstruction. Having witnessed buildings and living traditions become ruins seemingly overnight, England had established by the late 1580s the Elizabethan Society of Antiquaries, with which Spenser was well familiar.[10]

As Anthony Grafton has emphasized, new questions were emerging about the relationship of book learning to the things of the world. A c.1591 engraving shows a humanist keeping his place in a book with one hand while measuring with a compass in the other hand, as though he were testing these two different realms of knowledge against each other.[11]

In such contexts, objectivity was often seen as opposed to the subjectivity associated with literary experience. In his epistle dedicatory of the *Great Instauration*, Bacon claims that his new natural and experimental history is "true and severe"—by which he means, he explains, that it is "unencumbered with literature and book-learning."[12] This new epistemological paradigm emphasized a detached relation of subjects to objects, of the kind that undergirds much of our own current scholarly practice. In regard to literary-historical scholarship, for example, Margreta de Grazia probes in a recent article our shared working understanding of anachronism, defining

9. Bacon, *Works* 4:303.

10. For recent work on Spenser's involvement with antiquarianism, see Tom Muir, "Specters of Spenser: Translating the *Antiquitez*," *Spenser Studies* 25 (2010): 327–61; and Bart van Es, *Spenser's Forms of History* (Oxford: Oxford University Press, 2002). For the history of English antiquarianism, see Joan Evans, *A History of the Society of Antiquaries* (Oxford: Oxford University Press by Charles Batey for the Society of Antiquaries, 1956), 1–32; Arthur B. Ferguson, *Clio Unbound: Perception of the Social and Cultural Past in Renaissance England* (Durham: Duke University Press, 1979), 78–125; F. J. Levy, *Tudor Historical Thought* (San Marino: Huntington Library, 1967), 124–66; Kevin Sharpe, *Sir Robert Cotton, 1586–1631: History and Politics in Early Modern England* (Oxford: Oxford University Press, 1979); Angus Vine, *In Defiance of Time: Antiquarian Writing in Early Modern England* (Oxford: Oxford University Press, 2010); C. E. Wright, "The Elizabethan Society of Antiquaries and the Formation of the Cottonian Library," in *The English Library before 1700*, ed. Francis Wormald and C. E. Wright (London: Athlone Press, 1958), 176–212.

11. See Anthony Grafton, with April Shelford and Nancy Siraisi, *New Worlds, Ancient Texts: The Power of Tradition and the Shock of Discovery* (Cambridge, MA: Harvard University Press, 1992), 78.

12. Bacon, *Works* 4:12.

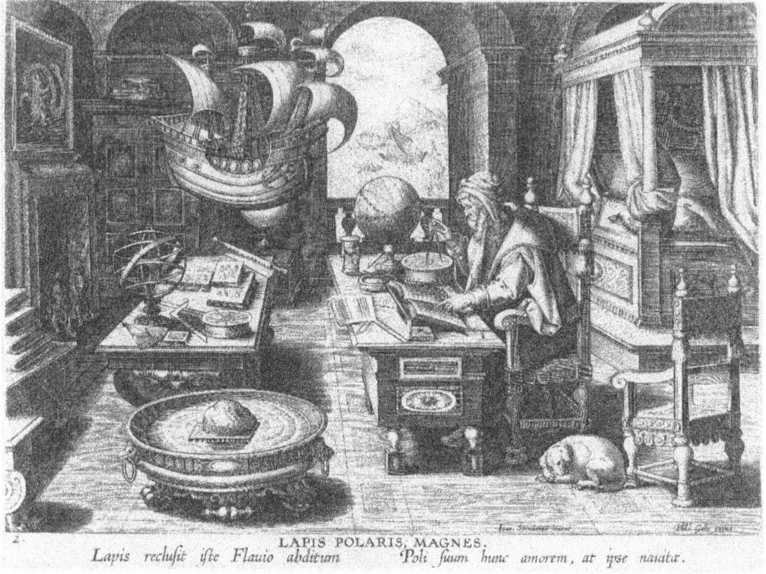

FIGURE 2. Jan Collaert, *Lapis polaris, magnes* (c. 1591). By permission of the Folger Shakespeare Library.

it as "a violation of the basic principle of epistemology: the viewing subject must remain distinct from the viewed object. When one collapses into the other, knowledge cannot take place."[13] This understanding of scholarly knowledge goes back to the sixteenth century, when learning was no longer supposed to entail immersing oneself in the object, but rather required holding oneself apart from it. The old reign of πάθει μάθος (Aeschylus's "suffering is knowledge") seemed to be ending.[14]

In this chapter, my exploration of these issues focuses on a sequence of ekphrases of art objects at the end of the 1590 edition of Edmund Spenser's *The Faerie Queene*. These ekphrases, I argue, offer insight into the historical process by which artworks began to be viewed as mere objects in the sixteenth century. In the first room of the House of Busirane, Britomart encounters a tapestry that, as the romance's longest ekphrasis, illustrates a viewer's immersive relationship to a work of art. In the second room, however, Spenser treats art differently. The art objects there are no longer ani-

13. Margreta de Grazia, "Anachronism," in *Cultural Reformations: Medieval and Renaissance in Literary History*, ed. Brian Cummings and James Simpson (Oxford: Oxford University Press, 2010), 13.

14. See Aeschylus, *Agamemnon* 11.177, 250–51.

mated by the viewer's imaginative involvement; Spenser distances his readers from what he perceives as the imagination's dangers by presenting the art as antiquarian refuse from a dead past. In so doing, he draws on concrete aspects of the material culture of the period, as well as on the larger paradigmatic shift toward scientific objective detachment with which material culture can be associated. However, at the same time as Spenser's sequence leads his reader from immersion to detachment, paralleling the larger historical development in the period, his highly imaginative poetics also resists this process. This complex conflict between immersion and detachment, far from debilitating his poetry, ultimately animates it in novel ways.

THE FIRST ROOM OF THE HOUSE OF BUSIRANE AND THE THREAT OF IMMERSIVE IMAGINATIVE EXPERIENCE

The first room of the House of Busirane raises questions about immersive imaginative experience. Spenser's elaborate tapestry in this evil house offers a world where everything is shifting around in a single, continuous, protean medium, with the effect that the line between subjects and objects blurs. The tapestries in the House of Busirane at the end of book 3 are highly eroticized, depicting the varied, often bestial forms the pagan gods adopted in order to gratify their lusts for mortals:

> Therein was writt, how often thondring *Ioue*
> Had felt the point of his hart percing dart,
> And leauing heauens kingdome, here did roue
> In straunge disguize, to slake his scalding smart;
> Now like a Ram, faire *Helle* to peruart,
> Now like a Bull, *Europa* to withdraw:
> Ah, how the fearefull Ladies tender hart
> Did liuely seeme to tremble, when she saw
> The huge seas vnder her t'obay her seruaunts law. (3.11.30)[15]

In this ekphrasis, which draws on Ovid's ekphrasis of Arachne's tapestry in the *Metamorphoses* book 6,[16] nothing preserves its own autonomy: peo-

15. All citations of Edmund Spenser's *The Faerie Queene* refer to the revised edition edited by A. C. Hamilton, Hiroshi Yamashita, Toshiyuki Suzuki, and Shohachi Fukuda (Harlow, UK: Longman, Pearson Education, 2007).

16. See John Hollander, *The Gazer's Spirit: Poems Speaking to Silent Works of Art* (Chicago: University of Chicago Press, 1995), 15ff. See also Leonard Barkan, *The Gods Made Flesh: Metamorphosis and the Pursuit of Paganism* (New Haven: Yale University Press, 1986), 1–6.

ple, things, and gods morph into and out of one another. This is a world of mutual interpenetration on many levels. The sea moves by the pulse of Jove, whom we see also metamorphosing into a ram and a bull. Fear makes Europa's heart move in a kind of correspondence with the movement of the sea, and the sea's heaving seems like both a subjective account of the disorienting experience of her terror and an objective account of what causes her terror. Spenser melds subjects with objects by creating reciprocal formal relationships between inner states of feeling and external actions of things.[17]

But at the same time, he calls into question this amorphous subject-object interplay—most obviously by setting it within the House of Busirane, a place of dark magic and destructive sexuality. The poetry of the tapestry itself is insidious, especially in the way that it blurs the boundaries between things:

> Wouen with gold and silke so close and nere,
> That the rich metall lurked priuily,
> As faining to be hidd from enuious eye;
> Yet here, and there, and euery where vnwares
> It shewd it selfe, and shone vnwillingly;
> Like to a discolourd Snake, whose hidden snares
> Through the greene gras his long bright burnisht back declares. (3.11.28)

Subjective and objective meanings fold tightly around one another. The adverbs expressing negations, "vnwares" and "vnwillingly," link the viewer's subjective experience with an imaginative version of the *material*'s subjective experience: "euery where vnwares[18] / It shewd it selfe, and shone vnwillingly." It is as if the viewer's surprise at what she sees is projected into the work, so that it seems that the work is what lacks awareness—it shines "vnwillingly"—which is also a realization of the objective fact: the work does, of course, shine unwillingly. But then this negation immediately implies the reverse, for to say that the material shines unwillingly is also, paradoxically, to suggest that this object has a will or subjectivity. Spenser's language presupposes animistic magic at the very moment that he denies it. And he implicitly questions—even demonizes—this magic's seductive

17. Michael Murrin writes that Spenser's fairyland is "the literary expression of a complex mental experience"; instead of just expressing external reality, the poem "includes both perceiver and the thing perceived." See "Spenser's Fairyland," in Murrin, *The Allegorical Epic: Essays in Its Rise and Decline* (Chicago: University of Chicago Press, 1980), 143.

18. Hamilton glosses "vnwares" as "unexpectedly" (393).

effect by, in his long sinuous last line, likening the way the gold moves through the tapestry's weave to the way a snake moves through grass.

Just as the metamorphosing gods can seduce mortals, so, too, can verisimilar art seduce its viewers. The poetry ensnares the subject in the object and obviates the distance between them. In describing Jove's transformation into an eagle and his abduction of Ganymede from Mount Ida, for example, Spenser considers the shepherds looking at the rape, who inevitably mirror the audience looking at the tapestry:

> Wondrous delight it was, there to behould,
> How the rude Shepheards after him did stare,
> Trembling through feare, least down he fallen should
> And often to him calling, to take surer hould. (3.11.34)

Through this doubling of onlookers, the text sets up a mirror by which the spectator of the tapestry finds her activity of looking represented within the tapestry. We stare, just as the shepherds stare. In so doing, we become so drawn into the picture that we seem to hear the shepherds' voices as they call to Ganymede from down below. As an artwork within an artwork, this elaborate ekphrasis reflects back on the subjectively immersive experience of Spenser's own poetics.

However, Spenser makes problematic such effects of illusionistic art at the same time as he uses them. In Spenser's lines, the similarity between the gazes of audience and shepherds reveals a difference: our ecstatic pleasure as spectators of the tapestry contrasts with the shepherds' genuine concern for the boy. They want Ganymede to hold on more tightly so that he does not fall. Implicit in this contrast between our "wondrous delight" in the artistic image and their concern for what will happen is Augustine's moral criticism of mimetic art in the *Confessions*, where he complains that it encourages us hedonistically to enjoy the spectacle of other people's suffering rather than to do anything about it.[19] In Spenser's critical rendering of this tapestry, boys and girls are raped, yet we are enraptured.[20]

19. In book 3 of the *Confessions*, trans. R. S. Pine-Coffin (London: Penguin, 1961), 56, Augustine describes the solipsism entailed in an Aristotelian cathartic response to the theater: "But what sort of pity can we really feel for an imaginary scene on the stage? The audience is not called upon to offer help but only to feel sorrow, and the more they are pained the more they applaud the author." Augustine's criticism does not, however, indicate his rejection of all pagan art: in *On Christian Teaching*, he offers strategies for the moral reading of pagan literature, the "spoil of the Egyptians."

20. Page duBois, *History, Rhetorical Description and the Epic: From Homer to Spenser* (Cambridge: D. S. Brewer, 1982), 85.

As spectators of this aesthetically animated ("liuely") tapestry, we are drawn into its moral corruption—and, in being so drawn, our faculties of judgment are suspended. The ekphrasis concludes: "So liuely and so like, that liuing sence it fayld" (3.11.46).[21] The object's apparent aliveness has been mistaken for the viewer's real aliveness, and her powers are thereby undermined. The viewing subject seems to have no distance from the illusory object—but, as Bacon would warn his readers against doing, mingles dangerously with it, forfeiting any individual agency.

Britomart herself seems not to exist for this part of the poem; the experience of looking is expressed in an impersonal form that denies the looker any specific identity—"Wondrous delight *it was,* there to behould . . ."—as if Britomart has forgotten herself and disappeared into the world of the tapestry's images.[22] Spenser refers to Britomart again only later in the scene, in the description of Cupid's statue, in front of which she appears in an altered condition without self-possession:

> That wondrous sight faire *Britomart* amazd,
> Ne seeing could her wonder satisfie,
> But euermore and more vpon it gazd,
> The whiles the passing brightnes her fraile sences dazd. (3.11.49)

In the first line quoted above, the grammatical subject is the "wondrous sight," which acts on Britomart. In the second line, the agent of action becomes "seeing," and, oddly enough, it is this seeing that is doing the gazing in the third line. Britomart's own agency has been peculiarly circumvented.[23]

Spenser's critical exploration of fused subjects and objects evokes what Ernst Cassirer once called, in paradigmatic terms, "the subject-object problem" of Renaissance thought. Students of the Renaissance will recall that Cassirer described how, for European thinkers of the fifteenth and sixteenth centuries, the world began to take on a "strong, strictly 'objective' character" evident in a newly emergent methodology of empirical investigation.[24] This methodology developed among European intellectuals work-

21. As Hamilton notes, "fayld" means "deceived; caused to fail" (396).

22. My italics. Earlier passages of the poem suggest that these images represent a version (a very dark version) of Britomart's own erotic desires. For example, likening the sea's violent tempests to her own, she says: "At length allay, and stint thy stormy stryfe, / Which in thy troubled bowels raignes, and rageth ryfe" (3.4.8).

23. Paul J. Alpers associates Britomart's seeming disappearance with the reader's intensified involvement in this scene. See his *The Poetry of "The Faerie Queene"* (Princeton: Princeton University Press, 1967), 15–16.

24. Ernst Cassirer, *The Individual and the Cosmos in Renaissance Philosophy*, trans. Mario Domandi (Chicago: University of Chicago Press, 2010), 123–91.

ing in a wide variety of fields (including, perhaps surprisingly, the study of magic[25]). In regard to Spenser's treatment of art in the House of Busirane, important work has been done focusing mostly on Protestant anxieties about idolatry;[26] I will concentrate instead on the impact of objectivity on Spenser's aesthetics.

The deceptiveness of these tapestries specifically concerns their relation to their own expensive materiality as objects. Although the costly "gold and silke" wish, or pretend to wish, not to be seen—"As faining to be hidd from enuious eye" (3.11.28)—Spenser exposes this apparent indifference to costliness as one of the tapestry's almost coquettish techniques of seduction. Indeed, tapestries made with gold-wrapped silk were, in this period, specifically associated with the display of wealth—so expensive that hardly anyone but royalty could own them in any number.[27] Edward Hall, who witnessed Henry VIII's displays, writes of the "riche and marveilous clothes of Arras wroughte of golde and silke, compassed of many auncient stories, with which . . . every wall and chamber were hanged, and all wyndowes so richely covered, that it passed all other sightes before seen."[28] The moral message of some tapestries' images, such as of the one depicting the sin of avarice in the series known as the *Seven Deadly Sins*, does not appear to have been as compelling as the expense of the object. Hall relates in copious detail the extravagant decorations accompanying one masque in which it was debated whether love or riches is better. The conclusion that both are good, at least for a prince, may have been reinforced by the fact that the "hanginges and all other thinges" were left standing for three or four days so that "al honest persones might see and beholde the houses and riches, and thether came a great nombre of people, to see and behold the riches and costely devices."[29] Although such tapestries were praised for

25. For example, Tommaso Campanella's *De sensu rerum et magia* was a major work on natural philosophy that concluded with a treatise on magic; ibid., 54.

26. See Ernest B. Gilman, *Iconoclasm and Poetry in the English Reformation: Down Went Dagon* (Chicago: University of Chicago Press, 1986), 61–83; Linda Gregerson, *The Reformation of the Subject: Spenser, Milton, and the English Protestant Epic* (Cambridge: Cambridge University Press, 1995); Kenneth Gross, *Spenserian Poetics: Idolatry, Iconoclasm, and Magic* (Ithaca: Cornell University Press, 1985); John N. King, *Spenser's Poetry and the Reformation Tradition* (Princeton: Princeton University Press, 1990); James A. Knapp, *Image Ethics in Shakespeare and Spenser* (New York: Palgrave Macmillan, 2011).

27. Tapestries made with gold and silk threads were approximately fifty times more expensive than those made with coarse wool. Thomas P. Campbell, *Henry VIII and the Art of Majesty: Tapestries at the Tudor Court* (New Haven: Yale University Press, 2007), 94.

28. Edward Hall, *The Triumphant Reigne of Kyng Henry the VIII* (London: T. C. & E. C. Jack, 1904), 1:191.

29. Ibid. 2:88.

their verisimilitude,[30] Spenser suggests that the illusion of life-likeness does not really make anyone forget the expense of the material object. In contrast to Angelo Poliziano, who, in a closely related Ovidian ekphrasis, celebrates the power of illusionist art to seem alive or real,[31] Spenser is a more anxious guest in the house of the imagination, and can be heard pacing back and forth as he employs its image-making capacities at the same time as he criticizes them.

TRODDEN IN DUST: GROTESQUES AND THINGS IN THE SECOND ROOM

In the second room, art has suddenly become less vivid. The "passing brightnes" (3.11.49) that dazzled Britomart's frail senses in the first room has, for the most part, passed. The second room is as fair as the first—in fact, all overlaid with gold, it is "much fayrer" (3.11.51)—but the objects seem to have receded into the status of artifacts. The reader is given, instead of an immersive experience, only brief allusions to the subject matter of the paintings and to the types of old weapons on the walls. This new sense of distance is like what Aby Warburg describes as the "mental space" that logical or scientific thought posits between internal and external worlds.[32] Subjects no longer cavort with objects in a dangerous and unlawful realm of imaginative interplay but stand apart from them and observe them. The price, though, for this new detachment is that art threatens to become a dusty artifact—a mere *thing* from a dead past.

The second room's artworks do not seem animated, the way the first room's tapestry did. Spenser has shifted into a mode of objectifying detachment:

> Much fayrer, then the former, was that roome,
> And richlier by many partes arayd:
> For not with arras made in painefull loome,

30. Campbell, *Henry VIII and the Art of Majesty*, 145.

31. In the *Stanze*, Poliziano describes without ambivalence the illusionistic images of metamorphosis that decorate the golden palace of Venus: "You would call the foam real, the sea real, real the conch shell and real the blowing wind" (1.100). Poliziano explains that this lifelike effect results from the viewers' imaginative involvement in what they see: "Whatever the art in itself does not contain, the mind, imagining, clearly understands" (1.119). *The "Stanze" of Angelo Poliziano*, trans. David Quint (University Park: Pennsylvania State University Press, 1993), 51, 61. I discuss these lines in more detail in chapter 5.

32. Aby Warburg, *The Renewal of Pagan Antiquity: Contributions to the Cultural History of the European Renaissance*, trans. David Britt (Los Angeles: Getty Research Institute for the History of Art and the Humanities, 1999), 599.

But with pure gold it all was ouerlayd,
Wrought with wilde Antickes, which their follies playd,
In the rich metall, as they liuing were:
A thousand monstrous formes therein were made,
Such as false loue doth oft vpon him weare,
For loue in thousand monstrous formes doth oft appeare.

And all about, the glistring walles were hong
With warlike spoiles, and with victorious prayes,
Of mightie Conquerours and Captaines strong,
Which were whilome captiued in their dayes,
To cruell loue, and wrought their owne decayes:
Their swerds and speres were broke, and hauberques rent
And their proud girlonds of tryumphant bayes,
Troden in dust with fury insolent,
To shew the victors might and mercilesse intent.

The warlike Mayd beholding earnestly
The goodly ordinaunce of this rich Place,
Did greatly wonder, ne could satisfy
Her greedy eyes with gazing a long space,
But more she meruaild that no footings trace,
Nor wight appear'd, but wastefull emptinesse,
And solemne silence ouer all that place:
Straunge thing it seem'd, that none was to possesse
So rich purueyaunce, ne them keepe with carefulnesse. (3.11.51–53)

The actual description of the artwork and objects is immediately subordinated to the overall richness of the room—the word "rich" is used four times in the space of two stanzas (stanzas 51 and 53). And the space for whatever Ovidian amorphous mingling there may be is shut down by being quickly and neatly allegorized: "A thousand monstrous formes therein were made, / Such as false loue doth oft vpon him weare, / For loue in thousand monstrous formes doth oft appeare." None of these thousand forms is named; in fact, they are kept sealed in Spenser's self-enclosed, chiastic lines (thousand monstrous forms : love :: love : thousand monstrous forms). These lines might remind the reader of the "thousand shapes" in which Cupid disguises himself (3.6.11), or the "thousand thoughts" that Britomart has of her future lover (3.4.5). Yet Spenser leaves entirely undeveloped these connections, which could provide the ground for the subject's involvement in the object; in doing so, the lines seem to close down the possibility of that entwinement, rather than actualize it in any way.

I noted earlier that Britomart's agency in looking at the things in the first room was peculiarly eclipsed: Spenser constructed the lines so that the wondrous sight acted on her. However, here in the second room, objects no longer seem like subjects, and subjects no longer like objects. No less fascinated by what she sees, Britomart is the active grammatical subject who looks at objects, "beholding [them] earnestly" (3.11.53).[33]

The paintings in the second room seem more like material objects partly because Spenser has made them continuous, in the second stanza quoted above, with the "warlike spoiles" displayed on the same wall—a possible reference to the Roman practice of depositing spoils in the Temple of Jupiter.[34] In Leonard Barkan's language, spoils are "alienated" from their cultural context,[35] quite literally stripped (*spolium* originally referred to skin stripped from an animal). Barkan shows that Roman collections of spoils, both as displayed at the time in triumphal processions and as then found in the Renaissance represented on monuments, often appeared randomly heaped and torn from context.[36] In the third painting (figure 3) of his late-

33. Compare the sequence of ekphrases of pavement designs in Dante's *Purgatorio* canto 11. Dante begins the ekphrases of the first four images by saying "I saw" (vedea); the next four by exclaiming to the represented figures, "O . . . !"; the last four by writing "It showed . . ." (mostrava); and then finally by returning to "I saw" again in the last ekphrasis. John Hollander (*The Gazer's Spirit,* 12) argues that the Dantean progression in this scene is toward objectivity, but the case may be the reverse. Dante, unlike Spenser, is moving his readers toward a state of increasing absorption by making his poetic persona disappear into the images. After all, Dante interrupts the sequence by having Virgil admonish him, "There is no more time to go thus absorbed" (sospeso) (11.78). Dante Alighieri, *The Divine Comedy: Purgatorio,* trans. John D. Sinclair (New York: Oxford University Press, 1939).

34. Livy 40.51. In medieval literature, broken bows can be found on the wall of the Temple of Venus in Chaucer's *Parliament of Fowls,* ll. 281–4.

35. Leonard Barkan, *Unearthing the Past: Archaeology and Aesthetics in the Making of Renaissance Culture* (New Haven: Yale University Press, 1999), 129.

36. Ibid., 130. Barkan illustrates his point by quoting Josephus, who describes the Romans' spoliation of Jerusalem after the destruction of the Second Temple (an event well-known in the Renaissance, both from Josephus's text and from the often-reproduced image carved into the Arch of Titus in the Roman Forum): "The rest of the spoils were borne along in random heaps. The most interesting of all were the spoils seized from the temple of Jerusalem: a gold table weighing many talents, and a lampstand, also made of gold" (7.5.148). But in this example, the decontextualization goes even further, for this "lampstand" (λυχνία) is actually the Temple's seven-branched menorah. The complete quotation continues: "[The lampstand] was made in a form different from that which we usually employ. For there was a central shaft fastened to the base; then spandrels extended from this in an arrangement which rather resembled the shape of a trident, and on the end of each of these spandrels a lamp was forged. There were seven of these, emphasizing the honor accorded to the number seven among the Jews." Josephus specifically records that this gold "lampstand" used to have a different meaning for the conquered people: in explaining what this meaning used to be, he cannot but translate it into terms comprehensible to his own conquerors. Thus,

fifteenth-century series *The Triumphs of Caesar*,[37] for example, Andrea Mantegna visually emphasizes how a triumph jumbles spoils together. He shows a pile of armor and gold bullion, mixing together things of different scales and straining our ability to understand exactly what we're seeing. It takes a moment to figure out whether, for example, that tiny gold figure near the frame's right edge is a man in the distance or part of a decorative lid. The point is that these objects, in being plundered, are deprived of their culturally accrued meaning. Such spoil is now understood in terms of its material value as gold. What makes an artwork have life is that we project into it; these projections are personal and social. In contrast, when things are cut off from the culture that produced them and gave them meaning, they are dead.

Conquering involves desecrating a culture's things—which means, in a sense, making things of its things, as well as of its people. In this context, Barkan's explanation is especially helpful that the term *spolia* was used not only in the ancient Roman context, but also commonly in the Middle Ages and Renaissance to describe pagan art used as material for Christian buildings whenever marble was in high demand.[38] In Spenser's England, the dissolution of the monasteries produced a new experience of spoliation, comparable to that described in the pages of Livy and Josephus. Keith Thomas writes vividly of the Reformation's impact on the lives of ordinary people: "Altar-stones were turned into paving stones, bridges, fireplaces, or even kitchen sinks. Dean Whittingham of Durham used two ex-holy-water stoups for salting beef and fish in his kitchen, and his wife burned St Cuthbert's banner."[39] At the same time as this disturbing experience of sudden cultural desacralization galvanized a desire on a new scale for antiquarian conservation,[40] this experience also, in Margaret Aston's words, "reached out beyond the work of antiquarians and historical researchers into more indefinable areas of literary consciousness."[41]

Josephus emphasizes the menorah's value in gold, and describes its shape as a trident (τριαίνης), the same word typically used for Poseidon's pronged weapon. I am quoting from J. J. Pollitt, *The Art of Rome, c. 753 B.C.–337 A.D.: Sources and Documents* (Englewood Cliffs, NJ: Prentice-Hall, 1966), 159. A reproduction of this famous image from the Arch of Titus can be found online: http://commons.wikimedia.org/wiki/File:Arch_of_Titus_Menorah_22.jpg.

37. For a fuller exploration of the first painting of this series, see the introduction (chapter 1).

38. Barkan, *Unearthing the Past*, 132.

39. Keith Thomas, *Religion and the Decline of Magic: Studies in Popular Beliefs in Sixteenth- and Seventeenth-Century England* (New York: Charles Scribner's Sons, 1971), 75.

40. Margaret Aston, "English Ruins and English History: The Dissolution and the Sense of the Past," *Journal of the Warburg and Courtauld Institutes* 36 (1973): 231–55; Ferguson, *Clio Unbound*, 84.

41. Aston, "English Ruins and English History," 254.

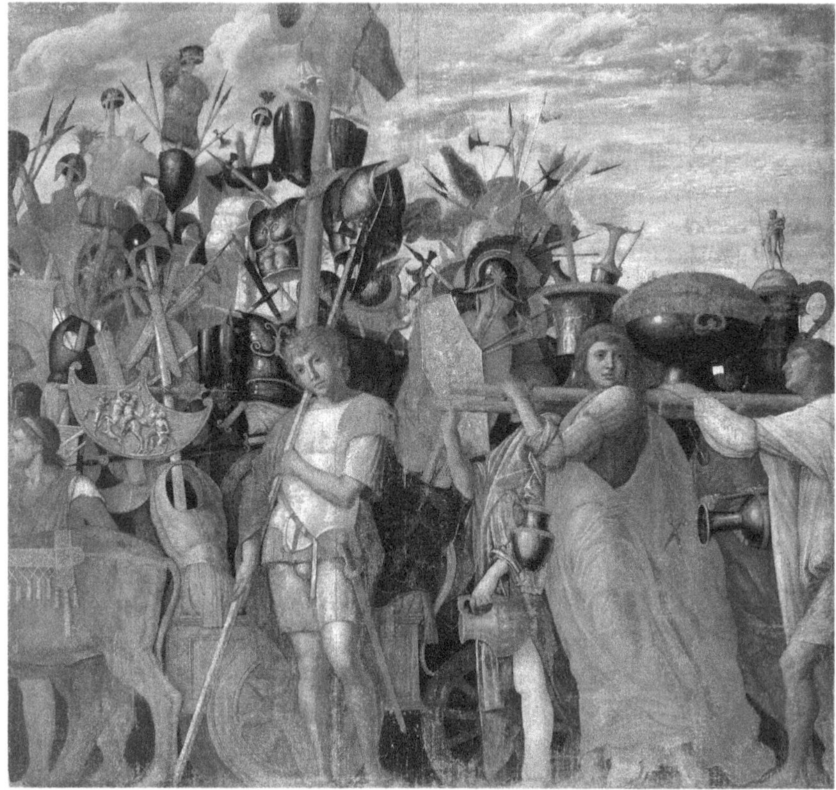

FIGURE 3. Andrea Mantegna, *The Triumphs of Caesar, III: The Bearers of Trophies and Bullion* (c. 1484–92). Hampton Court Palace. Royal Collection Trust © Her Majesty Queen Elizabeth II, 2016 / Bridgeman Images.

For Britomart, what's especially mysterious is the fact that the room seems to have been abandoned. Spenser emphasizes the place's "solemne silence," its "wastefull emptinesse," and the absence of any "footings trace." The room seems like an archaeological site requiring decipherment: the weapons are from the past; their original users are nameless; the material's value is impressive; no one is around; things are dusty; it is not clear who owns the place.

If this second room seems like an archaeological site, that is because it is based, at least partly, on an archaeological site, the Domus Aurea, Nero's Golden House, rediscovered in the late fifteenth century.[42] Barkan notes

42. It is now known that these grottos were part of Nero's palace, but there was significant confusion about this point in the sixteenth century. Many people, including Giorgio Vasari (see

this connection—and remarks on the pun: the "wilde Antickes" referred to in stanza 51 ("Wrought with wilde Antickes, which their follies playd, / In the rich metall, as they liuing were") are antic figures with a specifically antique origin: "a quite particular set of antique antics," Barkan writes.[43] Before Nero's palace was completely unearthed, a generation of painters had descended on ropes to study by candlelight these painted grotesques (the word *grotesque* derives from the erroneous belief that these buried rooms were grottos), which were the best-preserved ancient paintings yet found.[44]

In order to understand Spenser's grotesques in connection with the historical emergence of objectivity, we need to try to recover their culturally accrued meaning—and, in this way, to reverse their spoliation. Following the discovery of the Domus Aurea at the end of the fifteenth century, grotesques started to generate a great deal of excitement. In the early sixteenth century, Raphael and his circle decorated the Vatican's loggia with colorful, flowing, fanciful grotesques. The influence of the grotesques increased outside Italy after the sack of Rome in 1527, an event that dispersed Raphael's pupils into the "diaspora" of Europe.[45] In England, some walls of Henry

---

especially his life of Giovanni da Udine), incorrectly believed that the buried rooms containing the grotesques were part of the Baths of Titus. As Nicole Dacos explains, the rooms presented an archaeological puzzle partly because the Domus Aurea, which became almost immediately a symbol of imperial decadence (as is obvious in Suetonius's and Tacitus's accounts of the villa), was abandoned so soon after Nero's death and used as the foundation for the Baths of Trajan. The erroneous identification of the grotesques as part of the Baths of Titus was widespread and not generally corrected until the end of the seventeenth century. Yet evidence shows that at least some people in the sixteenth century did have the correct information. Most convincingly, a 1538 watercolor by the Portuguese artist Francisco de Holanda depicts the Domus Aurea's so-called Volta Dorata with the following inscription in the margin: "Domus aureae Neronis." The image with the full inscription can be found in Elías Tormo y Monzó, *Os desenhos das antigualhas que vio Francisco d'Ollanda, pintor portugués, 1539–1540* (Madrid: Ministerio de Asuntos Exteriores, 1940), 37–38. I am grateful to Nicole Dacos for kindly answering my questions about this matter, and I mourn the passing of this generous scholar. As is the case with most accounts of Renaissance grotesques, my discussion of these images depends heavily on her seminal *La découverte de la Domus Aurea et la formation des grotesques à la Renaissance* (London: Warburg Institute; Leiden: E. J. Brill, 1969).

43. Leonard Barkan, *The Gods Made Flesh*, 234.

44. Francis Ames-Lewis, *The Intellectual Life of the Early Renaissance Artist* (New Haven: Yale University Press, 2000), 128–29. David Evett reviews the Renaissance history of the grotesque and discusses the grotesque's possible importance for the "esthetic of *The Faerie Queene* as a whole" (181). In this context, he mentions "the poem's unresolved concern with the proper relationship between nature and art, its fascination with the ambiguities of visual experience, and its deep and incessant dualism" (204). His ultimate focus is on the structure of the poem, which, he says, could have evolved from the grotesques as a mnemonic system that disposes vivid images around an edifice (205). See his "Mammon's Grotto: Sixteenth-Century Visual Grotesquerie and Some Features of Spenser's *Faerie Queene*," *English Literary Renaissance* 12, no. 2 (Spring 1982): 180–209.

45. Nicole Dacos, *The Loggia of Raphael: A Vatican Art Treasure*, trans. Josephine Bacon (New York: Abbeville Press, 2008), 10.

VIII's Nonsuch Palace seem to have been decorated with grotesques by Italian artists,[46] and, most importantly, grotesques were integral to many designs of Henry VIII's massive tapestry collection. In 1542, the king acquired a duplicate set of the series of tapestries called *Grotesques of Leo X*, inspired by the Domus Aurea and based on Raphael-school cartoons probably by Giovanni da Udine.[47] And Italy was not the only source. The pseudo-Rabelaisian *Les songes drolatiques de Pantagruel* (Paris, 1565), with its pages filled with woodcuts of wonderfully bizarre grotesque figures, was also in circulation. Before Inigo Jones used these figures as the basis for costuming the antimasque of the 1640 production of Sir William Davenant's *Salmacida Spolia*,[48] they had appeared in 1581 ceiling decorations in Prestongrange in East Lothian.[49] Also important was Netherlandish work: Jacob Floris's grotesque cartouches were starting to make their way into England;[50] and Jan Vredeman de Vries's architectural treatises of the 1560s and '70s, with prints showing grotesque architectural details, were well-known.[51]

A critical conversation about the grotesques became especially intense during the forty years immediately preceding the first edition of *The Faerie Queene*.[52] It is hard, if not impossible, to know exactly how closely Spenser

46. Ibid., 308. Nonsuch was destroyed in the late seventeenth century, but some panels with grotesques that are believed to be from the palace are preserved in Loseley Park, Surrey. These are reproduced in Edward Croft-Murray, *Decorative Painting in England, 1537–1837*, vol. 1 (London: Country Life, 1962), figs. 17–20. It is not known who painted these panels, but one likely candidate is Toto del Nunziata, who was working in the English court and who was, according to Vasari, responsible for Henry VIII's "principale palazzo"—a likely reference to Nonsuch, Henry's last major building project, as Croft-Murray notes (18). Dacos concurs with Croft-Murray but adds that the panels are also related to popular engravings by Agostino Veneziano, which were based on the Raphael-school grotesques in the Loggia (*The Loggia of Raphael*, 313).

47. These tapestries, which are also referred to as the *Triumphs of the Gods*, each depict a god in a fanciful architectural setting, "obviously inspired by those in the Domus Aurea," writes Thomas P. Campbell, *Tapestry in the Renaissance: Art and Magnificence* (New Haven: Yale University Press, 2002), 228. Leo X's original series is now lost, but from Henry's seven-piece set two pieces survive at Hampton Court Palace, as well as three pieces from a later weaving in the Mobilier National in Paris (225–29).

48. See Anne Lake Prescott, "The Stuart Masque and Pantagruel's Dreams," *ELH* 51, no. 3 (Autumn 1984): 407–30. Prescott finds suggestions of the *Songes*'s influence on masques as early as Ben Jonson's 1617 *Vision of Delight*.

49. M. R. Apted and W. Norman Robertson, "Four 'Drollities' from the Painted Ceiling Formerly at Prestongrange, East Lothian," *Proceedings of the Society of Antiquaries of Scotland* 106 (1974–75): 158–60.

50. Anthony Wells-Cole, *Art and Decoration in Elizabethan and Jacobean England: The Influence of Continental Prints, 1558–1625* (New Haven and London: Yale University Press, 1997), 52.

51. L. E. Semler, "Breaking the Ice to Invention: Henry Peacham's *The Art of Drawing* (1606)," *Sixteenth Century Journal* 35, no. 3 (Fall 2004): 744–45.

52. André Chastel, "Sens et non-sens à la Renaissance. La question des chimères," *Archivio di filosofia* (1980): 188.

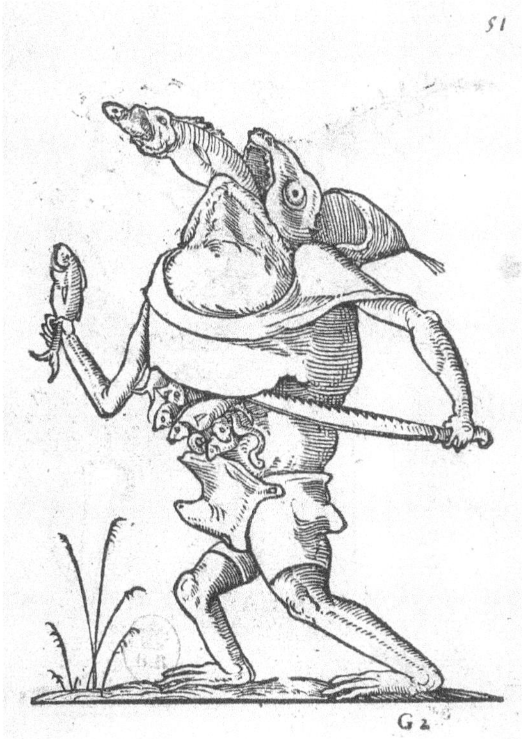

FIGURE 4. From *Les songes drolatiques de Pantagruel, où sont contenues plusieurs figures de l'invention de maistre François Rabelais, et dernière oeuvre d'iceluy, pour la récréation des bons esprits* (Paris, 1565). Bibliothèque nationale de France.

followed this debate, but his usage of the grotesques, as we'll see, draws on this intellectual history.

Grotesques were intimately linked with the imagination. David Summers has called them fantasy's "symbol,"[53] and Dacos says that grotesques and the imagination were in some contexts "almost synonymous."[54] Even outside artistic circles, it is not unusual to find Renaissance depictions of the imagination that sound like descriptions of grotesques. For example, in his *De anima et vita* of 1538, Juan Luis Vives describes the imagination as "prodigiously unrestrained and free; it can form, reform, combine, link

53. David Summers, *Michelangelo and the Language of Art* (Princeton: Princeton University Press, 1981), 139.

54. Dacos, *La découverte de la Domus Aurea*, vii.

together and separate; it can blend together the most distant objects or keep apart the most intimately connected objects."[55] In England, Timothy Bright writes in his 1586 *A Treatise of Melancholy* that the imagination, swayed by melancholy, "compoundeth, and forgeth disguised shapes."[56] Especially important is the composite nature of the imagination's means of production, i.e., it makes new forms by putting together parts of things and animals found in the world.

These associations were equally strong among those who revived the use of the grotesques as among those who were adamantly *against* their use: Gregorio Comanini defines the grotesque as an "image of an imaginary thing, something that existed only in the mind," which, following 1 Corinthians 8:4, he equates with "an idol [idolo], nothing that exists in this world."[57] But the rejection of the grotesques on such a basis also predates Christianity. Comanini is drawing on the ancient authority of Vitruvius, who questions and explicitly condemns grotesques in book 7 of *De architectura* for their lack of fidelity to the real:

> How is it possible for a reed to support a roof, or a candelabrum to bear a house with the ornaments on its roof, or a small and pliant stalk to carry a sitting figure; or, that half-figures and flowers at the same time should spring out of roots and stalks? And yet the public, so far from discouraging these falsehoods, are delighted with them, not for a moment considering whether such things could exist.[58]

As the only surviving ancient critical manual on architecture and sculpture, such a condemnation held enormous authority in the Renaissance. Further, Vitruvius's position seemed to be supported by the negative reference to a grotesque in the opening of Horace's so-called *Ars poetica*, which proved no less programmatic for Renaissance readers.[59]

In this way, grotesques became an arena for a long-standing argument

55. Juan Luis Vives, *De anima et vita*, ed. Mario Sancipriano (Torino: Bottega d'Erasmo, 1959), 32–33, quoted in Summers, *Michelangelo and the Language of Art*, 113.

56. Quoted in William Rossky, "Imagination in the English Renaissance: Psychology and Poetic," *Studies in the Renaissance* 5 (1958): 57.

57. See Gregorio Comanini, *The Figino; or, On the Purpose of Painting: Art Theory in the Late Renaissance*, ed. and trans. Ann Doyle-Anderson and Giancarlo Maiorino (Toronto: University of Toronto Press, 2001), 16; Summers, *Michelangelo and the Language of Art*, 140.

58. Vitruvius 7.5.4. I am quoting the text provided in William James Audsley and George Ashdown Audsley, *Popular Dictionary of Architecture and the Allied Arts*, vol. 2 (New York: G. P. Putnam's Sons, 1881), 6.

59. *De arte poetica* 1–5; Horace, *Satires. Epistles. Ars poetica*, trans. H. Rushton Fairclough (Cambridge, MA: Loeb Classical Library, 1929), 450.

about the imaginative basis of art. Not only do grotesques blur together external things; they also blur together external worlds with internal ones. Renaissance writers stressed the grotesques' unsettlingly ambiguous relationship with dream. Anton Francesco Doni determined in a 1549 dialogue on art that they exist only "in the chaos of my mind."[60] And Daniele Barbaro first compared them to a person's dreams—and then, as though to position them even further from reality, to the painting's dreams:

> They are like animals which carry Time, columns of straws, claws of monsters, deformities of natures, mixtures of varied species: Certainly, as the Fantasy in the dream represents to us confusedly the images of things and often puts together diverse natures, things that, we could say, would make the Grotesques, which without doubt we could name "the dreams of the painting."[61]

While expressing disapproval of grotesques, Barbaro's language seems, almost despite itself, to toy with their fecundity and strangeness; his line mimetically does for a moment what the grotesques do: through the paratactic string of its first five phrases, the sentence engenders a line of fantasy-beings that follow each other according to no order, or according only to the anarchic creative order of more on more.

Grotesques represent what logic pushes to the margins. Like the gigantomachia that decorates the outer wall of the Pergamon Altar, the grotesques serve as the counter-principle to the rationality celebrated at the center. For certain Renaissance artists, they were a fecund amalgamation, "an intermediate world," as Leo Spitzer describes Rabelais's poetics, "between reality and irreality, between the nowhere that frightens and the 'here' that reassures."[62] So unstable were these figures that Renaissance thinkers seemed to hesitate even to determine a name for them: some called them *chimere*, *grottesche*, or *mostri*.[63] Spenser, perhaps emphasizing their historicity, called them *Antickes*—from *antico grottesco*.[64]

60. Anton Francesco Doni, *Disegno* (Venice, 1549), 3:20; see Paola Barocchi, ed., *Scritti d'arte del cinquecento*, vol. 1 (Milan and Naples: R. Ricciardi, 1971), 585; Chastel, "Sens et non-sens à la Renaissance," 185.

61. "Come sono animali, che portano Tempi, colonne di cannuccie, artigli di mostri, difformita di nature, misti di varie specie: Certo si come la Fantasia nel sogno ci rappresenta confusamente le imagini delle cose, e spesso pone insieme nature diverse, cosi potremo dire, che facciano le Grottesche, le quali senza dubbio potemo nominare sogni della pittura." Cited in Dacos, *La découverte de la Domus Aurea*, 123–24. My translation from the Italian. I am grateful to Susan Tombel for her correction.

62. Leo Spitzer, *Linguistics and Literary History: Essays in Stylistics* (Princeton: Princeton University Press, 1948), 16–17.

63. Chastel, "Sens et non-sens à la Renaissance," 183–89.

64. In *Henry VIII*, Edward Hall uses the same word when describing grotesques in Henry

HISTORICIZING THE IMAGINATION

If, for sixteenth-century Renaissance artists and writers, grotesque figures represent the imagination's ambiguous relation with the world, so, too, do they for Spenser—but, for him, with a distinctly negative valence. In the House of Alma, there is a room where sits, among the buzzing flies, Phantastes, an unappealing character who is described as beetle-browed, beady-eyed, melancholy, mad, and foolish. As David Evett has pointed out, Phantastes's room is decorated with grotesques,[65] or, at the very least, is heavily associated with grotesques:

> His chamber was dispainted all with in,
> With sondry colours, in the which were writ
> Infinite shapes of thinges dispersed thin;
> Some such as in the world were neuer yit,
> Ne can deuized be of mortall wit;
> Some daily seene, and knowen by their names,
> Such as in idle fantasies doe flit:
> Infernall Hags, *Centaurs*, feendes, *Hippodames*,
> Apes, Lyons, Aegles, Owles, fooles, louers, children, Dames. (2.9.50)

In this chamber of fantasy, Spenser distinguishes between two categories of images. Some images are of things which have never existed and cannot by a mortal mind be described or possibly contrived (in *The Faerie Queene*, the word *deuized* carries both meanings). And there are some images that are regularly seen since they flit as "idle fantasies" and have names. The list that follows is a confusing jumble that mixes the unreal with the real, and, as Hamilton suggests, the absence of conjunctions creates the impression, at least upon first reading, that all the figures are connected with one another. The Lyons almost combine with the Aegles, he says, to make a griffin. With *Hippodames*, Spenser even offers his own version of the mixed objects he describes. Hamilton suggests that it is a variant spelling of *hippopotamus*, sometimes spelled *hippotame*; however, I suspect that, while punning on *hippotame*, Spenser is actually creating a female version of the centaur

VIII's tapestries and other palace decorations. Henry Peacham's *The Art of Drawing* (London, 1606) also employs versions of this word to mean "an vnnaturall or vnorderly composition for delight sake, of men, beasts, birds, fishes, flowers, &c without (as wee say) Rime or reason, for the greater variety you shew in your inuention, the more you please . . . you cannot bee too fantastical" (36).

65. See Evett, "Mammon's Grotto," 200.

mentioned just before (from the Greek *hippos* = horse + *dames*). Like Barbaro, Spenser seems to be creating in this passage his own paratactic line of strange beings, some that seem monstrous in and of themselves, and others that become monstrous when linked together without reason in his list.

Spenser's portrait of Phantastes may offer an oblique glimpse of himself as the poet. In *The Defense of Poesy*, Sir Philip Sidney had portrayed poets in similar terms, depicting them "making things either better than Nature bringeth forth, or, quite anew, forms such as never were in Nature, as the Heroes, Demigods, Cyclops, Chimeras, Furies, and such like."[66] However, the inventiveness that Sidney celebrated Spenser endows with an ambiguous if not downright negative quality. In this respect, Spenser's use of grotesques seems closer to Michel de Montaigne's description of his own tortured mental fecundity. Retiring to his family estate in the early 1570s, Montaigne finds that his mind "gives birth to so many chimeras and fantastic monsters, one on top of another, without order and without aim" (m'enfante tant de chimeres et monstres fantasques les uns sur les autres, sans ordre et sans propos) that he decides to record in writing this clambering riotous nothingness, "hoping in time to make my mind ashamed of itself" (esperant avec le temps luy en faire honte à luy mesmes).[67]

Like Montaigne, who compares his essays to grotesques,[68] Spenser associates the literary imagination with grotesque paintings. But, in Spenser's case, the paintings on the walls of Phantastes's chamber are of a particular kind: Spenser explicitly mentions the "sondry colours" and the "Infinite shapes of thinges dispersed thin." These qualities may refer specifically to the vibrant, flowing paintings found in the Domus Aurea. Previous to this discovery, Renaissance artists had to rely largely on recovered sculptures for their understanding of ancient art. Painterly qualities of color and brush handling were matters for speculation, tantalizingly alluded to in incomplete and sometimes contradictory ancient verbal descriptions of the work of such "immortal" painters as Apelles, of whom nothing survives.[69] In this situa-

66. Philip Sidney, *An Apology for Poetry (or The Defence of Poesy)*, ed. Geoffrey Shepherd; revised and expanded for 3rd ed. by R. W. Maslen (Manchester: Manchester University Press, 2002), 85.

67. Michel de Montaigne, *Essais*, vol. 1 (Paris: Garnier-Flammarion, 1969), 70.

68. Ibid., 231.

69. For example, Pliny wrote in regard to color that Apelles used only four pigments (*Naturalis historia* 35.32.50), but Cicero suggested that Apelles was more advanced than those who used only four colors (*Brutus* 70). In regard to paint handling, Pliny attributed the ineffable charm of Apelles's work to the fact that he "knew when to take his hand away from a picture" (*Naturalis historia* 35.36.80).

tion, it is hard to overestimate the importance of the Domus Aurea, as Hetty Joyce explains: "The discovery of ancient relics was of course no novelty. But in place of the stained, abraded, monochrome surfaces of old marbles, artists could see here [in the Domus Aurea] the fresh, vivid, and abundant revelation of the ancient artistic consciousness. Here, at last, was ancient Rome *in color*."[70] This color was soon registered in the more polychromatic, looser grotesques of certain Renaissance painters, such as Pinturicchio.[71]

The possible association of the colorful paintings in the Domus Aurea with the multicolored paintings on the walls of Phantastes's chamber is important because one of the ways that Spenser detaches his reader from the imagination is by historicizing its symbol, as we'll see below. He thereby pushes this symbol into the past as an antiquarian object from which the spectator can, by the end of book 3, claim an objective distance. In doing so, Spenser's poem reflects larger changes in the understanding of history.

History had previously been a largely literary study, based on the writings of authors from bygone eras. Now attention was shifting to a new form of history, based on the material records of events and institutions. Ancient history or literature was starting to become, in the language of Mark Pattison, an "object of science."[72] Like scientists, sixteenth-century antiquarians needed to remain detached from what they studied in order to aspire to, in Lorraine Daston and Peter Galison's words, "the viewpoint of angels."[73]

Spenser was deeply familiar with antiquarian methods of inquiry and even committed to them. In "The Ruines of Time," he praises the antiquarian William Camden, "the nourice of antiquitie," for rescuing from oblivion the old Roman settlement of Verlame, and Spenser uses as a direct source for this poem Camden's *Britannia*.[74] But Spenser was also aware that antiquarianism could conflict with poetry. In his *A View of the State of Ireland*, Eudoxus and Irenaeus discuss the problem of extracting historical truth from the accounts of Irish bards:

70. Hetty Joyce, "Grasping at Shadows: Ancient Paintings in Renaissance and Baroque Rome," *Art Bulletin* 74, no. 2 (June 1992): 219.

71. Dacos, *La découverte de la Domus Aurea*, 64.

72. Mark Pattison, *Isaac Casaubon, 1559–1614* (London: Longmans, Green, 1875), 509, cited by H. J. Erasmus, *The Origins of Rome in Historiography from Petrarch to Perizonius* (Assen: Van Gorcum, 1962), 32. See also Evans, *A History of the Society of Antiquaries*, 11.

73. Lorraine Daston and Peter Galison, "The Image of Objectivity," *Representations* 40, Special Issue: Seeing Science (Autumn 1992): 82.

74. Edmund Spenser, "The Ruines of Time," line 169, in *The Yale Edition of the Shorter Poems of Edmund Spenser*, ed. William A. Oram, Einar Bjorvand, Ronald Bond, Thomas H. Cain, Alexander Dunlop, and Richard Schell (New Haven: Yale University Press, 1989).

EUDOXUS: You doe very boldly Iren. adventure upon the histories of auncient times, and leane too confidently on those Irish Chronicles which are most fabulous and forged, in that out of them you dare take in hand to lay open the originall of such a nation so antique, as that no monument remaines of her beginning and first inhabiting; especially having been in those times without letters, but only bare traditions of times and remembrances of Bardes, which use to forge and falsifie every thing as they list, to please or displease any man.

IRENAEUS: Truly, I must confess I doe so, but yet not so absolutely as you suppose. I do herein rely upon those Bardes or Irish Chroniclers, though the Irish themselves through their ignorance in matters of learning and deepe judgement, doe most constantly beleeve and avouch them, but unto them besides I adde mine own reading; and out of them both together, with comparison of times, likewise of manners and customes, affinity of words and names, properties of natures, and uses, resemblances of rites and ceremonies, monuments of churches and tombes, and many other like circumstances, I doe gather a likelihood of truth, not certainly affirming anything, but by conferring of times, language, monuments, and such like, I doe hunt out a probability of things, which I leave to your judgment to believe or refuse.[75]

Bart van Es describes the historiographical interest of this passage as Spenser's "defense of antiquarian practice": it is through Irenaeus, van Es says, that "Spenser channels his knowledge of, and enthusiasm for, antiquarian research."[76] What's important to note for my purposes is the way in which this expression of Spenser's antiquarian commitments also articulates a tension with imaginative poetry. Spenser sounds like a conventional detractor of poetry, like Stephen Gosson, for example,[77] when he says of the bards

75. Edmund Spenser, *A View of the State of Ireland: From the First Printed Edition (1633)*, ed. Andrew Hadfield and Willy Maley (Oxford: Blackwell, 1997), 46.

76. See van Es, *Spenser's Forms of History*, 89; Ferguson, *Clio Unbound*, 83. Aspects of antiquarian methodology evident in this passage include antiquarianism's emphasis on nonliterary remains, its cautious suspension of judgment, and its typically multi-tiered process of collection, observation, and comparison. I am drawing from Peter N. Miller's account of antiquarian methodology in *Peiresc's Europe: Learning and Virtue in the Seventeenth Century* (New Haven: Yale University Press, 2000).

77. Peter C. Herman, *Squitter-wits and Muse-haters: Sidney, Spenser, Milton and Renaissance Antipoetic Sentiment* (Detroit: Wayne State University Press, 1996), 145–72.

that they "use to forge and falsifie every thing as they list, to please or displease any man."[78]

In the second room of the House of Busirane, Spenser depicts the grotesque figures, which represent the imagination, as historical objects. In so doing, he objectifies the imagination and detaches the viewer from the spell cast in the first room. The "wilde Antickes" may have been wrought "in the rich metall, as they liuing were," but they are now seen from a new distance that cuts short any immersion of the viewer in their riotous follies. Britomart, adopting a stance that Jeff Dolven calls one of "exemplary detachment,"[79] sees the artworks for the things that they are—but when they are perceived in this way, they become less like artworks and more like artifacts. The artwork here has lost any dialectical relationship with its own condition as an object and has become instead *simply* an object—one more thing in a world of things.

What's most striking in this second room of the House of Busirane is the sense of hiatus, of caesura, of aporia. Here is the poetry of the *un*filled: "ne could satisfy," "a long space," "no footings trace," "Nor wight appear'd," "wastefull emptinesse," "solemne silence," "none was to possesse." Rather than describing the grotesques, or listing their forms, or in some manner engaging us in their varied play of images (for example, by recreating a version of the grotesque in language, as in book 2's House of Alma, as well as in Barbaro's condemnation), Spenser objectifies them as historical artifacts in a room that has all the stillness, desolation, and uncertainty of an archaeological site heaped with spoliated fragments. Artworks no longer represent intersubjective imaginative worlds; instead, mere deteriorating artifacts.

HALFE ENUYING THEIR BLESSE: ON HERMAPHRODITES

Near the end of the 1590 edition of *The Faerie Queene*, there is an image that, I will argue, uniquely crystallizes the poem's dynamic relation to the process of epistemological detachment that I have been considering.

Immediately after the scene I have been discussing, Britomart endures the

78. Van Es, *Spenser's Forms of History*, 78–84, relates the publication history of this text: the antiquarian Sir James Ware included it in a 1633 volume of Irish history, *The Historie of Ireland, Collected by Three Learned Authors*, presenting Spenser's text as though it were itself an antiquarian treatise.

79. Jeff Dolven, *Scenes of Instruction in Renaissance Romance* (Chicago: University of Chicago Press, 2007), 171.

ultimate display of enargeic art, Busirane's sadistic masque of love, and survives the test unfazed: "Nether of ydle showes, nor of false charmes aghast" (3.12.29). She progresses into the next room, where she unchains Amoret and forces Busirane to undo his spell. In so doing, Britomart overcomes both the seductions of immersive art and, as scholars have extensively explored, problems of sexuality.[80] Finally, she emerges from the now-disenchanted house, where the rich display has vanished (3.12.42), and she observes the joyful reunion of Amoret and Scudamour:

> Lightly he clipt her twixt his armes twaine,
> And streightly did embrace her body bright,
> Her body, late the prison of sad paine,
> Now the sweet lodge of loue and deare delight:
> But she faire Lady ouercommen quight
> Of huge affection, did in pleasure melt,
> And in sweete rauishment pourd out her spright:
> No word they spake, nor earthly thing they felt,
> But like two senceles stocks in long embracement dwelt. (3.12.45)

In the lovers' happiness, mutual physicality, and escape from linguistic mediation ("No word they spake"), Amoret and Scudamour seem to have returned to a golden state intimate with nature. Spenser in fact compares the loving couple to entwined branches of a tree, "two senceles stocks."[81]

But the description doesn't end there:

> Had ye them seene, ye would haue surely thought,
> That they had beene that faire *Hermaphrodite*,

80. This part of the House of Busirane episode, involving the masque and then Britomart's entrance into the third room, has received thorough critical attention. Most famously, Thomas P. Roche Jr. understands Busirane's violence against Amoret as the projection of female fears of sex, an analysis that has elicited significant reevaluation from a range of critics, including Harry Berger Jr. and Lauren Silberman, among others. For the purposes of my argument, Silberman's analysis is especially suggestive. She explores how the scene evokes problems of literalization: rather than letting Amoret's states of fear or desire emerge interpersonally, Busirane attempts "to transform her body into the *spoil* of Cupid" (my italics), and thereby to render her into his object. See Roche, *The Kindly Flame: A Study of the Third and Fourth Books of Spenser's "Faerie Queene"* (Princeton: Princeton University Press, 1964); Berger, "Busirane and the War between the Sexes: An Interpretation of *The Faerie Queene* III.xi–xii," *English Literary Renaissance* 1, no. 2 (Spring 1971): 99–121; Silberman, *Transforming Desire: Erotic Knowledge in Books III and IV of "The Faerie Queene"* (Berkeley: University of California Press, 1995), 65ff.

81. As Hamilton notes, this metaphor connects Spenser's lines with Ovid's version of the story of Hermaphroditus; Arthur Golding translates Ovid's description of the union of Hermaphroditus and Salmacis: "Two twigges both growing into one and still togither holde" (4.379).

Which that rich *Romane* of white marble wrought,
And in his costly Bath causd to bee site:
So seemd those two, as growne together quite,
That *Britomart* halfe enuying their blesse,
Was much empassiond in her gentle sprite,
And to her selfe oft wisht like happinesse,
In vaine she wisht, that fate n'ould let her yet possesse. (3.12.46)

The lovers are now compared to a hermaphrodite, but not simply a hermaphrodite. They are compared, strangely, to a Roman statue of a hermaphrodite[82]—and, I would like to emphasize, one that has a pseudo-antiquarian quality. Spenser describes this statue (as he did Arthur's sword[83]) as if it were a real object that could be found somewhere, out there, in the world—that is, an object with an objective status: "*that* faire Hermaphrodite / Which *that* rich Romane of white marble wrought / And in his costly Bath causd to bee site" (my italics). Like those grotesques found in the Baths of Titus (or what was believed to be the Baths of Titus, but was really Nero's Domus Aurea[84]), this statue of the hermaphrodite purports to be an archaeological object depicted in situ near a Roman bath. And this antiquarian quality of the object distances Britomart from what she sees, as did the objects in the second room. The ecstasy of the lovers' embrace, which is associated first with happy primitivism through the reference to nature, is almost immediately pushed off to a distance with the metaphor of the Roman statue of the grotesque-like hermaphrodite.

The hermaphrodite metaphor suggests an erotic union of self with other, in opposition to a stance of detachment. The metaphor does so by associating this union with an object that is explicitly from the deep past. In fusing a man and a woman, the hermaphrodite becomes a composite figure not

82. Donald Cheney explores possible sources and meanings of the hermaphrodite image in "Spenser's Hermaphrodite and the 1590 *Faerie Queene*," *PMLA* 87, no. 2 (March 1972): 192–200. Rejecting any real Roman statue as the metaphor's source, he emphasizes how the image underscores "the limitations of our understanding of Amoret and Scudamour as lovers," positioning us as distanced spectators, who, like Britomart, must "see them [the lovers] from outside and try to make what we can of the spectacle" (196).

83. Of this sword, Spenser writes: "But when he dyde, the Faery Queene it brought / To Fairie lond, where yet it may be seene, if sought" (1.7.36). Arthur's sword, which, as Hamilton points out, is likened through a parallel passage to Caesar's sword (2.10.49), is precisely the kind of historical object that antiquarians prized. In fact, English antiquarians (such as John Leland) debated the question of whether Arthur was a real historical figure. See Ferguson, *Clio Unbound*, 104–9. Murrin, "Spenser's Fairyland," 133–34, makes a related argument about the objective existence of Fairyland.

84. See note 42.

unlike a grotesque. Spenser's hermaphrodite is, in fact, more grotesque-like than real Roman statues of hermaphrodites, which, as Donald Cheney has pointed out, were not of two people melding into one another but of one double-sexed individual.[85] The threat Spenser's hermaphrodite image poses is of the self's loss of differentiation from the world. It is certainly true that the hermaphrodite serves as an emblem of Christian marriage,[86] but Spenser brings out also the figure's association with older forms of thought by emphasizing the hermaphrodite's ancient origins. The image's ambiguous power belongs to the dual way it is both a superceded thing (the archaic) and an object of longing (the erotic).

The unreconciled dual quality of the hermaphrodite metaphor is brought to the surface through Britomart's "*halfe* enuying their blesse." While retaining a sense of her distance, Britomart also imagines herself participating in the couple's happiness. By employing an image of forms that lack separation (the embracing couple) to describe a position of separation (Britomart standing apart), the poem articulates for the reader an emergent historicized distance against a kind of prehistorical memory of undifferentiated union with the other in nature. Britomart desires the lovers' condition at the same time as she expresses her sense of difference from this condition. It is as though she were looking at intimacy—but an intimacy that is on display behind glass. This scene of Britomart looking at these embracing figures can be understood as an image of the tension of intellectual separation: the scene concretizes the conflictual process by which early modern consciousness defines itself in relation to that which it is in the process of renouncing. Britomart's ambivalent longing for that from which she is distanced speaks to the poem's conflicted relation to the historical process of detachment it has absorbed.

The doubleness of her position also describes Spenserian aesthetic experience, which entails both identification and detachment. Jane Grogan makes a related point about the "recursive movement between absorption

85. Cheney, "Spenser's Hermaphrodite and the 1590 *Faerie Queene*," 194.

86. Ibid. Roche has rightly drawn attention to the emblem tradition that lies behind this image: in Sambucus's and Reusner's collections of emblems of 1564 and 1591 respectively, one finds the ideal of male-female Christian union depicted in images of lovers who have physically grown into one another. The biblical source is probably Matthew 19:5, as C. S. Lewis has indicated, or Mark 10:8, both of which refer to a man cleaving to his wife and becoming one flesh with her. Or, as many commentators have suggested, the source might be Genesis 1:27 (which in the 1560 Geneva translation reads, "he created them male and female"), a version of creation that, to some, has implied an original hermaphroditic oneness of the sexes, not unlike the fantasy attributed to Aristophanes in the *Symposium*. See Roche, *The Kindly Flame*, 135–36.

and expulsion" in Spenser's poetry, especially in his ekphrases, which are constantly "transporting the reader sensually into Faeryland and then jolting him or her back out again."[87] That is, Spenser both immerses his readers within subjective experience, collapsing the boundaries between subjects and objects, and also creates distance from this immersion. This double identification undermines neither subjectivity nor objectivity, but rather holds on to the role of subjectivity in its ultimate relationship with objectivity, for the purpose of attaining cognizance in its fullest sense. A peculiarly complex aesthetic experience emerges, whereby neither subjective immersion nor objective detachment is treated as the end of aesthetic analysis, but both become irreducible moments in the ongoing process of interpreting the poem as it develops.

The poem is leading us through a kind of cognitive process that shuttles the reader between subjective and objective experience. Angus Fletcher describes a related dialectic with the image of a labyrinth and a tower. Spenser represents mortal life in its error and wandering, yet he also allows his readers to lift their heads periodically out of this maze-like experience and look around, as though from outside. Fletcher quotes W. B. Yeats's account of the double movements of his poem "The Second Coming," which, Yeats says, describe awareness of the world and the self, back and forth: "The human soul is always moving outward into the objective world or inward into itself," writes Yeats, "and this movement is double because the human soul would not be conscious were it not suspended between contraries, the greater the contrast the more intense the consciousness."[88] Spenser's poetry, too, offers the reader a heightened experience of this double movement. The very form of the Spenserian stanza—eight tightly interlocked lines and then a longer last line—has the effect of drawing the reader in and then pulling her out.[89]

Spenser has specifically marked the hermaphrodite scene as important for our understanding of the poem as a whole by using an ekphrastic convention to refer to the audience: "Had ye them seene, ye would haue surely thought. . . ."[90]—thus framing the scene with a meta-textual resonance (as

87. Jane Grogan, *Exemplary Spenser: Visual and Poetic Pedagogy in "The Faerie Queene"* (Burlington, VT: Ashgate, 2009), 114.

88. Quoted in Angus Fletcher, *The Prophetic Moment: An Essay on Spenser* (Chicago: University of Chicago Press, 1971), 48–49.

89. Gordon Teskey, "Thinking Moments in *The Faerie Queene*," *Spenser Studies* 22 (2007): 115.

90. This reference to what the audience would have seen has Virgilian origins and recurs throughout the ekphrastic tradition. In his ekphrasis of Aeneas's shield, Virgil marks the difference between the audience's ability to comprehend the depicted images of Roman history and

he did in his earlier ekphrasis of the tapestry, when he referred to what "ye mote haue liuely seene" [3.11.37]). As Lauren Silberman says, Britomart becomes, in her role as spectator, "the reader's surrogate as an onlooker."[91] The second-person references make the reader almost seem like a character within the poem. What results is a quivering, unstable, flickering relationship between the object and the person looking at it—and that becomes the new content of the work.

Spenser's poetry may ultimately entail a repeated renunciation of its own imaginative worlds. For James Nohrnberg, "it is precisely some capacity to betray, or qualify, or call into question its own mode of existence, that characterizes fictionality in literature."[92] This betrayal of the imagination is not the end of poetry but is integral to its core dynamic. Focusing on the unit of the poetic word, Thomas M. Greene writes that poetic language "seems to maintain a permanent conflict with archaic intuitions which persist despite all the well-intentioned logic of a society that considers itself modern." For Greene, words originally had a cultic power to affect the external world: by naming, we could create something, make it obey us, belong to us, or unite with us. If words have lost their originally magic vocation in the current more rational situation, this situation is also what has given birth to poetry. A poem "remains for us a text which carries itself *as if* [comme si] it were endowed with magical efficiency, the power of invoking, connecting and enchanting, but which at the same time implicitly renounces this power." It is by means of this as-if quality that a poem inscribes itself with the defeat of its longing for imaginative concretization. But this as-if quality is also that which we call "poetic."[93] In the end, an imaginative world is imaginative precisely because we see it as unreal. The historical development from subjective imaginative immersion to objective detachment is both a

Aeneas's inability to do so by three times addressing the audience with verbs in the second-person subjunctive: *aspiceres* (8.650), you would look at; *videres* (8.676), you would see; *credas* (8.691), you would believe. These verbs are in the subjunctive because they occur outside the context offered by the narrative.

91. Silberman, *Transforming Desire*, 67.

92. James Nohrnberg, *The Analogy of "The Faerie Queene"* (Princeton: Princeton University Press, 1976), 776. Nohrnberg argues that Spenser's decision to represent Nature in the *Mutabilitie Cantos* is, on one level, an act of disenchantment: "To represent a noumenon is in some sense to annul it" (775). In being represented, Nature becomes a discrete being, no longer magically interfused with the contemplating mind of the poem. But, on another level, the poem's unveiling of its own animating force is also what makes the artwork art: according to Nohrnberg, "if the gods be not gods, they may still be allegories" (776).

93. Thomas M. Greene, *Poésie et magie* (Paris: Julliard, 1991), 42, 52, 57. Translation from the French mine.

historical transition and also a dialectic preserved within the artwork. That is, the self-conscious fictionality of the poetry is produced by the tensions of the period—in this case, by the push-and-pull of poetry as subjective immersion (poetry as magic) and as objective detachment (poetry as artifact).

The scene with the hermaphrodite crystallizes in a single image the ambivalent relationship with pseudo-magical illusionism that is, in fact, scattered throughout the poem as a whole. We could speculate that Spenser had to eliminate the metaphor of the Roman statue of the hermaphrodite when he continued the poem for the 1596 edition not because, as various critics have long believed, Elizabeth's chief adviser, William Cecil, Lord Burleigh, found it too erotic.[94] Rather, the image concretizes a dynamic that energizes the self-problematizing forces of Spenser's poetic world. In forming this image, the poem overcomes the tension that had, in no small way, generated the poem; that is to say, the poem goes beyond the poem. The effect is that of closure, and for this reason, Spenser had to change the image in order to be able to continue the poem for the 1596 edition.

Donald R. Kelley is certainly right that no person can rise so far above his own cultural ocean as to become an oceanographer instead of a fish.[95] But the startling effect of the 1590 edition's final image is that, in it, the reader seems to witness Spenser for a moment leaping out of the mental waters of his own *Faerie Queene* and looking around with his bulbous eyes.

THINGS THAT AREN'T THINGS

For Adorno, authentic artworks are not objects in any stable or objective sense; they are more like dynamic processes that demand our interpretive involvement.[96] They cannot be taken literally because they do not mean what they overtly say. Rather, they are always pointing off beyond the explicit content of their words or images. What distinguishes aesthetic discourse from any other kind of discourse is that it constantly defers arriving at the closure of its meaning. Like the fabric that Penelope weaves and unweaves in Homer's *Odyssey*,[97] artworks are invested in delay. They put forward their assertions only to call them into question again.

94. See Hamilton, *The Fairie Queene*, 409; Anne K. Tuell, "The Original End of *Faerie Queene*, Book III," *Modern Language Notes* 36, no. 5 (May 1921): 309–11.

95. Donald R. Kelley, *Faces of History: Historical Inquiry from Herodotus to Herder* (New Haven: Yale University Press, 1998), xi.

96. Theodor W. Adorno, *Aesthetic Theory*, trans. Robert Hullot-Kentor, ed. Gretel Adorno and Rolf Tiedemann (Minneapolis: University of Minnesota Press, 1997), 3.

97. Ibid., 186.

The Faerie Queene is an artwork that knows what Adorno is talking about. The poem argues constantly with itself—making assertions and, at every turn, reflecting back on these assertions and waging a kind of rivalry between, in Dolven's terms, the voice of a schoolmaster and that of a poet.[98] As Augustine said about himself, so Spenser's poem seems to say, "I have become a problem to myself."[99]

In the proem to book 6, Spenser warns that "vertues seat is deepe within the mynd, / And not in outward shows, but inward thoughts defynd." If Spenser's romance is, in the words of one eighteenth-century reader, like a long picture gallery,[100] these words mark a moment when Spenser's work is seemingly rejecting its own pictorial strategies. Ernest B. Gilman understands these lines as having "something of the force of a retraction," in that they call into question the imagistic strategies of the poem itself.[101]

If we follow the implications of such a reading, the relationship of a poetic object to its own objective existence starts to look increasingly peculiar.[102] A retraction of the kind that Gilman, as well as David Lee Miller, discusses is an act fraught with ambiguities. This dynamic of retraction, which Miller describes as "a perpetually self-displacing mode of discourse,"[103] is most evident in *The Faerie Queene*'s relation to its own visual imagery.[104] Rather than slowly descending into a cloud of unknowing, the poem constantly reani-

98. Dolven, *Scenes of Instruction in Renaissance Romance.*

99. Augustine, *Confessions* 10.33.

100. Jean H. Hagstrum, *The Sister Arts: The Tradition of Literary Pictorialism and English Poetry from Dryden to Gray* (Chicago: University of Chicago Press, 1958), 76.

101. Gilman, *Iconoclasm and Poetry in the English Reformation,* 75. For Spenser's use of exegetical techniques of interpreting images *in bono [sensu] et in malo,* as well as of biblical *correctio,* see Carol V. Kaske, *Spenser and Biblical Poetics* (Ithaca: Cornell University Press, 1999).

102. Related questions have of course played an important role in criticism of twentieth-century art. See Bill Brown, *Other Things* (Chicago: University of Chicago Press, 2015); Michael Fried, "Art and Objecthood," in *Art and Objecthood: Essays and Reviews* (Chicago: University of Chicago Press, 1998), 148–72.

103. See David Lee Miller's discussion of Spenserian retraction as reinscribing what it intends to renounce, *The Poem's Two Bodies: The Poetics of the 1590 "Faerie Queene"* (Princeton: Princeton University Press, 1988), 11–14, 82–92.

104. There is a rich body of literature on this subject. For example, Gregerson in *The Reformation of the Subject* explores various ways that Spenser tries to avoid verbal idolatry. See also King, *Spenser's Poetry and the Reformation Tradition,* where he looks at iconoclastic scenes in which the narrator describes an attractive object just before "reporting its shattering, destruction, or death" (80). King associates these acts of destruction with bad art; for him, true art requires of Spenser no such destruction. My exploration is closer, in this regard, to that of Kenneth Gross, who finds Spenser calling into question his own poetics: "In every expansive progression toward a stable center, in every attempt to achieve something like visionary identification with a sacred emblem, the fear of fixation of subsequent misreading haunts the literary quest like a demon" (*Spenserian Poetics,* 17).

mates itself by shuttling between contradictory positions, neither of which can be maintained. Along with critics like Hamilton and Giamatti, Gilman emphasizes Spenser's rejection in *The Faerie Queene* of the external display and pageantry on which the work also relies: "*The Faerie Queene* grows centripetally, twining its various shows into a root sunk too deep for *pictura* to represent in its superficial analogy with *poesis*. Indeed, with Una as its inaugural symbol and its goal, the poem's redeeming search for its own integrity would issue, at some theoretical limit or vanishing point, in the collapse of all its intricate and proliferating workmanship into one dense word under the veil of its multiform plastic imagination."[105] In Gilman's evocative account, Spenser is reaching toward an ever-receding point of unity and integrity that would, if realized, defy all representation. What's important to me here is that the poem represents a state of conflict with its own mimetic strategies—pushing its readers to try to imagine (despite the impossibility built into that task) a meaning that lies somehow beyond the poem itself. The poem becomes, to use Adorno's language, "nonidentical" with itself.[106]

A kind of pulsing effect can be felt as the poem repeatedly tears down one show and puts up another.[107] As in several pictures printed alongside his poems in *The Theatre for Worldlings*, where the triumphal arch and monument are shown in two states at the same time, standing and wrecked, so, too, Spenser's elaborate visual edifices simultaneously stand tall and lie collapsed around their own foundations. Artworks like Spenser's do not simply destroy or renounce their own ongoing ideologies and modes of representation but, as I've been trying to show, continually interrogate them with intractable complexity.

Spenser's *The Faerie Queene* does not come to rest within itself; rather, it strives toward a completion of meaning at which it can never fully arrive. Far from dying of such failure, though, the poem would die of success if it ever overcame its own internal contradictions.[108] *The Faerie Queene* would at

105. Gilman, *Iconoclasm and Poetry in the English Reformation*, 75.

106. Adorno explains "nonidentity" as "the thing's own identity against its identifications," that is, its nonconceptual reality, which flashes up into consciousness through the process of what he calls negative dialectic. Theodor W. Adorno, *Negative Dialectics*, trans. E. B. Ashton (New York: Continuum, 1973), 161. See the final paragraph of Joe Moshenska's recent "Why Can't Spenserians Stop Talking about Hegel? A Response to Gordon Teskey," *Spenser Review* 44.1.2 (Spring-Summer 2014), where he refers to Adorno's concept of the "nonidentical" in regard to *The Faerie Queene*.

107. Teskey uses the metaphor of pulsing to describe the quality of thought in *The Faerie Queene*, specifically the poem's "continual oscillation between narrative movement and symbolic tableau." See his "Thinking Moments in *The Faerie Queene*," 115.

108. I am playing on the words of Gregg M. Horowitz, who is talking about art's unreconciled

last become the Letter to Raleigh. Happily, that is not what has happened. The poem remains in a state of internal conflict and irresolution, calling for our ongoing involvement. Just like Redcrosse, who no sooner completes his quest than he heads out again, so, too, Spenser's aesthetic meaning no sooner clarifies itself than it breaks through again to a renewed state of incompleteness, forestalling closure until the end of time[109]—at which point, we're told, subjectivity won't be subjectivity anymore. And art, I guess, won't be art.

---

struggle between determination and freedom. See his "Art History and Autonomy," in *The Semblance of Subjectivity: Essays in Adorno's Aesthetic Theory*, ed. Tom Huhn and Lambert Zuidervaart (Cambridge, MA: MIT Press, 1997), 276.

109. Susanne Lindgren Wofford writes that Spenser depends on "a consistently anti-apocalyptic poetics": through its gaps and fissures, *The Faerie Queene* poses problems that cannot be resolved during what she calls "the in-between time of interpretation." See her "Britomart's Petrarchan Lament: Allegory and Narrative in *The Faerie Queene* III, iv," *Comparative Literature* 39, no. 1 (Winter 1987): 54–55.

CHAPTER FOUR

Playing with Things: Reification in Marlowe's *Hero and Leander*

But what about when the poet himself, as though in opposition to the very argument I've been making in this book, associates poetry—or even poets—with *things*?

Such is the case with Christopher Marlowe, that most "decadent" of Elizabethan poets. Does not Marlowe call his poems, or at least his translations of Ovid's poems, "wanton toys"?[1] Does not Mycetes in *Tamburlaine I* declare that "'tis a prety toy to be a poet"?[2] Does not Marlowe play up the thingly qualities of the props in his plays so that, for example, even a crown starts to seem like a mere thing, passed back and forth between its rivals like a hot potato? Does not Marlowe fill his poems with lists and, most importantly, with elaborate descriptions of *things, things, things*?

Along these lines, Marlowe's 1593 *Hero and Leander* has been called a "fetishistic" poem for the way it combines an erotic story and a peculiar obsession with things. Falling from the pages of this poem is a confetti of buskins, baubles, trinkets, and toys. "Associated with wantonness, ornament, and excess,"[3] Marlowe's epyllion[4] seems to be a poem celebrating

1. *Elegia* 3.14.4. All citations of Marlowe's nondramatic works from *The Collected Poems of Christopher Marlowe*, ed. Patrick Cheney and Brian J. Striar (Oxford: Oxford University Press, 2006).

2. 2.2.54. All citations of Marlowe's dramatic works from Christopher Marlowe, *The Complete Plays*, ed. Frank Romany and Robert Lindsey (London: Penguin, 2003).

3. Georgia E. Brown, "Marlowe's Poems and Classicism," in *The Cambridge Companion to Christopher Marlowe*, ed. Patrick Cheney (Cambridge: Cambridge University Press, 2004), 116.

4. The meaning of the term *epyllion* has changed over time. I use it in the modern sense to mean a relatively short narrative poem that plays irreverently on the epic form. For the complex

stuff—so much so that the poem itself starts to seem like a thing. One critic says that the text becomes, in its ekphrases, a thing among things: "The text becomes a fetish, an object that is irrationally reverenced, and substitutes itself for erotic satisfaction."[5] So, how is it that I can say that Marlowe is not thingly, when he talks about things all the time?

If Marlowe is a poet of "wanton toys," he is not simply that. His work also resists the allures of its own potential trinketry. Sometimes this resistance manifests in a relatively direct way. When, for example, in *Tamburlaine I*, Mycetes says that "'tis a prety toy to be a poet," the Persian king does so in the context of inadvertently demonstrating his ineptitude—both as a king and as a rhetorician—and thereby putting up for critique this fetishistic attitude toward language. And in *Hero and Leander*, the narrator bemoans the fate of true scholars, who are so often reduced to poverty because their potential patrons are distracted—amazed by "every garish toy" (480). But on a more subtle and pervasive level, Marlowe resists his poetry's potential thingliness through his peculiarly elusive and mercurial style, which has proven so hard for criticism to grasp and describe.

This chapter is about a contradiction: how aesthetic form can be thingly and non-thingly at the same time. I will try to get at this elusive thingly/non-thingly Marlovian style by drawing out from within his epyllion a largely unexplored and surprising stylistic history—that of post-Augustan antiquity.[6] This late-ancient literature is characterized by a style that is thingly in overlapping senses: in constantly describing stuff, in using language and rhetorical ornament almost fetishistically, and in attempting through its aestheticism to seal itself off from history and flux.

We do not usually associate Marlowe's poetry with any Latin or Greek author after Ovid,[7] other than with his most immediate source, Musaeus.

history of this word's meaning, see Stefan Tilg, "On the Origins of the Modern Term 'Epyllion': Some Revisions to a Chapter in the History of Classical Scholarship," in *Brill's Companion to Greek and Latin Epyllion and Its Reception*, ed. Manuel Baumbach and Silvio Bär (Leiden: Brill, 2012), 29–54.

5. Brown, "Marlowe's Poems and Classicism," 117.

6. The period of the Roman Empire that I am calling the post-Augustan Empire is broad and does not entirely correspond with standard periodization. I am interested in stylistic features common to the largely neglected literature in the period after the fall of the Julio-Claudian emperors (starting approximately with Vespasian and the High Empire in 70 CE and extending just beyond the fall of the Late Empire in 410 CE). Within this broad period, I concentrate on the highly rhetorical culture of the Second Sophistic (the first through third centuries CE).

7. "Unanimously, critics identify *Hero and Leander* as an Ovidian narrative poem," writes Patrick Cheney in *Marlowe's Counterfeit Profession: Ovid, Spenser, Counter-Nationhood* (Toronto: University of Toronto Press, 1997), 240. For the central importance of Ovid to Marlowe, see also

The few critics[8] who allude to late antiquity when discussing Marlowe's style suggest that, in *Hero and Leander*, Marlowe repeats some qualities of the aesthetic of this era. In contrast, this chapter argues that while Marlowe has absorbed the stylistic peculiarities of this period's thingly aesthetic, he uses it in ways that subvert it. What's at stake is Marlowe's complex relation to the apparent thingliness of his own poetry.

Reification is another word for the problem I am talking about.[9] While in other chapters I have focused on objectivity and objects mostly in relation to antiquarianism and antiquarian artifacts, here I will widen the focus to consider the potential reifications of literary tradition itself, looping back in the end to consider a different kind of empiricist study emerging in the period, namely philology, which was changing Europe's understanding of its own past. I will argue that Marlowe used ekphrasis to create a style that could push out from within ever-congealing inherited traditions toward the dynamism of life.

So let's begin in the post-Augustan empire.

"HE NEVER STIRRED": POST-AUGUSTAN ANTIQUITY

A quality of rigid and aestheticized thingliness pervades post-Augustan literature and visual art. This quality can be immediately observed in many portraits, both pagan and Christian, of the period. Motion has largely lost its

---

William Keach, *Elizabethan Erotic Narratives: Irony and Pathos in the Ovidian Poetry of Shakespeare, Marlowe, and Their Contemporaries* (New Brunswick: Rutgers University Press, 1977), 85–116. Especially important for Marlowe's *Hero and Leander*, and the Ovidian history that lies behind the political importance of the poem's licentiousness, is Heather James, "The Poet's Toys: Christopher Marlowe and the Liberties of Erotic Elegy," *Modern Language Quarterly* 67, no. 1 (March 2006): 103–27.

8. Douglas Bush writes of the Greek romances that the "pictures of physical and artistic beauty sometimes suggest Marlowe's opulent brush." In a footnote, Bush quotes ekphrases in Longus's *Daphnis and Chloe* and Achilles Tatius's *Leucippe and Clitophon* to convey a sense of this heavily pictorial literature. See his *Mythology and the Renaissance Tradition in English Poetry* (Minneapolis: University of Minnesota Press, 1932), 124.

9. The concept of reification originates, as is well known, with Georg Lukács's interpretation of Karl Marx's account of commodity fetishism. Martin Jay explains that, for Lukács, reification means "the petrification of living processes into dead things"; *Marxism and Totality: The Adventures of a Concept from Lukács to Habermas* (Berkeley: University of California Press, 1984), 109. It is almost a truism that attempting to define reification runs the risk of reifying the term—that is, of slipping into the very kind of thinking that the term is meant to criticize. See Timothy Bewes, *Reification; or, The Anxiety of Late Capitalism* (London: Verso, 2002), 93. For an intellectual history of the term, see also Gillian Rose, *The Melancholy Science: An Introduction to the Thought of Theodor W. Adorno* (London: Macmillan, 1978). For an account of the term in early modern literary studies specifically, see Hugh Grady, *Shakespeare's Universal Wolf: Studies in Early Modern Reification* (Oxford: Oxford University Press, 1996).

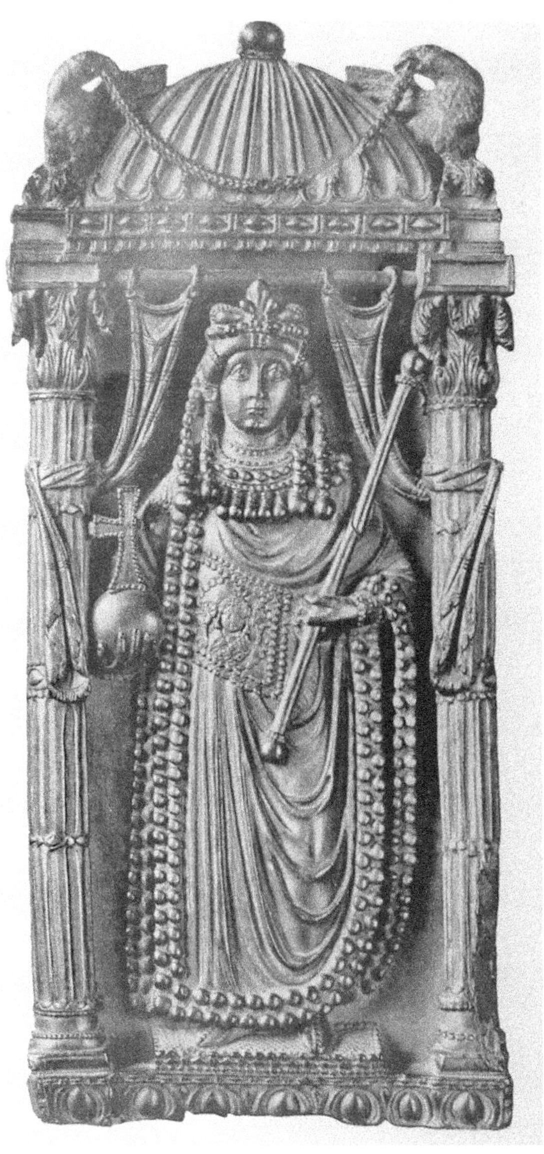

FIGURE 5. Ivory diptych panel of the Empress Ariadne (c. 500 CE). Museo Nazionale del Bargello, Florence.

value. The emphasis is on stability. The imperial portraits, which confront the viewer with insomniac eyes, often display a frontality and symmetricality that hinder the expression of movement by limiting the viewer's perception of dimensionality, and the figures' degree of rigor mortis can exceed that of any sepulchral portrait.

In the masterful ivory portrait of Empress Ariadne of approximately 500 CE, now in the Museo Nazionale del Bargello in Florence, for example, the Empress Consort of Zeno and then Anastasius looks straight ahead from the center of the composition. Pearls on the hem of her robe repeat the spherical form of the *globus cruciger* in her hand. These pearls have been arranged in a line that traces part of a rectangle following the frame of the composition and that thus downplays the movement of the form into the depth of the picture box. Adorned with all the insignia of imperial and religious power, Empress Ariadne is as rigid as the things around her, and her person appears almost indistinguishable from these things. For example, the line of pearls just mentioned extends to the empress's head, where jewelry continues the pattern into her hair and around her neck. Even the edifice in which she stands seems to be a rigid extension of her: the imperial eagles on the dome hold in their beaks a cord echoing the curve of her necklace. And the niche housing the empress's sculpted form is itself part of the sculpture; the "curtains" are made out of ivory. It is as though this ivory artwork depicted not a living woman but, rather, a sculpture of a living woman—Empress Ariadne has been made to appear as much as possible like a thing, or even *like a sculpture*.

This quality of rigid and aestheticized thingliness not only manifests itself in the visual art of the period but also pervades its literature, making ekphrasis a ubiquitous and representative rhetorical figure of this era. For example, the Antioch-born historian of the late Roman Empire, Ammianus Marcellinus (fourth century CE), portrays the emperor's *adventus*, or triumphant arrival at Rome in 357:

> [Constantius II] himself sat alone upon a golden car in the resplendent blaze of shimmering precious stones, whose mingled glitter seemed to form a sort of shifting light. And . . . he was surrounded by dragons, woven out of purple thread and bound to the golden and jeweled tops of spears, with wide mouths open to the breeze and hence hissing as if roused by anger, and leaving their tails winding in the wind. And there marched on either side twin lines of infantrymen with shields and crests gleaming with glittering rays, clad in shining mail; and scattered among them were the full-armoured cavalry . . . , all masked, furnished with protecting breastplates and girt with iron belts, so that

you might have supposed them statues polished by the hand of Praxiteles, not men. . . . [Constantius II] never stirred, but showed himself as calm and imperturbable as he was commonly seen in his provinces. For he both stooped when passing through lofty gates (although he was very short), and as if his neck were in a vice, he kept the gaze of his eyes straight ahead, and turned his face neither to right nor to left, but (as if he were a lay figure [figmentum hominis]) neither did he nod when the wheel jolted nor was he ever seen to spit, or to wipe or rub his face or nose, or move his hands about. (16.10.6–10)[10]

This ekphrasis has been most important to historians for its remarkable description of the bearing of the emperor: Constantius II is impressive to the degree to which he is inflexible, deliberate, and imperturbable. There may have been times when a leader's power was associated with agility, spontaneity, and passion, but these are not such times. Constantius II's extremely rigid behavior produces the effect that he is a statue of a man rather than an actual living man, in the same way that the Empress Ariadne was made to look like a sculpture.[11] This is not to say that he doesn't have an interiority—but that his interiority is characterized by an iron will that renders him able to keep all passing human impulses in check. His one movement, stooping for a high gate even though he's short, is evidently a purely symbolic gesture that indicates the stature of his imperial body.

In this era of late antiquity, objects seem to have absorbed an animation that human beings have renounced, and people take on an eerie, almost

10. ". . . insidebat aureo solus ipse carpento, fulgenti claritudine lapidum variorum, quo micante lux quaedam misceri videbatur alterna. Eumque post antegressos multiplices alios, purpureis subtegminibus texti, circumdedere dracones, hastarum aureis gemmatisque summitatibus illigati, hiatu vasto perflabiles, et ideo velut ira perciti sibilantes, caudarumque volumina relinquentes in ventum. Et incedebat hinc inde ordo geminus armatorum, clipeatus atque cristatus, corusco lumine radians, nitidis loricis indutus, sparsique cataphracti equites (quos clibanarios dictitant) personati thoracum muniti tegminibus, et limbis ferreis cincti, ut Praxitelis manu polita crederes simulacra, non viros; quos laminarum circuli tenues, apti corporis flexibus ambiebant, per omnia membra diducti, ut quocumque artus necessitas commovisset, vestitus congrueret, iunctura cohaerenter aptata. Augustus itaque faustis vocibus appellatus, non montium litorumque intonante fragore cohorruit, talem se tamque immobilem, qualis in provinciis suis visebatur, ostendens. Nam et corpus perhumile curvabat portas ingrediens celsas, et velut collo munito, rectam aciem luminum tendens, nec dextra vultum nec laeva flectebat et (tamquam figmentum hominis) nec cum rota concuteret nutans, nec spuens, aut os aut nasum tergens vel fricans manumve agitans visus est umquam." I am quoting from Ammianus Marcellinus, *The History*, trans. J. C. Rolfe (Cambridge, MA: Loeb Classical Library, 1950).

11. Ramsay MacMullen writes of a "curious rapprochement": "At the same time that imperial statues were coming to resemble their subjects by being borne about in processions, carried in chariots, wreathed and hailed and addressed as witnesses to oaths, the emperors themselves copied their own statues." See MacMullen, "Some Pictures in Ammianus Marcellinus," *Art Bulletin* 46, no. 4 (Dec. 1964): 439.

golem-like existence. The gold and gems glitter like a second daylight, and the tightly fitted armor on the cavalry moves as though on its own, making the men seem like statues by Praxiteles.

This objectification is important. By adopting a purely externalized viewpoint that downplays the men's internal experiences, the ekphrasis furthers the impression of nonhuman thingliness, producing what Erich Auerbach calls a "paralysis of the human."[12] Whereas in Petrarch's account of a procession in *Africa,* it was the conquered who were objectified, here it is the victors. The most alive parts of this procession are apparently the kite-like dragons, "woven out of purple thread and bound to the golden and jeweled tops of spears, with wide mouths open to the breeze and hence hissing as if roused by anger, and leaving their tails winding in the wind." In contrast to the emperor, who doesn't spit, show feeling, or touch his nose, these *dracones* hiss and whip about in the air.[13] *Notice that the description is thingly in that it focuses on things,* so much so that even the people seem like things.

But this ekphrasis is thingly in a second way as well. Edward Gibbon, who relies on Ammianus as a source for late antiquity, criticizes him for his overdone language, which is typical of late-antique style, and complains of "those turgid metaphors, those false ornaments, that perpetually disfigure the style of Ammianus."[14] In the twentieth century, Arnaldo Momigliano writes of the "extraordinary contortions and complications of his style,"[15] and Auerbach refers to the "rhetorically horripilating" quality of his work, which is characterized by a "whole gallery of gruesomely grotesque and extremely sensory-graphic portraits."[16] Ammianus's ekphrasis of Constan-

12. Erich Auerbach, *Mimesis: The Representation of Reality in Western Literature,* trans. Willard R. Trask (Princeton: Princeton University Press, 1953), 53.

13. Arrian (c. 86–160 CE), a Second Sophistic Greek historian of Rome, describes these dragons in *Ars tactica* 35.3 as windsocks that fill with air and hiss when those bearing them charge. It is generally believed that these *dracones* were introduced into the Roman imperial military by the Sarmatians, when they were absorbed into the Roman cavalry in the second century. The *dracones* were at first used for ceremonial purposes, as an object of impressive exotica, but had become a customary part of active units by the time of Vegetius, who indicates that each cohort carried one (2.13). See Graham Webster, *The Roman Imperial Army of the First and Second Centuries A.D.* (Norman: University of Oklahoma Press, 1998), 134–35.

14. Edward Gibbon, *The History of the Decline and Fall of the Roman Empire,* vol. 1, ed. David Womersley (London: Penguin, 1994), 1056n81, cited in Gavin Kelly, "Ammianus Marcellinus: Tacitus' Heir and Gibbon's Guide," in *The Cambridge Companion to the Roman Historians,* ed. Andrew Feldherr (Cambridge: Cambridge University Press, 2009), 356.

15. Arnaldo Momigliano, "The Lonely Historian Ammianus Marcellinus," in Momigliano, *Essays in Ancient and Modern Historiography* (Chicago: University of Chicago Press, 2012), 136.

16. Auerbach, *Mimesis,* 54. Auerbach talks about the "unrealistically refined tendency of the style," which begins to jar with the soberness of the content. "The diction grows mannered; the

tius II is a literary showpiece—itself as uneasily "static and stagy," to use one scholar's phrase, as anything it represents.[17] In other words, Ammianus does not just spell out what is in the procession but also, as a connoisseur might dwell on a fine object, lingers aesthetically over his own description.

This point is harder to make because it is less familiar. But the idea is that the entire description becomes an aestheticized object that is put on show. It is a purple patch, constituted of "rare lexical tidbits" that are put on "display like precious jewels."[18] The description as a whole is like an object, an object of literary connoisseurship. *Notice how the rhetoric itself becomes a thing.*

Sometimes these two qualities (one, that the language describes a lot of things, and two, that the language is so ornate as itself to seem a kind of thing) are hard to distinguish. For example, in describing the conversation at a lavish banquet at the house of Ulpian in Rome, Athenaeus's *Deipnosophists* (late second to early third century CE) provides a compendium of antiquarian details about food, furniture, and entertainment for the connoisseur. The excessive detail of the text's historical descriptions suits the extravagance of the imperial displays, which in one case includes an eighteen-foot Dionysus on an elephant, sixty satyrs and sileni, every kind of tree and dog and bird, tens of thousands of cavalry and infantry in full uniform, 3,200 gold crowns, hundreds of carefully costumed children, and a skin holding thirty thousand gallons of wine.[19] Throughout the conversation, Athenaeus's characters serve up abstruse delicacies of classical

---

constructions begin, as it were, to writhe and twist. The equable elegance is disturbed; the refined reserve gives way to a somber pomp; and, against its will as it were, the style renders a greater sensoriness than would originally have been compatible with *gravitas*, yet *gravitas* itself is by no means lost, but on the contrary is heightened. The elevated style becomes hyperpathetic and gruesome, becomes pictorial and sensory" (57).

17. MacMullen, "Some Pictures in Ammianus Marcellinus," 438.

18. Robert A. Kaster, *Guardians of Language: The Grammarian and Society in Late Antiquity* (Berkeley: University of California Press, 1988), 12.

19. Ruth Webb draws attention to the strange manner in which these long ekphrases depicting historical objects end: among all these wondrous goods, the narrator comments that he is sure that the host will ask about a certain obscure vessel stand. As Webb points out, the contrast is extreme between the "sensual extravagances of a lost age" and "the dusty preoccupations of the sophists at dinner." This vessel stand of scholarly minutiae, Webb writes, "serves to bring our attention back to the surface of the text." Ruth Webb, "Picturing the Past: Uses of Ekphrasis in the *Deipnosophistae* and Other Works of the Second Sophistic," in *Athenaeus and His World: Reading Greek Culture in the Roman Empire*, ed. David Braund and John Wilkins (Exeter: University of Exeter Press, 2000), 225. The antiquarian interest, in this case, works at cross-purposes to the enargeic vividness of the ekphrasis: readers are reminded of distance at the same time as they are asked to forget this distance.

knowledge, and then use these literary bits to settle questions of dining etiquette ("Homer has also taught us who need not be invited" [5.177c]) and to gratify demanding tastes ("Tell us, learned Ulpian, whether liver thus encased is mentioned anywhere," says one guest when this dish is brought out in book 3, to which the host counters, "Show us first in what author *epiplus* [wrapped fried liver] is used of the fatty caul" [3.106f]).[20] Written in the period's highly stylized prose, the gourmet language of the *Deipnosophists* takes to an extreme Socrates's criticism in the *Gorgias* that rhetoric is a kind of cookery (ἡ ὀψοποιική), designed to flatter sickly palates rather than cure the corrupting illness, as Socrates claims philosophy can do (465b).

Such highly artificial rhetoric reflects how the elite were trained. In Philostratus the Elder's third-century *Imagines*, the narrator initiates his host's ten-year-old son into his elite cultural world by offering a series of ekphrases of paintings based on classical literature. Looking at the panel paintings, the narrator instructs the boy:

> Have you noticed, my boy, that the painting here is based on Homer, or have you failed to do so because you are lost in wonder as to how in the world the fire could live in the midst of the water? Well then, let us try to get at the meaning of it. Turn your eyes away from the painting itself so as to look only at the events on which it is based. (1.1)[21]

Such scenes of rhetorical pedagogy will resonate strongly in the rhetorical literary culture emerging in the sixteenth-century English classroom. The first ekphrasis shown by Philostratus's narrator represents a painting of the *Iliad*'s burning River Scamander. As several scholars have noted, the emphasis of this pedagogical scene is not exactly on seeing ("turn your eyes *away* from the painting itself") but on developing a storehouse of mythical references shared among those initiated into the cult of the Muses.[22]

20. All citations of Athenaeus from *The Deipnosophists*, vols. 1–7, trans. Charles Burton Gulick (London: W. Heinemann; New York: Putnam, 1927–41).

21. Philostratus the Elder, *Imagines* (with Philostratus the Younger, *Imagines* and Callistratus, *Descriptions*), trans. Arthur Fairbanks (Cambridge, MA: Loeb Classical Library, 1931).

22. Zahra Newby points out that this suggestion (to look away from the painting and to think about the relevant passage from Homer) is "a direct corrective to the boy's *thauma*, wonder, provoked by the unexpected sight of fire in water. The boy does not seem to have realized that the image is based on Homer, precisely because he has been caught in awe at its visual effects." See Newby, "Absorption and Erudition in Philostratus' *Imagines*," in *Philostratus*, ed. Ewen Bowie and Jaś Elsner (Cambridge: Cambridge University Press, 2009), 326. The ekphrasis is here employed, albeit with playful self-consciousness, as a rhetorical figure that brings the scene clearly before our

Such literature, larded with ornate verbal forms[23] and garnished with classical allusions, helped bind together the emperor and the members of the ruling class in a common cult of classical beauty, as Peter Brown has argued. In this world of the vast late empire where the elite knew they were needed but also knew they were subject without recourse to the emperor's potentially capricious and violent decrees—where men of the ruling class were, in Auerbach's words, "lusting for power yet constantly trying to conceal the chattering of their teeth"[24]—the ruling class learned to speak in increasingly elaborate forms. For example, an appeal by a grammarian for an unpaid salary from the emperor engendered the following: "Your heavenly magnanimity and your fellowship with the Muses (for *Paideia* sits beside you on the throne) have given me confidence to offer a just and lawful petition . . . [etc]."[25] Covering their appeals with a "fine dust of ancient phrases,"[26] the members of the elite evoked a putatively timeless order of the Muses and thereby attempted to hide in their rhetoric that they were complicit in the power relations of the period. The flowery phrases typically came in large bouquets. *Notice how this literature, in its aestheticism, attempts to deny its own historical situation.*

With this background in mind, I'll now turn to Marlowe.

"AND WITH STILL PANTING ROCKED": THE MOVEMENT OF POETIC FORM IN *HERO AND LEANDER*

As we turn to consider Marlowe's relationship with this literature of late antiquity, we enter into unfamiliar critical territory. The neglect of late antiquity in Marlowe criticism is surprising for many reasons, not least because one of the primary ways in which Renaissance schoolboys like Marlowe learned literary techniques such as ekphrasis was though Aphthonius's

eyes but that simultaneously also distances us from this same scene through the emphasis on its rhetorical nature—on the ekphrasis *qua* ekphrasis, as a "literary jewel."

23. The allusions were accompanied by increasingly antiquated forms and elaborate verbal structures; in Latin, the sentences are cardhouses of carefully balanced appositional phrases, and the style in Greek is *attikismos*, utilizing outdated Attic words and grammatical forms (most notably, an unusual number of optatives). Among other factors, the rise of Latin may well have helped crystallize the task of the Greek grammarians. Simon Swain, *Hellenism and Empire: Language, Classicism, and Power in the Greek World AD 50–250* (Oxford: Clarendon Press, 1996), 17–42.

24. Auerbach, *Mimesis*, 55.

25. From the petition of Lollianus, a third-century Egyptian grammarian. Quoted in Peter Brown, *Power and Persuasion in Late Antiquity: Towards a Christian Empire* (Madison: University of Wisconsin Press, 1992), 35.

26. Ibid., 31.

fourth-century-CE *Progymnasmata*. This late-antique rhetorical handbook, which went through over ninety editions between 1542 and 1689, was heavily used in the English schoolroom in an edition that Reinhard Lorichius had expanded with classical examples.[27]

To the extent that *The Cambridge Companion to Christopher Marlowe* represents current scholarly consensus about Marlowe, it is noteworthy that the 2006 edition includes no substantial discussion of any author who was born after Augustus (other than, of course, Lucan and Musaeus, whom Marlowe translated).[28] The influence of post-Augustan antiquity has suffered a general neglect among scholars of early modern literature,[29] but awareness of *Hero and Leander*'s particular connections with this period may also have been hampered by the supplanting of L. C. Martin's 1931 edition of Marlowe's poems by Millar MacLure's 1968 edition, which subtly reinforces through its glosses a narrower sense of Marlowe's classicism.[30] One of the few scholarly accounts that addresses the importance of the ekphrastic style of post-Augustan antiquity for understanding *Hero and Lean-*

27. The section on ekphrasis is chapter 12, 305–28, "DE DESCRIPTIONE, QUAE Graecè ἔκφρασις dicta." See Lynn Enterline, *Shakespeare's Schoolroom: Rhetoric, Discipline, Emotion* (Philadelphia: University of Pennsylvania Press, 2012), 107.

28. Gabriel Harvey, we learn in one passing reference, calls Marlowe a "Lucian." The social context for Harvey's statement is discussed by David Riggs, *The World of Christopher Marlowe* (New York: Henry Holt, 2004), 280. If *we* don't think of Marlowe in relation to the literature of post-Republican antiquity, some of his contemporaries apparently did.

29. A recent exception, which focuses specifically on ekphrasis, is Elizabeth B. Bearden's *The Emblematics of the Self: Ekphrasis and Identity in Renaissance Imitations of Greek Romance* (Toronto: University of Toronto Press, 2012). Her focus is on the ways that ekphrasis involves the complex representation of identity in Renaissance prose imitations of Greek romances. She concentrates among British authors on Sir Philip Sidney, John Barclay, and Lady Mary Wroth—not Marlowe, who receives only a passing reference. While her focus is different from mine, her work helps affirm the importance of Greek romances as a neglected body of work necessary for understanding late sixteenth-century English literature. See also Samuel Lee Wolff, *The Greek Romances in Elizabethan Prose Fiction* (New York: Columbia University Press, 1912).

30. As Gordon Braden points out, Martin refers to Apuleius's second-century *Golden Ass* as a possible direct source both for Marlowe's description of the crowd's response to Hero and for the ekphrasis of Venus's temple, but MacLure omits mention of any post-Augustan author other than Musaeus. See Gordon Braden, *The Classics and English Renaissance Poetry: Three Case Studies* (New Haven: Yale University Press, 1978), 138. Reviewing MacLure's edition shortly after its publication, Roma Gill described it as an "inadequate re-working of L. C. Martin's edition" and a "disappointment"; *Review of English Studies* 21, no. 83 (Aug. 1970): 346–48. It may be no coincidence that one of the few references to the possible importance of post-Augustan antiquity to Marlowe's poem was published the year after Martin's edition, in Douglas Bush's 1932 *Mythology and the Renaissance Tradition in English Poetry*. In Patrick Cheney and Brian J. Striar's 2006 edition of Marlowe's poems, one of Martin's glosses of Apuleius reappears in the notes on Venus's temple, lines 133–57.

der is the central chapter of Gordon Braden's 1978 *The Classics and English Renaissance Poetry: Three Case Studies*. This text, however, focuses mostly on Renaissance translations of Marlowe's direct source, Musaeus (probably of the late fifth or early sixth century CE), and on the Nonnian school of which Musaeus was a part, rather than on the larger ekphrastic style of the post-Augustan Roman Empire, especially the Second Sophistic, as I will develop in this chapter.[31] I take as a jumping-off point Braden's suggestion that "Marlowe's hyperbolic style, and particularly his habit of insinuating hyperbole into the texts that he is imitating, suggest deep analogies of literary intent, not merely with Mousaios, but also with the even more extravagant tradition of which Mousaios was a relatively meek part."[32] My aim is to try to understand Marlowe's elusive style by looking at the influence of the literature just prior to Musaeus, focusing especially on the Second Sophistic Greek romances.

There is evidence of direct influence. Marlowe's conceit of the absurdly innocent lovers who don't know what sex is may originate in one of these romances, Longus's third-century-CE *Daphnis and Chloe*, which Jacques Amyot translates into French in 1559, removing the sexually most explicit parts, and which Angel Day translates into English in 1587, similarly censoring the text.[33] Also, Hero's agate and silver Temple of Venus, with its floor depicting images of the riotous pagan gods, may recall Athenaeus's description of the tessellated floor in *Hieron*'s great ship, "made of a variety

31. Musaeus is not my focus, but I will return to him briefly at the end of the chapter. I've limited my discussion of Musaeus in this way not only because Braden has already illuminated this aspect of the subject but, more importantly, because my concern is with the larger stylistic model of post-Augustan ekphrastic literature. Musaeus is in two ways problematic for this purpose. One is that, as Braden notes, Musaeus breaks with the stylistic mode of his time by *not* including any ekphrases; and, two, that Marlowe probably did not know that Musaeus was of the late fifth or early sixth century CE, and thus was not, as most Renaissance writers believed, the contemporary of Orpheus (pre-Homeric).

32. Braden, *The Classics and English Renaissance Poetry*, 136. Braden specifically discusses the importance of ekphrasis to the Nonnian school, saying that the form "eventually takes over the whole tradition" (72–75).

33. Day removes the opening ekphrasis and the story's most sexually explicit episodes, and he interpolates into the text his own pastoral poems. Amyot's translation is the more historically significant of the two; while reportedly only one copy of the Day text survives in any known public collection (in the British Library), Amyot's translation went through five editions before the end of the century (in 1559, 1578, 1594, 1596, and 1599). I discuss Amyot's changes below. See Heinz Hofmann, "The *Expositi* of Lorenzo Gambara di Brescia: A Sixteenth-Century Adaptation in Latin Hexameters of Longus' *Daphnis and Chloe*," in *Fictional Traces: Receptions of the Ancient Novel*, vol. 1, ed. Marília P. Futre Pinheiro and Stephen J. Harrison (Groningen: Barkhuis Publishing and Groningen University Library, 2011), 108–9.

of stones, in the pattern of which was wonderfully wrought the entire story of the *Iliad*" with, near the gangway, "a shrine of Aphrodite . . . with a floor made of agate and other stones" (5.207d–e).[34] Alternatively, this same temple may draw on another work of post-Augustan antiquity, Apuleius's *Golden Ass*, available in the popular Adlington translation of 1566. Cupid's bejeweled palace has a floor made "al of pretious stone, deuided and cut one from an other, whereon was carued diuers kindes of pictures" (book 5).[35]

In addition, Marlowe's text shares many features specifically with the Greek and Latin romances of the first few centuries CE. These romances constitute a remarkably cohesive body of literature with a common set of features,[36] many of which can also be found in Marlowe's poem: a preoccupation with virginity;[37] an emphatic demonstration of rhetoric especially

34. Athenaeus's *Deipnosophists* was available in Natale Conti's Latin translation of 1556. Tasso used this translation as a source for his *Discorsi del poema eroico*. See Dennis Looney, *Compromising the Classics: Romance Epic Narrative in the Italian Renaissance* (Detroit: Wayne State University Press, 1996), 69. In 1597–1600, the philologist Isaac Casaubon produced an edition of Athenaeus with commentary. Casaubon complained that, because of Athenaeus's triviality and lack of moral concern, his own efforts on this text were "catenati in ergastulo labores" (the labors of a man chained in prison). See Mark Pattison, *Isaac Casaubon, 1559–1614* (London: Longmans, Green, 1875), 123. However, despite Casaubon's distaste, table-talk books were a major genre in the Renaissance, and Athenaeus was "widely read," according to Michel Jeanneret, *A Feast of Words: Banquets and Table Talk in the Renaissance*, trans. Jeremy Whiteley and Emma Hughes (Cambridge: Polity Press, 1991), 65.

35. Apuleius, *The. xi. Bookes of the Golden Asse, conteininge the Metamorphosie of Lucius Apuleius, enterlaced with sondrie pleasaunt and delectable Tales, with an excellent Narration of the Mariage of Cupide and Psiches, set out in the. iiij. v. and vj Bookes*, trans. William Adlington (London: Henry Wykes, 1566), 46, Early English Books Online, http: //eebo.chadwyck.com. That this reference may be direct is supported, as L. C. Martin notes and Gordon Braden emphasizes, by the fact that Venus's temple is immediately preceded in the *Golden Ass* by a description of Psyche (4.28) that also resonates with Marlowe's account of Hero. Among various similarities linking Psyche and Hero, I would point especially to the idea of the heroine as a new Venus: Apuleius says that Psyche was "a newe Venus, endewed with the flower of virginitie" (44), and Marlowe says that Cupid "imagined Hero was his mother" (40). *Marlowe's Poems*, ed. L. C. Martin (New York: Dial Press, 1931), 34–35. See Braden, *The Classics and English Renaissance Poetry*, 137–39.

36. See Helen Morales's introduction to Achilles Tatius, *Leucippe and Clitophon*, trans. Tim Whitmarsh (Oxford: Oxford University Press, 2001), ix.

37. This virginity is defined not infrequently in relation to the love of a brother and sister. The plot in several Greek romances centers on the vigilant maintaining of the heroine's virginity until the end of the narrative. In Heliodorus, for example, the sexually unconsummated couple Charicleia and Theagenes sleep together chastely and pose as brother and sister until they can officially marry. In Achilles Tatius, Clitophon can tell Leucippe's father at the end of the book that he and his daughter have "became like brother and sister" (8.5). And in Longus, the lovers maintain until the last page a form of love "like brother and sister" (more or less)—not so much, in their case, because of a commitment to the institution of marriage but because they can't figure out how to have sex. Cf. Marlowe's Leander, who "as a brother with his sister toyed / Supposing nothing else

in the set speeches;[38] an exploration of problems of paideia or education;[39] and the presence of a peripheral male homosexual character who facilitates or obstructs the primary heterosexual narrative.[40]

What's key to my investigation is that these romances feature a proliferation of ekphrases, often occurring right at the beginning of the narrative. So begin Longus's *Daphnis and Chloe* and Achilles Tatius's *Leucippe and Clitophon*. And Heliodorus introduces an important ekphrasis, of Charicleia on the rock, within a few pages of the opening of his *Aethiopica*, which was especially popular in Underdowne's 1569 English translation. Also beginning in this manner are Lucian's *Heracles* and his *Calumny* and Cebes's *Pinax*; although these are not strictly romances, they are Second Sophistic works that share characteristics with these romances. Lucian's *Calumny* was especially well known, having been translated into Latin in 1518 by Philip Melanchthon and serving as the basis of an ekphrasis in Thomas Elyot's 1531 *Book of the Governor*.[41] These romances may lie behind Marlowe's three introductory ekphrases of Hero's clothing (9–50), Leander's body (51–90), and Venus's temple (135–60). By beginning in this manner, Marlowe utilizes a form of introduction that is characteristic of Second Sophistic literature.[42]

But more important for my purposes than tracking down the poem's

was to be done" (536–37). For Longus, see Moses Hadas's translation of *Daphnis and Chloe* in *Three Greek Romances* (Indianapolis: Bobbs-Merrill, 1964).

38. Rhetoric is a theme discussed among or practiced by the characters (through declamations, etc.); not infrequently, the rhetoric is specifically about erotic matters. At the end of book 5 of *Leucippe and Clitophon*, Melite gives an "exposition" to Clitophon, persuading him (successfully) to have sex with her; Achilles concludes this passage, "Eros is a resourceful, improvising sophist, who can turn any place into a temple for his mysteries" (5.27). Cf. Marlowe's Leander, who is "a bold sharp sophister" (197).

39. The principal characters undergo some process of education: in Longus, this is a sexual education; in the *Golden Ass*, Lucius is educated in professions and, eventually, comes into his own career as a priest of Isis and a lawyer. Cf. *Hero and Leander*, where experience eventually "taught" Leander "all that elder lovers know" (553).

40. In Longus, there is Gnathon; in Achilles Tatius, Clinias. These figures have the role of disrupting or facilitating the primary heterosexual narrative; their own story is subordinate to the romance's featured male-female couple. Cf. Marlowe's Neptune.

41. See Elyot's chapter called "Of Detraction, and the Image Thereby Made by the Painter Apelles."

42. Shadi Bartsch comments on the use of ekphrases at the beginning of Second Sophistic literary works; *Decoding the Ancient Novel: The Reader and the Role of Description in Heliodorus and Achilles Tatius* (Princeton: Princeton University Press, 1989), 40–41. See also Froma I. Zeitlin, "The Poetics of *Eros*: Nature, Art, and Imitation in Longus' *Daphnis and Chloe*," in *Before Sexuality: The Construction of Erotic Experience in the Ancient Greek World*, ed. David M. Halperin, John J. Winkler, and Froma I. Zeitlin (Princeton: Princeton University Press, 1990), 417–64; and "Figure: Ekphrasis," *Greece & Rome* 60, no. 1 (April 2013): 17–31.

profusion of multiple allusions, which often evoke more than one text at the same time, is recognizing that, in the cumulative effect of pictorial aestheticism, Marlowe's poem absorbs into itself an aesthetic that typifies the literature of post-Augustan antiquity. Douglas Bush alludes to the potential significance of the Second Sophistic to Marlowe's text[43] but, like other commentators, suggests that *Hero and Leander* repeats a post-Augustan aesthetic.[44] In contrast, I will argue that Marlowe's poetry works in a more dialectical way, absorbing this late-ancient literature's ekphrastic aesthetic into itself only to critique its fetishized reification by enlivening it with new tensions.[45]

Earlier in this chapter, I drew attention to three aspects of thingly post-Augustan literary style: a) how things are emphasized; b) how rhetoric becomes a thing; and c) how this aestheticism denies history. I now want to use these same categories to look specifically at how Marlowe challenges this reified literary inheritance, even as he uses it.

(a) A Streame of Liquid Pearle: Things Rendered Unthingly

Even outside the poem's ekphrastic moments, it is impossible to miss *Hero and Leander*'s pervasive thingliness. Gaudy and garish toys fill the lines of Marlowe's verse. Sometimes things in this poem play the role of sexual energy conductors and go-betweens. When Leander crawls into Hero's tower after swimming the Hellespont, it is her still-warm pillow and spot in bed that revive Leander's "drooping thoughts" (741). At other times, objects are not just conductors between people but substitutes for them; a man's possession of a woman's things represents his possession of her. After his first liaison with Hero, Leander sports her hair ribbon and ring and adorns his hat with myrtle (589–94), as if parading with spoils in a military triumph. In its preoccupation with things, the poem also explores the exchange of

43. Bush, *Mythology and the Renaissance Tradition in English Poetry*, 124.

44. Bush comments on the "anachronisms" that "never troubled an Elizabethan poet" (ibid., 129), but I think the insensitivity to anachronism is in this case partly our own in not recognizing the historically sensitive tensions than animate Marlowe's poetry. For example, Hero drops "her painted fan of curled plumes" (495) when leaving the temple not, as Bush suggests, because Marlowe imagined such an item could have been tucked into an ancient priestess's chiton but, on the contrary, because Marlowe wanted to exaggerate the tension between the historical layers of his poem by incongruously mixing the emphatically classical reference to Dido leaving the temple in book 1 of the *Aeneid* (1.495–504) with an object of contemporary fashion.

45. For *fetishism* I intend the same basic meaning that Georgia E. Brown offers in the passage cited on this chapter's opening page, where she refers to a fetish as "an object that is irrationally reverenced."

lovers' gifts. Neptune, upon seeing Leander naked, wants to make him his by giving him "gaudy toys to please his eye" (671), and the Destinies try to seduce Mercury with their own special gifts: "They offered him the deadly fatal knife / That shears the slender threads of human life" (447–48). Marlowe suggests that such lovers' gifts are odious for the sad reason that all rejected lovers' gifts are odious: because their gifts resemble them.[46] In Theocritus's Idyll 11, the Cyclops's rustic present of four bear cubs for the elegant nymph Galatea fares no better than the Destinies' morbid and pea-brainedly redundant "deadly fatal knife."

As Marlowe explores the commerce of objects, even people begin to seem like things. Hero apparently converts herself into a thingly state not only by donning an elaborate costume but also by striking poses both aestheticized and almost mechanistically coy: "Vailed to the ground, vailing her eyelids close, / And modestly they opened as she rose" (159–60); then, later, "Viewing Leander's face, [Hero] fell down and fainted" (486) and, upon recovering herself with humorous rapidity and popping back up after he kisses her, "Wherewith, as one displeased, away she trips. / Yet as she went, full often looked behind" (488–89). Hero is constructed, or constructs herself, as various coquettish images—several of which are recognizable as specifically *literary* images. The famous final image of her sliding naked out of bed with a blushing lack of self-possession plays on Ovid's ekphrasis of Corinna in *Elegies* 1.5. On account of such images, Claude J. Summers calls Hero "the ultimate commodity."[47]

Some of the poem's objects may recall the exotic objects that also fill the literature of late antiquity. Hero's famous buskins, with their chirping gold-and-pearl sparrows, evoke the kinds of things found in the ekphrases of Athenaeus, for example, one of which describes a procession that includes such wondrous objects as the statue of Nysa, which "could rise up automatically without anyone putting his hands to it, and after pouring a libation of milk from a gold saucer it could sit down again."[48]

However, even as Marlowe draws on this thing-packed tradition of late antiquity, his descriptions often seem to de-solidify the physical objects he is writing about. Consider his first ekphrasis of Hero. For all its emphasis

46. Cf. Tamburlaine's profession of love to Zenocrate: "My martial prizes, with five hundred men, / Won on the fifty-headed Volga's waves, / Shall all we offer to Zenocrate, / And then myself to fair Zenocrate" (1.2.102–5).

47. Claude J. Summers, "*Hero and Leander*: The Arbitrariness of Desire," in *Constructing Christopher Marlowe*, ed. J. A. Downie and J. T. Parnell (Cambridge: Cambridge University Press, 2000), 146.

48. Athenaeus 5.198f.

on thingliness—on Hero's hair and garments and jewelry and buskins—the ekphrasis also conveys a surprising lack of solidity:

> Many would praise the sweet smell as she passed,
> When 'twas the odour which her breath forth cast;
> And there for honey bees have sought in vain,
> And beat from thence, have lighted there again.
> About her neck hung chains of pebble-stone,
> Which lightened by her neck, like diamonds shone.
> She ware no gloves, for neither sun nor wind
> Would burn or parch her hands, but to her mind
> Or warm or cool them, for they took delight
> To play upon those hands, they were so white. (21–30)

The light flickers on Hero's hands; the bees, drawn by the sweetness of her breath, land and fly away and light again on her lips. Around her, everything seems to be hovering, playing, flickering, breathing. Marlowe's poetry, occupying an airy distance around Hero's surface, describes not her face but her hair; not her body but the material of her outer garments. And even these things are approached, more distantly still, by way of the unrequited desire they elicit from others: "Hero the fair, / Whom young Apollo courted for her hair" (5–6); "And there for honey bees have sought in vain" (23); and "for her the fairest Cupid pined" (37). Not unlike those bees, the reader is allowed to move toward Hero, to touch down upon her hair or blouse or buskins, but then is brushed away again. The objects Marlowe describes become the occasion for an unprecedented degree of motion and a frothy hyperbolic life. Like the bees, readers are kept hovering around Hero, who turns out to be not simply an object of beauty but a space for hypotheses about her that must be constantly revised. Marlowe describes her in this passage admiringly, yet at other moments with unsettling dark aspects that he never explains. Her kirtle, for example, has stains "made with the blood of wretched lovers slain" (16).

From within thingly images, Marlowe draws out unexpected forms of poetic motion. Consider his treatment of the reified image of tears as pearls. For the sake of comparison, here is Achilles Tatius's ekphrasis of tears in his Greek romance *Leucippe and Clitophon* (Achilles, although not translated into English until 1597, was available in Latin, 1554; Italian, 1560; and French, 1568):

> She was filled with tears on hearing this, and even her tears had their own distinctive beauty: for a tear swells the eye, making it more prominent. If the eye is vulgar and unattractive, it contributes to the ugliness; but if it is sweet, the black dye of the pupil softly garlanded with white, it resembles a fountain's

> generous breast whenever moistened by tears. When the salt water of tears floods around the eye, the outer part shines, while the black part turns deep crimson: the latter is like the violet, the former the narcissus. The tears laugh as they spin around the eyes. Such were Leucippe's tears: they overmastered her grief, and turned it into beauty. If they could have congealed as they fell, the earth would have had a novel kind of amber.[49]

In this ancient passage, elaborate though it is, the tears undergo just one phase transition (from liquid to solid), at the end of the description in the form of a conditional—a pretty phrase about a clearly imaginary event: "If they [the tears] could have congealed as they fell, the earth would have had a novel kind of amber." Like Achilles Tatius, Marlowe converts his heroine's tears into the hard commodity of precious stones. But in Marlowe's description, the first phase transition is just the beginning of a series that goes back and forth, each stage described as if real. There is no stable state: ". . . as she spake, / Forth from those two tralucent cisterns brake / A stream of liquid pearl, which down her face / Made milk-white paths, whereon the gods might trace / To Jove's high court" (295–99). And less than a hundred lines later, Marlowe turns Hero's tears back into hard pearls again: Hero "looked so dolefully, / As made Love sigh, to see his tyranny. / And as she wept, her tears to pearl he turned, / And wound them on his arm, and for her mourned" (373–76). As the tears shift back and forth between liquidity and solidity, the poetry shifts back and forth between suggesting, on the one hand, the ever-changing, flowing states of mind that constitute lived human experience and, on the other, aestheticized things.

Marlowe pushes his poetry toward aesthetic reification, but he does so to such an extreme that the poem as a whole starts to convey a lack of solidity. The poetry in its pulsations of meaning becomes like a living substance in a manner that is almost Hegelian insofar as it is in "the movement of positing itself, or is the mediation of its self-othering with itself."[50] Marlowe does not so much replicate the thingliness of post-Augustan antiquity as set his ear against this body of work and—through a kind of poetic auscultation—discover the unexpected life and movement that are buried in thingliness. Marlowe discovers a new poetic life that, "still panting rocked" (44), arises from within ekphrastic thingliness.

What has already started to emerge is not just the thingliness of things but also the thingliness of language itself. Let's probe this issue further.

49. I am quoting from Tim Whitmarsh's translation of *Leucippe and Clitophon*, 6.7.

50. G. W. F. Hegel, *Phenomenology of Spirit*, trans. A. V. Miller (Oxford: Oxford University Press, 1977), 10.

(b) *If Language Is a Thing, It Is Nothing*

Hero and Leander is studded with literary ornaments. As Bush observes, "Marlowe seems resolved to gather up all the pictorial conventions that tradition supplied and excel all predecessors in the luxuriant handling of them."[51] Flouting George Puttenham's advice concerning the "discrete using" of literary ornaments, which should be chosen by "all measure and just proportion,"[52] Marlowe's over-the-top poetry decorates itself in the most glittering garments of verse.[53]

Yet, in so doing, Marlowe's work also subverts this apparent literary fetishism. Across his corpus, he probes the relationship of words and things—and reveals how language can become empty when it is aestheticized. I have already referred to Mycetes, the ineffectual King of Persia in *Tamburlaine I*, who is a connoisseur of rhetoric. His rhetorical aestheticism becomes most evident when he concocts his own mini-ekphrasis:

> I long to see thee back return from thence,
> That I may view these milk-white steeds of mine
> All loaden with the heads of killed men,
> And from their knees even to their hoofs below
> Besmeared with blood, that makes a dainty show. (1.1.76–80)

A Renaissance reader would recognize the play of red on white (blood on milk-white steeds) as a Petrarchan trope of love poetry, repeated throughout

51. Bush, *Mythology and the Renaissance Tradition in English Poetry*, 128.

52. George Puttenham, *The Art of English Poesy: A Critical Edition*, ed. Frank Whigham and Wayne A. Rebhorn (Ithaca: Cornell University Press, 2007), 222.

53. Georgia Brown argues that this excessive adornment became part of a larger turn toward aestheticism in the literature of the period. She describes a new literary sensibility that was emerging among a generation of writers in the 1590s who embraced the "shameful" aspects of the literature they produced. Rejecting the grave moralism of the previous generation of humanists, these writers decorated their prose with ornaments—notably ekphrases—and used such figures to develop a poetry of the margins. Ribald, emphatically artificial, self-effeminizing poetry like Marlowe's epyllion demanded attention—not despite its triviality but precisely because of it, she argues. See Brown, *Redefining Elizabethan Literature* (Cambridge: Cambridge University Press, 2004). In "Breaking the Canon: Marlowe's Challenge to the Literary Status Quo in *Hero and Leander*," in *Marlowe, History, and Sexuality: New Critical Essays on Christopher Marlowe*, ed. Paul Whitfield White (New York: AMS Press, 1998), 59–75, Brown writes that Marlowe's epyllion "exploits its own guilty errors in order to promote a shamelessly self-indulgent authorial voice" (59) and, in embracing literary license, "defines a space for literature which is free from the strictures of morality" (62). Although I place greater emphasis on the moral aspects of Marlowe's work, I draw on her account of the hyperbolic qualities of his style. See also her "Gender and Voice in *Hero and Leander*," in *Constructing Christopher Marlowe*, ed. J. A. Downie and J. T. Parnell (Cambridge: Cambridge University Press, 2000), 148–63.

the period, usually in admiration of a beloved's blushing skin. Mycetes is following all the principles of classical rhetoric that he's been taught (other than perhaps decorum). By casting in aesthetic terms the dripping decapitated heads, his speech brings the described scene "clearly before the eyes," just as the *progymnasmata* say that a description should—but, with the pronoun "that" in the last line ("Besmeared with blood, that makes a dainty show"), the speech also reflects on itself as a speech, as an object of aestheticized pleasure.

The antecedent of "that" is the violent image Mycetes's speech has just evoked, the chopped-off heads, but the pronoun also refers to the speech itself *as a speech*, as a rhetorical object: "*that* makes a dainty show." It is as though Mycetes were taking a step back from the image he has just made to appreciate its rhetorical construction. This reification characterizes Mycetes's language: "And 'tis a pretty toy to be a poet. / Well, well, Meander, thou art deeply read, / And having thee, I have a jewel sure" (2.2.54–6). Poetry and poets are rendered as possessions—as toys and jewels—but in a manner that reflects on them as such, which makes their reification available for critical consideration.[54] For a moment, Mycetes seems as childish as a schoolboy, expecting approval for the rhetorical exercise he has just performed.[55]

In *Hero and Leander*, Marlowe similarly probes the problems of aestheticized language. The three ekphrases at the poem's opening are followed by Leander's three rhetorical declamations to Hero (199–294,

54. For the sake of contrast, recall the Occitan warrior poet Bertran de Born of the late twelfth through early thirteenth centuries. His astonishing images of the battlefield, just as sensorial, imply no such critique of the aestheticization of violence: "I tell you, eating or drinking or sleeping hasn't such savor [sabor] for me as the moment I hear both sides shouting 'Get 'em!' and I hear riderless horses crashing through the shadows, and I hear men shouting, 'Help! Help!' and I see the small and the great falling in the grassy ditches, and I see the dead with splintered lances, decked with pennons, through their sides." (E•us dic qe tant no m'a sabor / manjar ni beure ni dormir / cum a qand auch cridar, "A lor!" / d'ambas las partz, et auch bruir / cavals voitz per l'ombratge, / et auch cridar, "Aidatz! Aidatz!" / e vei cazer per los fossatz / paucs e grans per l'erbatge, / e vei los mortz qe pels costatz / ant los tronchos ab los cendatz.) Represented here is the brutality of the physical, but not submitted for critique—rather, the physical is rising toward its exaltation. See the fifth stanza of "Be•m plai lo gais temps de pascor," in *The Poems of the Troubadour Bertran de Born*, ed. William D. Paden Jr., Tilde Sankovitch, and Patricia H. Stäblein (Berkeley: University of California Press, 1986), 342–43.

55. Lynn Enterline (*Shakespeare's Schoolroom*, 113) notes that many of Lorichius's examples in the Renaissance edition of Aphthonius's *Progymnasmata* concern moments of brutality and violence, as this ekphrasis does. Such ekphrases may have resonated among the schoolboys who, frequently whipped by their schoolmasters, were enduring their own experiences of pedagogical violence. See also William P. Weaver, *Untutored Lines: The Making of the English Epyllion* (Edinburgh: Edinburgh University Press, 2012), who explores the fact that in most sixteenth-century editions, Musaeus's *Hero and Leander* was printed alongside Aesop's *Fables*, concretizing the connection between the Hero and Leander story and texts associated with grammar school education.

299–310, 315–28), in which he tries to convince her to have sex with him. His first attempts are described in terrifically overblown language:

> And now begins Leander to display
> Love's holy fire, with words, with sighs and tears,
> Which like sweet music entered Hero's ears,
> And yet at every word she turned aside,
> And always cut him off as he replied.
> At last, like to a bold sharp sophister,
> With cheerful hope thus he accosted her. (192–98)

A good student of Aphthonius, Leander attempts to "display" his passion through over-aestheticized words and gestures. He is the "bold sharp sophister"—a phrase where the last word "sophister" produces a sing-song double rhyme with the next line's "accosted her."

But Leander's language turns out to be weirdly empty. Marlowe subjects to scrutiny the ways in which such aestheticized language can reify people and experience, and, ultimately, turn language itself into an object. Leander reifies Hero by comparing her and her virginity to a long inventory of things: a diamond (215), a "stately builded ship, well-rigged and tall" (225), "untuned golden strings" (229), a brass vessel (231), treasure (234), "rich robes" (237), a palace (239), "empty houses" (242), "a mass of drossy pelf" (244), a "fair gem" (247), water (264), "base bullion" (265), an "idol" (269), and corn (327). Through language, Hero is made into a thing, and the physical rules that govern material objects then seem to govern her. If a brass vessel shines brighter by being "oft handled" (231), so, too, it seems, does a person. In acknowledging only things, Leander arrives at the conclusion that Hero's virginity—which has now been rendered a thing—is nothing: "Of that which hath no being, do not boast; / Things that are not at all, are never lost" (275–76). Marlowe shows the vapidity of the rhetoric of this "bold sharp sophister."

Marlowe's treatment of his characters' sexual explorations is a set of experiments in the simultaneously thingly and empty qualities of overly artful language. The poem seems to ask over and over: What do words have to do with physical experience? Hero and Leander's sexual explorations are described in terms that are simultaneously both overly pictorial and oddly empty, and create a confusing experience for the reader. The couple's first time in bed is described as follows:

> He asked, she gave, and nothing was denied;
> Both to each other quickly were affied.

Look how their hands, so were their hearts united,
And what he did she willingly requited.
(Sweet are the kisses, the embracements sweet,
When like desires and affections meet,
For from the earth to heaven is Cupid raised,
Where fancy is in equal balance peised.)
Yet she this rashness suddenly repented,
And turned aside, and to herself lamented,
As if her name and honour had been wronged
By being possessed of him for whom she longed;
Ay, and she wished, albeit not from her heart,
That he would leave her turret and depart. (509–22)

If it seems at first that we are going to be voyeurs of the sexual act, Marlowe immediately hinders this expectation. The first line makes us think that the couple has already had sex that we didn't get to see ("He asked, she gave, and nothing was denied"), but then, a couple of lines later, the pictorial language makes us think that, no, maybe we will, after all, get to see something ("Look how . . ."). However, our naughty peeping reveals nothing because, confusingly, what we see is only the lovers holding hands. Revising our initial impression that the lovers have had sex, we decide now they have not. But then, immediately, finding Hero repenting of "being possessed of him for whom she longed," we have to revise our hypothesis back: something *has* happened. And, wobbling our impression of what has happened back and forth between something and nothing, so the narrative goes:

Albeit Leander, rude in love, and raw,
Long dallying with Hero, nothing saw
That might delight him more, yet he suspected
Some amorous rites or other were neglected.
Therefore unto his body hers he clung;
She, fearing on the rushes to be flung,
Strived with redoubled strength; the more she strived,
The more a gentle pleasing heat revived,
Which taught him all that elder lovers know.
And now the same 'gan so to scorch and glow,
As in plain terms (yet cunningly) he craved it;
Love always makes those eloquent that have it.
She, with a kind of granting, put him by it,
And ever as he thought himself most nigh it,
Like to the tree of Tantalus she fled,
And, seeming lavish, saved her maidenhead. (545–60)

Leander is "rude in love, and raw." His fumblings are only a version, however, of the readerly interpretive fumblings that we have just been through, seeing at first *nothing that might delight us more,* but then suspecting that *some amorous rites or other were neglected.* At the heart of this passage is the discovery, to which Marlowe's poetry has led us, that extreme linguistic thingliness is actually linguistic emptiness. What we—or Leander—have been seeking ("it") lacks any referent. Repeated four times at the ends of lines 555–58, this word "it" presents itself as the thing in "plain terms," *ad rem,* and yet this thing expresses exactly nothing. As Judith Haber quips, "Now you have it, now you don't."[56] The word "it" is, after all, just a placeholder for experience.

The literary history of the Second Sophistic is important here. In *Daphnis and Chloe,* as in *Hero and Leander,* the young lovers have lain together physically but somehow haven't figured out what to do with their bodies other than hug and kiss. In Longus's original version of this scene, an older woman, Lycainion, promises to teach Daphnis how to have sexual intercourse with a woman, at which point:

> Daphnis could hardly restrain himself for pleasure, but like the rustic and goatherd and lover and callow youth that he was, he fell at Lycainion's feet and implored her to teach him as quickly as possible that art of love so that he might have his desire with Chloe. Moreover, as if he were going to learn some mystery great and heaven-sent, he promised to give Lycainion a suckling kid and soft cheeses made of the first milk and the she-goat with them. When Lycainion discovered such ingenuousness as she had never expected of a goatherd she began to tutor Daphnis after this fashion. She bade him to sit down by her directly and to bestow kisses upon her, of the customary quality and quantity, and in the midst of his kissing to embrace her and lie down on the ground. When he had sat down and kissed her and lain down, and she discovered that he was now able to act and was bursting with swollen energy, she raised him from his reclining position to his side and featly placed herself underneath, and then put him in the way of the desired path [ὁδὸν]. Nature provided instruction on what was next to be done. (3.18)[57]

Simon Goldhill observes that "as the narrative reaches the moment beyond which Daphnis has been unable to progress without explicit instruction, the description reverts to the most euphemistic expression. If it is knowledge

56. Judith Haber, "'True-loves Blood': Narrative and Desire in *Hero and Leander,*" *English Literary Renaissance* 28, no. 3 (Autumn 1998): 380.

57. I am quoting Moses Hadas's translation of *Daphnis and Chloe* in *Three Greek Romances,* 43.

for which you read this text, the narrative leads you down the path, but refuses—precisely—the information sought."[58] Longus's narrative, in other words, provides the most exacting pseudo-pornographic physical detail, but at the sought-for center reverts to a clichéd literary euphemism and, as does Marlowe with his "it," constructs a conspicuous blank: Lycainion puts Daphnis on the *road* (ὁδὸν). The curtain of discretion having dropped, the narrative then sententiously informs us that all the rest was left to the instinctive teachings of Nature.

Although it is unlikely that this specific scene in its original form could have directly influenced Marlowe, the language of sexual euphemism is, along with the obsession for virginity, a mainstay of these Second Sophistic romances. Day and the cleric Amyot cut from their translations the most explicit moments of the romance, which use language about sex that is curiously similar to Marlowe's poem. If Marlowe read the work in Amyot's French, he would have encountered the titillating euphemism of Longus's original language curiously magnified by Renaissance censorship. First published the same year as Paul IV's *Index librorum prohibitorum*, Amyot's translation deletes the romance's most erotic episodes but, in so doing, does not avoid making these deleted parts strangely conspicuous. Amyot includes the scene with Lycainion but eliminates the last three sentences of the passage I quoted above. In not otherwise modifying this passage, Amyot (or the publisher of the 1559 edition) makes the gap in the narrative evident as a gap: "Thus Lycoenion, finding in this young goatherd a simplicity greater than she had thought, began to convey the lesson in the following manner. Finished with this apprenticeship, Daphnis . . ." (Aussi Lycoenion trouuant en ce ieune cheurier vne simplicité plus grande qu'elle n'eust pensé, conmença à le passer maistre en cette maniere. Finy cest apprentissage, Daphnis . . .).[59] Thus, the translation in its own way constructs the sought-for "lesson" as an omission in the text. Amyot also deletes the erotic bathing scene in book 1. In this case, the entire scene has been removed, but the absence is marked by the following in all capital letters: "EN CEST ENDROIT Y A" (IN THIS PLACE THERE IS), and then, just below, in a smaller font and all lowercase letters, as though the text were leaning

58. Simon Goldhill, *Foucault's Virginity: Ancient Erotic Fiction and the History of Sexuality* (Cambridge: Cambridge University Press, 1995), 26.

59. Longus, *Les amovrs pastorals de Daphnis et de Chloé, escriptes premierement en grec par Longus, & puis traduictes en François* (Paris pour Vincent Sertenas, demeurant en le rue neuue nostre Dame, à l'enseigne sainct lehan l'Euangeliste: et en sa boutique au Palais, en la gallerie par ou on va à la chancellerie, 1559), Houghton FC5 Am987 559.

forward confidentially to whisper, "vne grande omission en l'original." This "omission" is the place-nonplace where, we are to imagine, the sexuality happens. In that sense, the text becomes fetishistic by constructing a gap that serves as substitute for erotic satisfaction.

Marlowe takes up this game but develops it in a new direction. If the language in romances like *Daphnis and Chloe* collapses into fetishism, the language in *Hero and Leander* promises to do the same—but never quite delivers. Haber reminds us that in modern editions, the poem is usually edited so that it builds more neatly toward sexual consummation; this requires moving twelve lines so that Leander enters the garden only *after* a period of struggle (rather than, as in the 1598 edition, in the reverse order). The text that Marlowe wrote may not have aligned narrative climax so unproblematically with sexual climax.[60] Destabilizing the fetishistic possibilities of the text, Marlowe calls up an end-directed narrative at the same time as he diverts his readers endlessly from it, as Haber says.[61]

When Hero and Leander do finally have intercourse, or seem to, near the end of the poem, the experience is—after all the elaborate rhetoric—described as something that exists both inside and outside rhetoric:

> She trembling strove; this strife of hers (like that
> Which made the world) another world begat
> Of unknown joy. Treason was in her thought,
> And cunningly to yield herself she sought. (775–78)

Even at this moment, where the action seems to belong finally to the physical, to bodies, Marlowe immediately reinscribes this assertion of elemental physical reality that lies outside thought back into the realm of thought: "Treason was in her thought." The thing, the "act," the "*it*" lies both inside and outside the realm of mental constructs in a highly unstable fashion—the erotic becoming almost a metaphor for this fluctuation between inner and outer realities.

60. Haber, "'True-loves Blood,'" 381–83. What are called lines 763–74 in most modern editions ("Wherein Leander on her quivering breast" to "Forth plungeth, and oft flutters with her wing") were originally printed immediately *after* what we now call line 784 ("That pulls or shakes it from the golden tree"). This emendation dates from C. F. Tucker Brooke's edition in 1910. Until this correction, Hero seemed to resist Leander only after he had entered the Hesperides.

61. For an exploration of how ekphrases and other forms of rhetorical performance in *Hero and Leander* constitute "Marlowe's cheeky reaction to the social teleology laid down by schoolmasters," see Lynn Enterline, "Elizabethan Minor Epic," in *The Oxford History of Classical Reception in English Literature*, vol. 2, *1558–1660*, ed. Patrick Cheney and Philip Hardie (Oxford: Oxford University Press, 2015), 253–71; 260 quoted.

(c) *While the Virgins of Damascus Are Slaughtered*

Whereas the literature of late antiquity attempted to cloak itself with aestheticism, Marlowe's poetry constantly alludes to the history that this aestheticism conceals. In some cases, he does so through creating an effect of dissonance, or a lack of fit, between the poem's historical layers. In this light, consider again the ekphrasis of Hero's buskins:

> Buskins of shells all silvered used she,
> And branched with blushing coral to the knee,
> Where sparrows perched, of hollow pearl and gold,
> Such as the world would wonder to behold:
> Those with sweet water oft her handmaid fills,
> Which as she went would chirrup through the bills. (31–36)

The emphatically English words with which the ekphrasis ends—the onomatopoeic "chirrup" (which, having only recently become a verb in English, would have sounded emphatically modern[62]) and the "bills" (derived from the Old English *bile*)—are enough in themselves to make the reader feel the incongruity between the early modern English context and the over-the-top classical costume.

In other cases, Marlowe emphasizes the historical reality that underlies ornate objects by suggesting their economic value as commodities. In the sixteenth century, luxury goods were becoming increasingly available and beginning to threaten class distinctions—to the point in England where sumptuary laws had to be reinforced on a class basis.[63] This fashion produced, in the words of Philip Stubbes, a "mingle mangle" of class distinctions. Stubbes complained that "you shall haue those, which are neither of the nobylitie gentilitie, nor yeomanry, no, nor yet anie Magistrat or Officer in the common welth, go daylie in silkes, veluets, satens, damasks, taffeties, and such like, notwithstanding that they be both base by byrthe, meane by estate, & seruyle by calling. This is a great confusion & a general disorder, God be mercyfull vnto vs."[64] Hero's "purple silk" (10),

62. The *OED* states that the first usage of this word as a verb is implied in Spenser's *Shepheardes Calender* ("June"): "Thy rymes . . . Whose Echo . . . taught the byrdes . . . Frame to thy songe their cheerefull cheriping."

63. N. B. Harte, "State Control of Dress and Social Change in Pre-Industrial England," in *Trade, Government and Economy in Pre-Industrial England: Essays Presented to F. J. Fisher*, ed. D. C. Coleman and A. H. John (London: Weidenfeld & Nicolson, 1976), 139.

64. Philip Stubbes, *The Anatomie of Abuses* (London: Richard Jones, 1583), 10r, Early English

which was associated with Tyrian purple and decadence in Latin literature, was specifically restricted to the royal family by the 1533 sumptuary laws.[65] Hero, in her tawdry splendor, comically exceeds any vestige of aristocratic *sprezzatura* or repose. Whereas Spenser's Belphoebe, who also wears buskins, is an unambiguously aristocratic maiden clad in gold, costly Spanish leather, and "rich iewell,"[66] Hero can only hope to be such a maiden. But her kirtle is stained with blood, and her jewels are only pebble-stones. Hero's garish costume shows its seams through the slippage between intention and effect,[67] as though anticipating what Norbert Elias calls "kitsch style."[68] What differentiates Marlowe is that he *seeks* this quality of slippage or ill-fittedness.

Not dissimilarly, in the ekphrasis of Leander (51–90), Marlowe casts Leander as an overdone classical commodity. The narrator likens his blond "dangling tresses" to the Golden Fleece, that most famous luxury object of the East, the quest for which marked the end of the Golden Age. And Neptune wants to give Leander "gaudy toys": the word *gaudy,* which was not exclusively negative as in the modern usage, may nonetheless carry class-based implications of bourgeois ostentation. This usage is suggested by the aristocratic Polonius's advice to Laertes in *Hamlet,* wherein "gaudy" is contrasted with the truly "rich": "Costly thy habit as thy purse can buy / But not express'd in fancy; *rich, not gaudy*" (1.3.69–70).[69] Whether such comments are parodying parvenu bourgeois ostentation or depicting anxi-

Books Online, http://eebo.chadwyck.com. This text went through five editions between 1583 and 1595. See Harte, "State Control," 141–42.

65. Ibid., 143. See also Christopher J. Berry, *The Idea of Luxury: A Conceptual and Historical Investigation* (Cambridge: Cambridge University Press, 1994).

66. "Below her ham her weed did somewhat trayne, / And her streight legs most brauely were embayld / In gilden buskins of costly Cordwayne, / All bard with golden bendes, which were entayld / With curious antickes, and full fayre aumayld: / Before they fastned were vnder her knee / In a rich iewell, and therein entrayld / The ends of all the knots, that none might see, / How they within their fouldings close enrapped bee" (2.3.27). See Edmund Spenser, *The Faerie Queene*, ed. A. C. Hamilton, Hiroshi Yamashita, Toshiyuki Suzuki, and Shohachi Fukuda (Harlow, UK: Longman, Pearson Education, 2007).

67. Spenser probably chose to conceal the ends of Belphoebe's boot in order, as Hamilton says, to suggest so-called virgin knots symbolizing her maidenhood.

68. Norbert Elias, "The Kitsch Style and the Age of Kitsch," in *The Norbert Elias Reader*, ed. Johan Goudsblom and Stephen Mennell (Oxford: Blackwell, 1998), 26–35. For the literary manifestation of anxieties about the conflict between the desire for economic prosperity and the moral danger of luxuriousness, see Joshua Scodel, *Excess and Mean in Early Modern English Literature* (Princeton: Princeton University Press, 2002), 111–41. See also Maurice Dobb, "The Beginnings of the Bourgeoisie" in his *Studies in the Development of Capitalism* (London: George Routledge & Sons, 1946), 83–122.

69. Cited in the *OED*, "gaudy," adj. 2, def. 3.

eties about aristocratic splendor, the attention is directed at these objects as economic signifiers.[70]

Late antiquity aspired toward the "timeless order of the Muses" through the use of objects. These things often conveyed the promise of innocence and a return, even, of a lost paradise. Marlowe, by contrast, repeatedly reveals throughout his corpus realities that this regressive Golden Age fantasy of things excluded.

By bringing out the history of suffering that aestheticism represses, Marlowe challenges this aestheticism. For example, in *Tamburlaine I*, Marlowe frames with violence Tamburlaine's famous ode to Zenocrate's beauty (5.1.135-90). It is while the citizens of Damascus are being slaughtered that the audience hears Tamburlaine lovingly compare his beloved to Flora "in her morning's pride / shaking her silver tresses in the air, / [who] Rain'st on the earth resolved pearls in showers," imagining that "Beauty, mother to the Muses, sits / and comments volumes with her ivory pen." Marlowe uses the emphatically artful metaphor of tears as pearls, but now the violent framing of the scene begins to suggest their real-world material existence as spoils of war.[71] By asserting the brutality of the context, Marlowe shows, as the literature of post-Augustan antiquity did not, that the order of the Muses is born under the pressures of the current world order's accumulated sufferings—sufferings that, in this case, Tamburlaine himself is inflicting.

It is the *fantasy* of ahistoricity that Marlowe constantly exposes through his attention to objects. In *Dido, Queen of Carthage*, just after Aeneas has told his tale of escaping Troy at the end of act 2—a scene that represents,

70. In "Marlowe's Poems and Classicism," in *The Cambridge Companion to Christopher Marlowe*, Brown explores how *Hero and Leander* reflects on conditions of economic exchange. For her, Marlowe undermines the idealized incorporeal text by showing how his own writing is implicated in capitalist exchange (the Bourdieu-ish "symbolic capital [that] Marlowe accrues through his poetic accomplishments," 119). She writes: "His text is structurally and thematically scandalous, but at least it does not lie, nor advance claims to disinterestedness and moral purity that cannot be maintained" (118).

71. Pearls are commonly listed in ekphrases of triumphs. The most spectacular example is the portrait head of Pompey. Made entirely of pearls, it was carried in his September 29, 61 BCE triumph, which celebrated Pompey's victory over the East (especially over King Mithradates Eupator of Pontus). This triumph "first inclined our taste toward pearls and gems," according to Pliny, *Naturalis historia* 37.6.14. See J. J. Pollitt, *The Art of Rome, c. 753 B.C.–337 A.D.: Sources and Documents* (Englewood Cliffs, NJ: Prentice-Hall, 1966), 65. In the sixteenth century, pearls were luxury goods of significant economic importance, coveted as symbols of power and wealth. Shipped in large numbers from the New World via Seville, they were part of the "traffick of Pearles and Pepper" that Montaigne lamented for the consequent destruction inflicted on tribal peoples. Quoted in R. A. Donkin, *Beyond Price: Pearls and Pearl-Fishing: Origins to the Age of Discoveries* (Philadelphia: American Philosophical Society, 1998), 279.

on many levels, historical suffering—Dido says that the story has made her sad. Hoping to find "some pleasing sport, / To rid me from these melancholy thoughts" (2.1.302–3), she exits the stage. It is as if the play then responds to her desire for diversion when Venus and Cupid enter and try to win over Ascanius by listing sweet things and shiny trinkets that they will give him: "sugar-almonds, sweet conserves, / A silver girdle and a golden purse" (2.1.305–6). Venus lulls Ascanius to sleep by promising him ever more things, which soon prove as soporific as Cerberus's honey-soaked sop:

> Such bow, such quiver, and such golden shafts,
> Will Dido give to sweet Ascanius.
> For Dido's sake I take thee in my arms
> And stick these spangled feathers in thy hat;
> Eat comfits in mine arms, and I will sing.
> Now is he fast asleep, and in this grove,
> Amongst green brakes, I'll lay Ascanius,
> And strew him with sweet-smelling violets,
> Blushing roses, purple hyacinth;
> These milk-white doves shall be his sentinels,
> Who, if that any seek to do him hurt,
> Will quickly fly to Cytherea's fist. (2.1.311–22)

These things, which seem so supercharged with sensation, are actually only minimally described—it is the list-like form that conveys the sense of excess. If things in Marlowe's poetry express a desire for innocence, Marlowe frames this desire with the awareness of history (the fall of Troy).[72] Marlowe's materiality expresses the desire for escape, for "some pleasing sport," but Marlowe also makes the reader constantly aware of what the characters are trying to escape.

72. A related poetic effect can be found at the end of the *Aeneid* book 1, just before Aeneas recounts the story of Troy's fall: "Cupid went forth, carrying the royal gifts for the Tyrians. As he enters, the queen has already, amid royal hangings, laid herself on a golden couch, and taken her place in their midst. Now father Aeneas, now the Trojan youth gather, and the guests recline on coverlets of purple. Servants pour water on their hands, serve bread from baskets, and bring smooth-shorn napkins. There are fifty serving-maids within, whose task it is to arrange the long feast in order and keep the hearth aglow with fire. A hundred more there are, with as many pages of like age, to load the board with viands and set out the cups. The Tyrians, too, are gathered in throngs throughout the festal halls; summoned to recline on the embroidered couches, they marvel at the gifts of Aeneas, marvel at Iulus, at the god's glowing looks and well-feigned words, at the robe and the veil, embroidered with saffron acanthus" (1.695–711). This description of the banquet similarly works by overcharging Virgil's audience with sensations and inducing a blurry effect almost of intoxication. I am quoting H. R. Fairclough's translation, Virgil, *Eclogues. Georgics. Aeneid 1–6*, rev. G. P. Goold (Cambridge, MA: Loeb Classical Library, 1999).

In a similar manner, objects offer a Golden Age fantasy for Dido in her speech of love. This speech, too, is a fantasy of escape that Marlowe counters with an awareness of history. Dido's speech, which plays on Marlowe's much-quoted pastoral poem "Come Live with Me and Be My Love,"[73] is a Golden Age fantasy. But the stuff evoked by this fantasy is associated with later stages of civilization that the Golden Age explicitly precludes: gold, trade (ivory), money, and ships.[74]

> I'll give thee tackling made of rivelled gold,
> Wound on the barks of odoriferous trees;
> Oars of massy ivory, full of holes,
> Through which the water shall delight to play.
> Thy anchors shall be hewed from crystal rocks,
> Which if thou lose shall shine above the waves;
> The masts whereon thy swelling sails shall hang,
> Hollow pyramides of silver plate;
> The sails of folded lawn, where shall be wrought
> The wars of Troy, but not Troy's overthrow;
> For ballast, empty Dido's treasury,
> Take what ye will, but leave Aeneas here. (3.1.115–26)

Golden Age fantasies have, of course, nothing to do with the actual origins of humankind; they are, among Marlowe's characters, the afterimage of historical anxieties. Most interestingly, Dido explicitly promises to leave out from her ekphrastic image any reference to Troy's fall. On the sails "shall be wrought / The wars of Troy, but not Troy's overthrow."[75] The fantasies of humankind's earliest origins (the Golden Age) and of time's end (heaven) are so similar possibly because the desires that underlie them are alike[76]; both fantasies express historical weariness (the loss of Troy in this case), which would be inconceivable in an age without historical awareness. Mar-

73. Riggs, *The World of Christopher Marlowe*, 108, 124–25.

74. In the *Metamorphoses*, Ovid describes the Golden Age by listing all the things that have not yet corrupted the era: "Not yet had the pine-tree, felled on its native mountains, descended thence into the watery plain to visit other lands; men knew no shores except their own" (1.94–96; Nondum caesa suis, peregrinum ut viseret orbem,/ montibus in liquidas pinus descenderat undas, / nullaque mortals prater sua litora norant). Ovid, *Metamorphoses*, books 1–8, trans. Frank Justus Miller, rev. G. P. Goold (Cambridge, MA: Harvard University Press, 1977).

75. The Virgilian precedent is the ekphrasis of Daedalus's gates at the entrance to the Sibyl's cave. Virgil describes the painful event that Daedalus has *omitted* from his image—the death of his son, Icarus: "twice he had tried to fashion the fall in gold, twice the hand of the father fell" (6.32–33; bis conatus erat casus effingere in auro, / bis patriae cecidere manus). My translation.

76. See Harry Levin, *The Myth of the Golden Age in the Renaissance* (Bloomington: Indiana University Press, 1969).

lowe's poetry is not materialist or sensualist or "decadent"—to return to a word that recurs in Marlowe criticism[77]—but, rather, produces a critique of materialism by showing the ways that materialist fantasies are, despite themselves, related to history. This is why, in Marlowe's poetry, lists of things are so often related to regressive states, like childhood, the pastoral, and sleep. Marlowe is not regressive; rather, he has framed the regressive as such. In so doing, his poetry critiques or subverts the stance of ahistoricity or timelessness associated with "the timeless order of the Muses."

In undermining aestheticism, Marlowe develops a radically critical poetics. C. S. Lewis is right to emphasize what he calls Marlowe's "material imagination"—his insistence on things ("he writes best about flesh, gold, gems, stone, fire, clothes, water, snow, and air")—but I think Lewis is wrong to suggest that this emphasis makes Marlowe a sensualist on "holiday from all facts and all morals."[78] Marlowe's poetry is much more dialectical than such criticism acknowledges, in that his poetry of things consistently undermines its own potential escapism. His poetry proceeds by an emphatically critical process of reevaluation, a process that late antiquity's intensely aestheticized thingliness, and its time-frozen emotional concomitant, sentimentality, cannot endure.

Working against post-Augustan antiquity's fantasy of the so-called uncontaminated spring of the Muses, Marlowe's poetry subjects this fantasy of virginal aestheticized innocence to a scrutiny that demythologizes it. Hero and Leander have their own tawdry charm that never entirely escapes an inverse sense of the darkness and brutality of the world. In place of post-Augustan antiquity's effete aesthetics, I find in Marlowe a spirit of insistent criticalness and a disquieting humor.

Marlowe's *Hero and Leander* resists its own reification. If this dynamic self-opposition is hard to describe, it is also what interests me. It interests

77. The word *decadent* is also a turn-of-the-century "code word" for homosexual. In her *Fathers and Daughters in Shakespeare and Shaw* (Westport, CT: Greenwood Press, 2001), 33, Lagretta Tallent Lenker refers to Marlowe's supposed "decadence" in the criticism and cites, for the association of the word with homosexuality in the fin de siècle, Elaine Showalter, *Sexual Anarchy: Gender and Culture at the Fin de Siècle* (New York: Viking, 1990), 171. The history of Marlovian criticism is imbued with chastising attitudes toward homosexuality—even when, or particularly when, Marlowe's own sexuality is not directly discussed. Bush, for example, observes in 1932 that Leander "is supposedly a strong and bold swimmer, but many of the descriptive lines have a taint of effeminacy" (*Mythology and the Renaissance Tradition in English Poetry*, 130), which gives rise in 1977 to Keach's protest, "but it is apparent from the narrator's praise of Leander's back that there is nothing weak or unmasculine about his musculature" (*Elizabethan Erotic Narratives*, 96).

78. See C. S. Lewis, *English Literature in the Sixteenth Century, Excluding Drama* (Oxford: Clarendon Press, 1954), 486.

me because this inner movement of form, as the poem works both with and against the history it has embodied, is what ultimately makes an art object unlike any other kind of object—in other words, what makes it never simply a thing. I have tried to bring out some of the dynamic inner life of *Hero and Leander* through comparison with the late-antique literature against which Marlowe is responding. If reification results from a kind of forgetting, as Adorno famously claimed,[79] then *de*-reification may require perceiving history, and thereby entering into the unresolved historical dynamics that constitute and energize literary form. For Adorno, aesthetic tensions are historical: "The unsolved antagonisms of reality return in artworks as immanent problems of form," he writes. "This, not the insertion of objective elements, defines the relation of art to society."[80] In other words, understanding a poetry's links to a period requires not only working out its references to contemporary matters but also working through the poetry's inner tensions. It is in this sense that I understand Adorno's idea that "to analyze artworks means no less than to become conscious of the history immanently sedimented in them."[81]

A POETRY OF REEVALUATION: LEAVING THE PRISTINE SPRING OF THE MUSES

This chapter has been asking, in effect, where Marlowe's style comes from. For all the ways in which Marlowe's *Hero and Leander* works against tensions contained in the literature of post-Augustan antiquity, it is striking that Marlowe may not have known that Musaeus, his most direct source, was from late antiquity. In the Renaissance, this late fifth- or early sixth-century-CE writer was generally conflated with an earlier Musaeus (after whom the later Musaeus probably named himself), a prophet-poet who appears evocatively in a wide variety of classical sources as a legendary figure surrounded by the mists of prehistory.[82]

79. Max Horkheimer and Theodor W. Adorno, *Dialectic of Enlightenment: Philosophical Fragments*, ed. Gunzelin Schmid Noerr, trans. Edmund Jephcott (Stanford: Stanford University Press, 2002), 191.

80. Theodor W. Adorno, *Aesthetic Theory*, ed. Gretel Adorno and Rolf Tiedemann, trans. Robert Hullot-Kentor (Minneapolis: University of Minnesota Press, 1997), 6.

81. Ibid., 85.

82. Plato was not unusual in linking Musaeus with Orpheus; he calls them "hierophants and prophets" in *Protagoras* (316d), and "the offspring of the Moon and the Muse, *as they say* [ως φασι]" in the *Republic* (364e). In his *Bibliotheca historica* (4.25), Diodorus Siculus mentions Musaeus in an account of the labors of Hercules: before trying to drag Cerberus up from Hades, Hercules purifies

For early Renaissance humanists, it had been enchanting to encounter Musaeus's *Hero and Leander* along this path of associations. Opening Aldus Manutius's first edition of 1494, they felt they had reached the place where literary history began—where, in Callimachus's phrase, poetry's "unworn paths"[83] first emerged from the pastures and where the pure notes of man's earliest songs might have mixed with the songs of birds. In a gesture of what Braden calls "neat symbolism," the Aldine Press printed Musaeus at (or near)[84] the inception of its series of ancient Greek texts because the publisher thought he came first in the literary tradition; in his Greek preface, Aldus calls him "the most ancient poet."[85] In 1598, when George Chapman produced his "continuation" of Marlowe's poem, Chapman heralds Musaeus as the "first Author" and honors Hero and Leander's tragic deaths in his closing lines as "the first that ever Poet sung." And in 1616, when Chapman wrote his own version of the complete poem, he foregrounds this claim to Musaeus's priority in the title: "The Divine Poem of Musaeus. First of all Bookes."

However, philologists were sounding doubts about Musaeus's place in literary history throughout the century. As early as 1518, Johannes Froben referred in his Latin preface to "those among the learned" (in doctis) who deny that Musaeus is the author of the poem.[86] While Froben claimed to *withhold* judgment (he uses the Greek ἐπέχομεν for its association with Sextus Empiricus[87]), he nonetheless suggested that he sided with the believers.[88] The

himself by taking part in the rites of Demeter at Eleusis, which are presided over by Musaeus, the son of Orpheus. In the *Aeneid*, Virgil situates Musaeus among the blessed, towering over the other souls gathered around him (his size perhaps associating him with men of an earlier age, who were often thought to be taller). Virgil clearly endows Musaeus with a privileged status: "before all" (ante omni) (6.667), the Sibyl addresses him as the "best prophet" (optime vates) (6.669). It is Musaeus who explains to Aeneas the conditions in which the blessed live, and this prehistorical prophet-poet seems colored by the Golden Age qualities of Elysium that he describes: "'For no one a fixed home; we live in shady woods and abide on soft riverbanks and on the fresh meadows with brooks'" (6.673–75, nulli certa domus; lucis habitamus opacis / riparumque toros et prata recentia rivis / incolimus).

83. Callimachus, *Aetia* 1.27–28.

84. Curt F. Bühler thinks Musaeus was the Aldine Press's second text, as Braden notes (*The Classics and English Renaissance Poetry*, 81). See Bühler, "Aldus Manutius and His First Edition of the Greek Musaeus," in *Scritti sopra Aldo Manuzio*, ed. Roberto Ridolfi (Florence: L. S. Olschki, 1955), 3–7, 106–7.

85. Quoted in Braden, *The Classics and English Renaissance Poetry*, 81.

86. Ibid.

87. Sextus writes, "As for the objects in the external world, we suspend judgment insofar as it is a matter of reason" (ἐπέχομεν ὅσον ἐπὶ τῷ λόγῳ), *Outlines of Pyrrhonism* 1.215. See *The Original Sceptics: A Controversy*, ed. Myles Burnyeat and Michael Frede (Indianapolis: Hackett, 1998), 10–11.

88. Thanks to Tobias Joho for supplying me with his translation of the preface.

criticisms became more rigorous as philological techniques and knowledge of Greek improved.[89] The century's most "decisive case" against Musaeus's pre-Homeric origin appeared tucked away in Isaac Casaubon's 1583 commentary to Diogenes Laertius.[90]

It is impossible to know whether Marlowe, in exaggerating the rhetorical effects of post-Augustan antique style in his version of *Hero and Leander*, is aware of this scholarly reevaluation of Musaeus's dating. In *Doctor Faustus*, at least, Marlowe seems to have associated Musaeus with the legendary archaic poet who holds first rank in the underworld of the *Aeneid*.[91] The situation may be that Marlowe and the philologists were thinking on "parallel" tracks.[92] If the philologists were making discoveries about literary history by thinking about stylistic clues in one way, Marlowe may have been making discoveries of his own by thinking about literary form in another. Although it is impossible to know for sure, the evidence suggests that Marlowe probably didn't know as a factual matter the correct dates of Musaeus, but he seems to have associated him on stylistic grounds with other writers of post-Augustan antiquity and their ekphrastic or thingly style. Marlowe's *Hero and Leander* may be a case of an artist's having moved an inherited artistic

89. Departing from the opinion of his father (who infamously argued that, although Musaeus was born before Homer, his style was nonetheless better than Homer's because it was more polished), Joseph Scaliger in 1566 notes privately in the margin of Willem Canter's *Novae lectiones* that Canter is wrong to suggest that Ovid imitated Musaeus in *Heroides* 17.149ff., since "that Musaeus" (iste Musaeus) was of a later age. And, more publicly, Scaliger declared to his students that Musaeus "n'est pas cet ancien qui estoit du temps d'Homere" but has the "style de Sophiste"—a style that Scaliger had disliked since his youth. See Anthony Grafton, *Joseph Scaliger: A Study in the History of Classical Scholarship*, 2 vols. (Oxford: Clarendon Press, 1983–1993), 2:65, 691–92.

90. Braden, *The Classics and English Renaissance Poetry*, 82. Mark Pattison's account suggests the essentially positivist orientation of Casaubon's scholarship: Casaubon, he writes, had "the enviable gift of presenting the object as it is [Veranschaulichung]. This was due not to the possession of a poetic imagination, but to its absence" (*Isaac Casaubon*, 518).

91. Recalling Virgil's account of Musaeus as a primeval poet in the underworld, Faustus explains how his brilliance "made the flow'ring pride of Wittenberg / Swarm to my problems as the infernal spirits, / On sweet Musaeus when he came to hell" (1.116–18).

92. Braden writes of the similarities between Marlowe's style and that of the school of Nonnos: "Many of the specific tricks of the Nonnian style in general have direct analogues in late Renaissance style—sometimes very direct ones, such as the duBartasian craze for compound adjectives. There cannot be any question of large-scale causality, but there is a sense of parallel enterprise that could conceivably cause ignition in particular cases, such as Marlowe's. For encoded into the Nonnian techniques is a relation to the main body of classical literature, a relation curiously similar to that in which the Renaissance stood: hypnotized by the prestige of the great names, minutely familiar with their works, and eager to surpass them, as much as possible, on their own terms. The sixteenth century picks up where Nonnos leaves off; antique detumescence intersects Renaissance exuberance" (*The Classics and English Renaissance Poetry*, 84–85).

form forward by carrying through with the implications found imbedded in this form—by, in Adorno's words, "see[ing] with the work's own eyes."[93]

The best literature of post-Augustan antiquity had already begun to turn on its own ekphrastic style and reveal its latent contradictions. Apuleius's *Golden Ass*, for example, wonderfully defies its own genre by overturning the hierophantic solemnity that fetishism requires.

But in Marlowe's work, this self-antagonistic turn is consistently brought to the point of utter subversion. Throughout his oeuvre, Marlowe's poetry produces critique in the way that Adorno ascribes to an artwork that "pushes its situation so far that it becomes the critique of this situation."[94] The characters in *The Jew of Malta*, for example, unlike most characters in world literature, lose rather than gain their human dimensionality as the play goes on; by the end, the Jew and the Turk and the Catholic are nothing but the projections of Marlowe's own culture's crude fantasies.[95] By immersing his audience in such fantasies, Marlowe's work criticizes these fantasies—a peculiarly edgy and uncompromising kind of criticism, which emerges from within a history that has been made to work against itself. Marlowe is a thinker who, to borrow the words of Charles Baudelaire (writing at the advent of modernism about Edgar Allan Poe), is "like a slave determined to make his master blush."[96]

In the case of *Hero and Leander*, Marlowe develops the literary form of ekphrasis, but not by returning to this ancient form as to some mythically pure starting point. Rather, he reevaluates it and activates the tensions that are contained in the form's history but not yet known in the Renaissance. "Through contemplative immersion the immanent processual quality of the work is set free," Adorno writes. "Whatever in the artifact may be called the unity of its meaning is not static but processual, the enactment of antagonisms that each work necessarily has in itself."[97] The artwork posits a unity of meaning but also constantly suspends the closure of this meaning

93. Adorno, *Aesthetic Theory*, 267.

94. Ibid., 260. Lewis may gesture toward a related impression when he describes Marlowe's having put us on the *inside* of the poem's erotic experience: "We do not see their [the lovers'] frenzy from outside as we see that of Shakespeare's Venus. We are at the centre and see the rest of the universe transfigured by the hard, brittle splendor of erotic vision" (*English Literature in the Sixteenth Century, Excluding Drama*, 487).

95. Stephen Greenblatt, *Renaissance Self-Fashioning: From More to Shakespeare* (Chicago: University of Chicago Press, 1980), 193–221.

96. Charles Baudelaire, *"The Painter of Modern Life" and Other Essays*, trans. Jonathan Mayne (London and New York: Phaidon Press, 1995), 95.

97. Adorno, *Aesthetic Theory*, 176.

through the form's tensions and contradictions. In this sense, an artwork's spirit is not "something that exists; rather it is something in a process of development and formation."[98] Marlowe's poetry undertakes this process of development and, in so doing, offers a model for literary criticism—as a process of thought that speaks for the unfolding of historical meaning held in tension by the artwork's form. This process de-reifies inherited forms, and reintroduces them into the flow of intellectual reevaluation, while at the same time preserving their history in the form of critique.

98. Ibid., 91.

CHAPTER FIVE

Feeling like a Fragment: Shakespeare's *The Rape of Lucrece*

In this chapter, I am going to consider aesthetic experience in tension with one last kind of thingliness: the material fragment. As I began to explore in regard to Petrarch's account of Roman ruins in chapter 1, the fragment is closely linked with antiquarianism. Despite its emphasis on subjectivity, Petrarch's ekphrasis of Roman ruins helped initiate a tradition of studying material remains. We'll see in this chapter how, through the antiquarian lens, the material artifact was soon understood in its brokenness, rather than serving as a catalyst for imagining a past world brought to life. We will see also how fragments could be used to reveal what it *feels* like to exist in a fractured world—an experience that empiricism leaves out. By focusing on fragments in Shakespeare's 1594 *The Rape of Lucrece*, this chapter will explore the question of what happens to subjectivity when it encounters that from which it has been split. In this poem, Shakespeare uses ekphrasis to show how historical fragments can become animated by a new and peculiarly modern kind of subjectivity.

This chapter unfolds in three parts. The first briefly reviews the increasing awareness of material historical fragments in Renaissance intellectual life. The second looks at the importance of these fragments to Shakespeare's poem, especially to its ekphrasis of the picture showing the fall of Troy. Finally, the third focuses on how Shakespeare represents Lucrece experiencing these material remains of the past. The same empiricist artifacts that were supposed to provide a detached way of understanding the past now serve, paradoxically, as the screen onto which a new kind of subjectivity is projected.[1]

1. For a recent exploration of an English Renaissance poet's use of ruins, see Rebeca Helfer, *Spenser's Ruins and the Art of Recollection* (Toronto: University of Toronto Press, 2012).

HISTORY AS FRAGMENTS

By the end of the sixteenth century, the emphasis on factual accuracy in European historiography was increasing. The project of historical reconstruction entailed a growing involvement with material remains. However, in trying to bridge the present to the past, humanists ended up with an unexpected result: a heightened awareness of the temporal gap that separated them from the ancient world.

This emphasis represented a general departure from earlier years of the Renaissance, when many humanists were less concerned with anachronism.[2] As an example of this earlier mode of thought, the fifteenth-century poet Angelo Poliziano described his efforts to resurrect the past by analogy to Aesculapius: just as the mythical doctor used his healing art to rejoin the parts of Hippolytus's dismembered body, so the humanist would use philological techniques to reconstruct the badly damaged corpus of Cicero's works.[3] For collectors of fragments of ancient sculpture, these metaphors of reconstitution and revivification could seem literal.[4] Especially in regard to the world of the ancient Romans, the desire underlying this project of restoration was to bring the ancient world to life. "Indeed," wrote Petrarch in his 1341 letter from Rome, "who can doubt that Rome would right then rise [surrectura sit], if she began to know herself [si ceperit se Roma cognoscere]?"[5] In order to evoke this ancient world so vividly that Romans could begin to know themselves, Petrarch searched for lost manuscripts of authors like Cicero, while writing letters to him and other ancient authors as though they were living people.

2. The tension between a sense of the irrecoverable distance of the ancient world and a fantasy of its resurrection recurred throughout the Renaissance. For early Renaissance concerns with the distance of the past, see Thomas M. Greene's discussion of Petrarch in *The Light in Troy: Imitation and Discovery in Renaissance Poetry* (New Haven: Yale University Press, 1982). For the ongoing resurrectionist aspects of English antiquarianism, see Angus Vine, *In Defiance of Time: Antiquarian Writing in Early Modern England* (Oxford: Oxford University Press, 2010).

3. Poliziano wrote, "The second book of Cicero's *De deorum natura* is just as mangled in all ancient and modern manuscripts as was Hippolytus once, pulled apart by frightened horses. The legends tell how Aesculapius later gathered the torn members, pieced them together and restored them to life, for which act he is said to have been struck by lightning as a result of the gods' jealousy. But what jealousy will deter me, what lightning bolt, from daring to restore the very father of the Roman language and philosophy, whose head and hands have been lopped off again by I know not what Antony?" Quoted in Greene, *The Light in Troy*, 169.

4. See Leonard Barkan, *Unearthing the Past: Archaeology and Aesthetics in the Making of Renaissance Culture* (New Haven: Yale University Press, 1999).

5. Petrarch, *Lettres familières, IV–VII. Rerum familiarum, IV–VII*, ed. and trans. Ugo Dotti, Christophe Carraud, Frank La Brasca, and André Longpré (Paris: Les Belles Lettres, 2002), 6.2.14, 251.

Ekphrasis often exemplified this resurrectionist drive. Valentine Cunningham has proposed that ekphrasis "grants a demonstration of literature's persistent resurrectionist desires—the craving to have the past return livingly, to live again, to speak again."[6] This desire was especially evident during the early Renaissance. In Poliziano's celebrated ekphrasis of images carved on the doors of Venus's golden palace in his 1494 *Stanze*, for example, the reader is described as mistaking the represented scenes for reality: "You would call the foam real, the sea real, real the conch shell and real the blowing wind" (1.100).[7] Thus, for twenty-three descriptive stanzas, Poliziano elaborates this Renaissance fantasy of the pagan world's rebirth:

> You could swear that the goddess had emerged from the waves, pressing her hair with her right hand, covering with the other her sweet mound of flesh; and where the strand was imprinted by her sacred and divine step, it had clothed itself in flowers and grass; then with happy, more than mortal features, she was received in the bosom of the three nymphs and cloaked in a starry garment. (1.101)[8]

Poliziano describes the carved doors as if this artwork makes the goddess herself appear, brought to life. This ekphrasis attempts in this instance to overcome the described art image's necessary incompletion. Only briefly does Poliziano acknowledge that the image is not in itself whole, insisting that the viewer's imagination makes it seem whole: "Whatever the art in itself does not contain, the mind, imagining, clearly understands" (1.119).[9] His ekphrasis describes the feeling of complete experience that an art object can produce in the mind.

6. Valentine Cunningham, "Why Ekphrasis?" *Classical Philology* 102, no. 1 (Jan. 2007): 63.

7. "Vera la schiuma e vero il mar diresti, / e vero il nicchio e ver soffiar di venti." *The "Stanze" of Angelo Poliziano*, trans. David Quint (University Park: Pennsylvania State University Press, 1993).

8. "Giurar potresti che dell'onde uscissi / la dea premendo colla destra il crino, / coll'altra il dolce pome ricoprissi; / e, stampata dal piè sacro e divino, / d'erbe e di fior l'arena si vestissi; / poi, con sembiante lieto e peregrino, / dalle tre ninfe in grembo fussi accolta, / e di stellato vestimento involta."

9. "E quanto l'arte intra sé non comprende, / la mente imaginando chiaro intende." In the sixteenth century, Ludovico Dolce theorized about this participation of the imagination: when figures in a painting are behaving as if they were alive, this perception "is not an effect or property of the painting" (e non effeto o proprietà della Pittura) but, rather, is "plain imagination on the spectator's part, prompted by different attitudes [i.e., postures of the figures in the painting] that serve that end" (certa imaginatione di chi mira, causata da diverse attitudini, che a cio servono). See Mark W. Roskill, *Dolce's "Aretino" and Venetian Art Theory of the Cinquecento* (Toronto: University of Toronto Press in association with the Renaissance Society of America, 2000), 98–99.

The central humanist concept of exemplarity was based, after all, on the idea that past figures could be brought to life again by living people imitating them in the present. This pseudo-resurrection depended on a sense of historical models as "living texts" (textos animados), in the words of the Spanish Jesuit Baltasar Gracián.[10] Petrarch, for example, presented his *De viris illustribus* to Charles IV along with a collection of Roman coins portraying ancient rulers, offering the emperor this advice: "Here, O Caesar, . . . are the men whom you have succeeded, here are those whom you must try to imitate and admire, whose ways and character you should emulate."[11] If Petrarch hoped that Charles IV would eventually bring to life the ancient exemplars by imitating them, Petrarch first needed to restore their representations to the greatest possible effect of life-likeness.

The desire to restore the past often led humanists to imagine beyond what the artifacts actually represented. A c. 1350 edition of Suetonius's *De vita Caesarum* is the first known instance to use replications of actual ancient coins to illustrate the rulers portrayed. While this use of coins indicates an interest in pieces of historical evidence, it is suggestive that these portraits show not only the heads actually represented on the coins but also arms and torsos. In addition, the figures are made to seem even more complete by being portrayed holding identifying objects like the Roman imperial standard,[12] suggesting that the whole man was being restored. In contrast, as Sean Keilen has explored, some later humanists like Andrea Fulvio in the sixteenth century may have attempted to heighten the evidential effect of their sequences of numismatic portraits, despite these series being partly imaginary, by *leaving out* certain portraits—the assumption then being that a *real* record is fragmented and incomplete.[13]

The sense of the past was changing. The turn toward objectivity meant that the fragments of manuscripts and bits of sculpture no longer faded into an imagined resurrection of the past in its wholeness but now tended to remain before the eyes as things in themselves, in all their brokenness and fragmentation—what the English antiquarian William Camden called

10. See Timothy Hampton, *Writing from History: The Rhetoric of Exemplarity in Renaissance Literature* (Ithaca: Cornell University Press, 1990), 11.

11. Petrarch, *Letters on Familiar Matters, Rerum familiarum libri*, vol. 3, *Books XVII-XXIV*, trans. Aldo S. Bernardo (New York: Italica Press, 2005), 19.3, 79. See Sean Keilen, "Exemplary Metals: Classical Numismatics and the Commerce of Humanism," *Word & Image* 18, no. 3 (July–Sept. 2002): 284.

12. Francis Haskell, *History and Its Images: Art and the Interpretation of the Past* (New Haven: Yale University Press, 1993), 26–27.

13. Keilen, "Exemplary Metals," 287ff.

the "rude rubble and out-cast rubbish" of the material historical record.[14] The sculptures depicted in Maarten van Heemskerck's meticulous c. 1532–36 drawing of Jacopo Galli's garden were not of goddesses floating over the waves on their conch shells but of sculptures shown in their brokenness.[15]

Glenn W. Most has characterized the search for fragments in the Middle Ages and Renaissance as "somewhat aesthetic and antihistorical in character, inasmuch as attention is paid preferentially to finer fragments." He writes that humanists were not reluctant "to improve, supplement, correct, modify, or even invent" so that the objects would appear "more beautiful."[16] Indeed, Western European medievals often sought out ancient artifacts more on the basis of the fine craftsmanship of their precious material than on their worth as historical evidence. For example, an ancient ivory diptych of consuls at Monza, Lombardy, seems to have been adapted in the eighth or ninth century to become King David and St. Gregory.[17] Many medievals were like Aeneas with his shield insofar as they rejoiced in images without knowing what they once represented (8.730).

While Most suggests that only significantly later, in the eighteenth, nineteenth, and twentieth centuries, did an interest in the fragment as historical evidence become central,[18] other scholars have dated this turn significantly earlier, in the Renaissance. Anthony Grafton writes that the first systematic use of textual fragments was made not by nineteenth-century German philologists like Friedrich August Wolf, Friedrich Creuzer, and Karl Müller but, rather, by late sixteenth- and early seventeenth-century scholars like Joseph Scaliger and Isaac Casaubon.[19] These scholars developed their work on chronology and their editions of Athenaeus and Theophrastus and Diogenes Laertius by accumulating and comparing the most complete possible collection of fragments related to a textual discrepancy.[20] One major feature that distinguishes a Renaissance sense of the past, as Peter Burke

14. Quoted in Scott L. Newstok, *Quoting Death in Early Modern England: The Poetics of Epitaphs beyond the Tomb* (Houndmills, Basingstoke, Hampshire, and New York: Palgrave Macmillan, 2009), 61.

15. See Barkan, *Unearthing the Past*, 121.

16. Glenn W. Most, "On Fragments," in *The Fragment: An Incomplete History*, ed. William Tronzo (Los Angeles: Getty Research Institute, 2009), 11.

17. Roberto Weiss, *The Renaissance Discovery of Classical Antiquity* (Oxford: Blackwell, 1969), 3. See also *The Catholic Encyclopedia*, vol. 5, ed. Charles G. Herbermann, Edward A. Pace, Condé B. Pallen, Thomas J. Shahan, and John J. Wynne (New York: Robert Appleton, 1909), 23.

18. Most, "On Fragments," 11–12.

19. Anthony Grafton, "*Fragmenta Historicorum Graecorum*: Fragments of Some Lost Enterprises," in *Collecting Fragments/Fragmente sammeln*, ed. Glenn W. Most (Göttingen: Vandenhoeck & Ruprecht, 1997), 124–43.

20. Mark Pattison, *Isaac Casaubon, 1559–1614* (London: Longmans, Green, 1875), 484.

has explained, is the new emphasis on evidence.[21] The interest in fragments is reflective of this emphasis.

The very attempt to take hold of the past and bring it to life was producing, ironically, a new experience of its distance and deadness. As Leonard Barkan has emphasized, a tension between an anachronistic understanding of the past and a new historicism was growing. As humanists learned more about the ancient world in its historical specificity, the past seemed increasingly elusive. Barkan describes antiquity as "the essential unresponsive *donna crudele*,"[22] always eliciting desire but never offering satisfaction. Thomas M. Greene similarly describes the Renaissance longing for a bygone age in terms of the pain of an "incomplete embrace."[23] The image is almost Ovidian, evoking the moment when Apollo finally reaches Daphne just as she has begun to transform into an object, in this case a tree, so that, throwing his arms around her body, all he can do is feel her heart still fluttering beneath the bark[24]—a figure of her (and the past's) ultimate unreachability.

There was, of course, no one decisive tipping point in the treatment of historical evidence, no single moment when the fragment shifted from being in the background of an imaginatively reconstructed sense of the past to being in the forefront as an object regarded as evidence. Rather, there was an increased awareness of the fragmentary incompletion of the historical record. This awareness affected literature. For A. C. Dionisotti, "the true triumph of the fragment in the sixteenth century" comes at the beginning of the second chapter of *Gargantua*, when François Rabelais describes how some farmers find inside a buried tomb a moldy pamphlet written on elm bark and "so timeworn that one could hardly recognize three [letters] in a row" (tant toutesfoys usées par vetusté, qu'à poine en povoit on troys recongnoistre de ranc). For the reverence he bears antiquity (par reverence de l'antiquaille), the narrator faithfully transcribes the nonsense verses, including the beginnings of the first five lines that, he says, rats and cockroaches or other pernicious beasts have nibbled: "Les ratz et blattes ou (affin que je ne mente) aultres malignes bestes avoient brousté le commencement."[25]

Commenting on the "cryptic wisps of letters" in the original print edition, Dionisotti writes that "Rabelais' printers knew better than today's how to

21. Peter Burke, *The Renaissance Sense of the Past* (New York: St. Martin's Press, 1969), 7.

22. Leonard Barkan, *Mute Poetry, Speaking Pictures* (Princeton: Princeton University Press, 2013), 113.

23. Greene, *The Light in Troy*, 43.

24. "Trepidare . . . sub cortice pectus." Ovid, *Metamorphoses*, books 1–8, trans. Frank Justus Miller, rev. G. P. Goold (Cambridge, MA: Loeb Classical Library, 1977), I.554.

25. François Rabelais, *Gargantua* (Paris: Éditions du Seuil, 1973), 56–58. My translation.

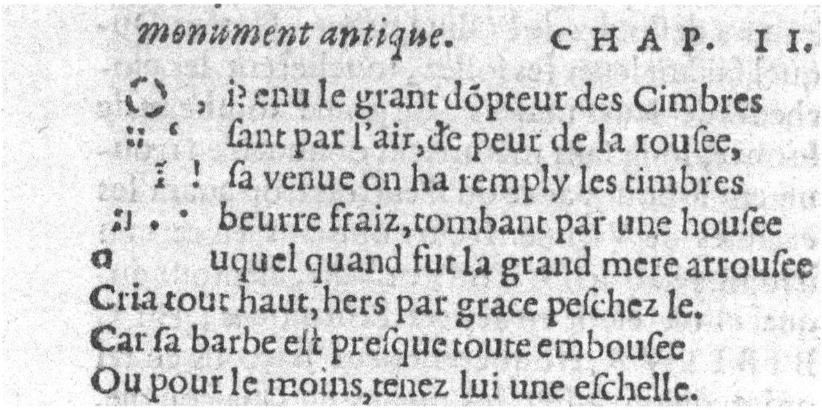

monument antique. CHAP. II.
, i? enu le grant dōpteur des Cimbres
ſant par l'air, de peur de la rouſee,
ſa venue on ha remply les timbres
beurre fraiz, tombant par une houſee
uquel quand fut la grand mere arrouſee
Cria tout haut, hers par grace peſchez le.
Car ſa barbe eſt preſque toute embouſee
Ou pour le moins, tenez lui une eſchelle.

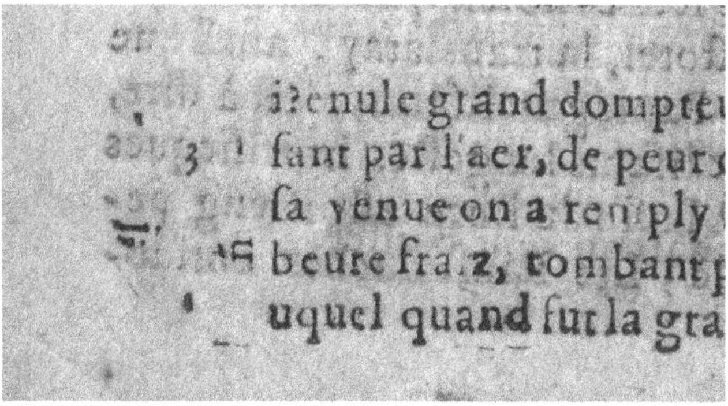

i?enule grand dompte
ſant par l'aer, de peur
ſa venue on a remply
beure fra.z, tombant
uquel quand fut la gra

FIGURES 6 AND 7. From two Renaissance editions of Rabelais. The detail above is from *Les oevvres de M. François Rabelais, docteur en medecin: contenans la vie, faicts & dicts heroïques de Gargantua & de son filz Pantagruel: auec la prognostication Pantagrueline* (France [?], 1556), 54C-800, Houghton Library, Harvard University. The detail below is from *La plaisante, et ioyeuse histoyre du grand geant Gargantua / prochainement reueue & de beaucoup augmentée par l'au[t]heur mesme* (Valence: Chéz Claude La Ville, 1547,[s.l., s.n., c. 1600]), John Davis Batchelder Collection, Rare Book and Special Collections Division of the Library of Congress, Washington, DC.

make a fragment look like a fragment."[26] And Rabelais's printers weren't alone. Another text from this same period reveals a similar interest in letters that have been broken to look historically accurate: Gabriele Simeoni's 1558 *Les illustres obseruations antiques* prints some monument inscriptions with damaged letters that show their timeworn condition.

26. A. C. Dionisotti, "On Fragments in Classical Scholarship," in *Collecting Fragments / Fragmente sammeln*, 33.

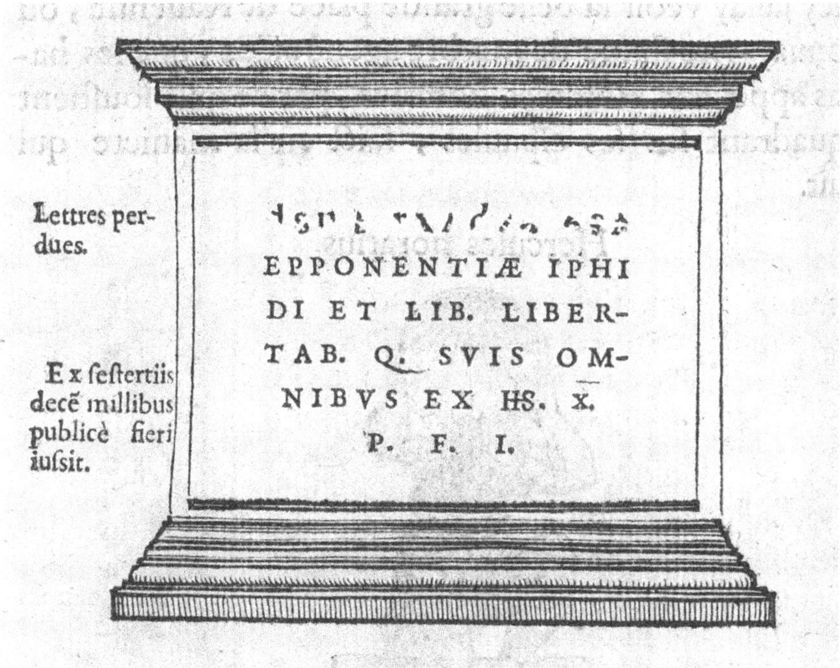

FIGURE 8. Detail from Gabriele Simeoni, *Les illustres obseruations antiques* (Lyon: Ian de Tournes, 1558), The Huntington Library, San Marino, California (132559).

But such examples were still relatively rare. While most statues were fragmentary, most ekphrases continued to evoke the subject magically restored to wholeness and come to life.[27] In the literary sphere, the desire for a fantasized fullness of history remained strong, even under the pressure of a rising awareness of history's material fragmentation. This was the context in which Shakespeare began to reimagine the story of Lucrece.

"ART GAVE LIFELESS LIFE": FRAGMENTS, RUINS, AND TOMBS IN *THE RAPE OF LUCRECE*

Shakespeare's *The Rape of Lucrece* narrates an oft-told-tale of Roman history: that of the rape of a Roman woman, Lucrece, by the king's son, Tarquin. As the ancient historian Livy recounted, her ensuing suicide served as the

27. See Barkan, *Unearthing the Past*, 4–7. Renaissance ekphrases often stood, he says, "in ambiguous relation to the actual objects emerging from the ground."

impetus for a major change of regime: the Romans expelled the royal family and thereby initiated the Roman republic.

Of his many changes to this ancient story, Shakespeare added a 209-line ekphrasis of a picture showing the fall of Troy. The fall of this city was of course a favorite subject of many poets, from Virgil to Chrétien de Troyes to Geoffrey Chaucer to George Peele. Through his version of this story, Shakespeare evokes the ekphrastic tradition of revivification, maintaining a familiar tone of credulous admiration for the wonders of a verisimilar artwork (i.e., an artwork that seems real): the depicted scene "beguiled attention, charmed the sight" (1404).[28] He employs the stock motif of art outdoing nature, reworking a trope that had been reworked over and over in the Renaissance:[29] "A thousand lamentable objects there, / In scorn of Nature, Art gave lifeless life" (1373–74). So familiar is this motif in Renaissance ekphrases that a reader might hardly notice the important paradox that Shakespeare draws from it. The art object endows the "thousand lamentable objects" it depicts with a kind of "life" that is "lifeless"—whether because so much of the depicted scene of horror is associated with death (Shakespeare mentions dying eyes, ashy lights, dying coals, and reeking blood), or because these images of death are merely a lifeless art object's mimetic representations. From within the ekphrastic assertion of a resuscitated reality, Shakespeare draws out an awareness of fragmented thingliness.

While appearing to celebrate the idea of an illusionistic experience that makes the past seem fully alive as a vivid fantasy in the present, Shake-

28. All citations of *The Rape of Lucrece* from William Shakespeare, *The Complete Sonnets and Poems*, ed. Colin Burrow (Oxford: Oxford University Press, 2002).

29. Shakespeare's claim that this picture was "in scorn of Nature" (1374) ultimately derives from Pliny's anecdote about Zeuxis's painting of grapes which appeared so real that the birds pecked at them (*Naturalis historia* 35.36.65). Variations on this theme reappear throughout Renaissance descriptions of art and were still common in the sixteenth century: for example, Giorgio Vasari wrote of Raphael's work that no one could look at his painting of Mount Parnassus without being amazed that he had "brought painted objects to life," and that the weapons in his painting of the imprisonment of St. Peter "shine so resplendently that their burnished lustre appears more lifelike than the real thing." Vasari, *Lives of the Artists*, vol. 1, trans. George Bull (London: Penguin, 1965), 294, 300. But the motif is not unique to the West. Ernst Kris and Otto Kurz allude to Asian and Indian examples: the connoisseur who tries to flick away a painted fly or who breaks his fingernails attempting to pick up a painted peacock feather. Kris and Kurz trace these legends to their prehistorical foundations: the artist's ability to create something that *seems* alive emerged from a more archaic belief in the artist's ability to create something that *is* alive: "Motion and life, which in mythology had a literal meaning, became pale metaphors, and the simile, 'So true to nature that the work of art creates the illusion of life and movement,' was retained in the legend." Ernst Kris and Otto Kurz, *Legend, Myth, and Magic in the Image of the Artist: A Historical Experiment* (New Haven: Yale University Press, 1979), 65, 71.

speare's ekphrasis of the falling city increasingly draws his audience's attention to the *things*—the "thousand lamentable objects" in their disjointed thingliness—that supposedly evoke this fantasy. Toying with creating the illusionistic effect of fullness, he seems to allude to the sound of Nestor's speech, for example, when he writes, "In speech it seemed his beard, all silver-white, / Wagged up and down, and from his lips did fly / Thin winding breath, which purled up to the sky" (1405–7). Yet even here the fantasy stays surprisingly tethered to the concrete bits from which it should rise into dream-like fullness. The lips and wagging beard release not the full resonance of a voice but "thin winding breath, which purled up to the sky." For Renaissance readers, this description may have evoked not so much the illusionistic experience of a voice but rather a curling speech scroll, also known as a banderole (commonly used in the period to represent speech in tapestries, book illustrations, etchings, paintings, and stained glass windows).

Shakespeare's attention is directed at the object itself, instead of at the illusion this object is supposed to create:

> About him [Nestor] were a press of gaping faces . . .
> Some high, some low, the painter was so nice.
> The scalps of many, almost hid behind,
> To jump up higher seemed to mock the mind.
>
> Here one man's hand leaned on another's head,
> His nose being shadowed by his neighbor's ear . . .
>
> . . . for Achilles' image stood his spear,
> Gripped in an armed hand, himself behind
> Was left unseen, save to the eye of mind:
> A hand, a foot, a face, a leg, a head
> Stood for the whole to be imagined. (1408; 1412–16; 1424–28)

As E. H. Gombrich noticed, Shakespeare's version of the battle at Troy seems to draw on the late-antique Greek rhetorician Philostratus.[30] Philostratus's *Imagines*, which was available in Latin and French translations, was part of the curriculum at St. John's College, Cambridge, where Thomas Jenkins, the principal master of Stratford Grammar School, studied.[31] In his ekphra-

30. E. H. Gombrich, *Art and Illusion: A Study in the Psychology of Pictorial Representation* (Princeton: Princeton University Press, 1960), 211.

31. Burrow, *The Complete Sonnets and Poems*, 318.

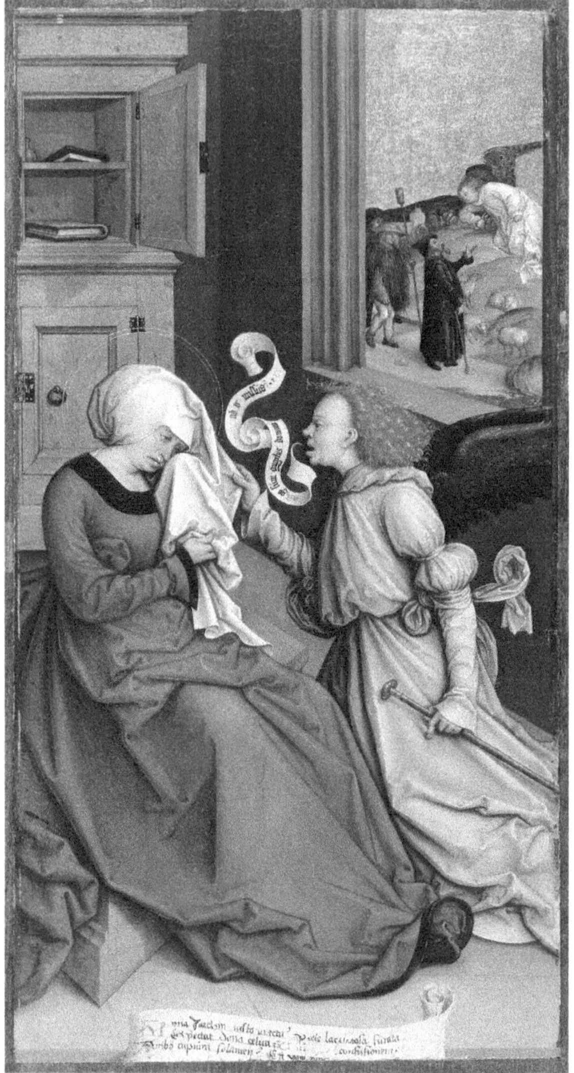

FIGURE 9. A banderole in Bernhard Strigel, *The Annunciation to Saint Anne* (c. 1505–10). Museo Thyssen-Bornemisza / Scala / Art Resource, New York.

sis of a painting showing the siege of Thebes, Philostratus explained that the figures in front are shown in full figure, but those behind only from the waist up; then, going back, heads only; and finally just the spearpoints. As things move higher up on the picture plane, they seem to recede back into space: "The problem is to deceive the eyes as they travel back along with the proper receding planes of the pictures," Philostratus writes (1.4.32–33).[32] Shakespeare's version of the battle at Troy seems to recall this explanation of how figures can be overlapped to create an illusion of depth: Shakespeare repeats Philostratus's itemization of the body parts; he even includes Philostratus's detail of the spear. But in his enthusiasm for pictorial artifice, Shakespeare's narrator displays a humorous naivety: "Some high, some low, the painter was so nice. / The scalps of many, almost hid behind, / To jump up higher seemed to mock the mind." Shakespeare's poem playfully misconstrues the intended effect that Philostratus describes. The intended effect is not, of course, that some figures are jumping, but rather that they are deeper back in space.[33]

In pretending to celebrate the picture's lifelike illusionistic effect, Shakespeare actually describes with exaggerated realism or literal-mindedness the arrangement of the art object itself and, specifically, the way its figures (specifically their heads or even just their scalps) are located at different heights on the picture plane, as Catherine Belsey and Richard Meek have also recently emphasized.[34] The image does not fuse into an illusion of reality; rather, it remains fragmented.

So literal is the description that an earlier generation of scholars conjectured that Shakespeare was thinking of actual fifteenth-century Netherlander tapestries depicting the fall of Troy,[35] such as the tapestry from the Tournai series known as *The War of Troy*, which is now at the Victoria and Albert Museum in London. This set once belonged to Charles VIII of France, although several sets were made of this series, including one owned by Henry VII of which only parts now survive.[36]

Similarly, Shakespeare's description of the picture representing Troy as "so compact" (1423) probably means, as Colin Burrow notes, that the picture is "made up of a complex intermingling of elements." But Shakespeare

32. I am quoting the translation included in Philostratus the Elder, *Imagines* (with Philostratus the Younger, *Imagines* and Callistratus, *Descriptions*), trans. Arthur Fairbanks (Cambridge, MA: Loeb Classical Library, 1931).

33. Burrow notes, "Viewers know that they [the figures] are not actually higher, but are deceived by the perspective" (318).

34. Catherine Belsey, "Invocation of the Visual Image: Ekphrasis in *Lucrece* and Beyond," *Shakespeare Quarterly* 63, no. 2 (Summer 2012): 192; Richard Meek, *Narrating the Visual in Shakespeare* (Burlington, VT: Ashgate, 2009), 75.

35. Sidney Colvin, "The Sack of Troy in Shakespeare's 'Lucrece' and in Some Fifteenth-Century Drawings and Tapestries," in *A Book of Homage to Shakespeare*, ed. Israel Gollancz (Oxford: Humphrey Milford, Oxford University Press, 1916), 88–99. Colvin mentions specifically the problem of perspective in the depiction of the crowd around Nestor (97).

36. Thomas P. Campbell, *Tapestry in the Renaissance: Art and Magnificence* (New Haven: Yale University Press, 2002), 55–64.

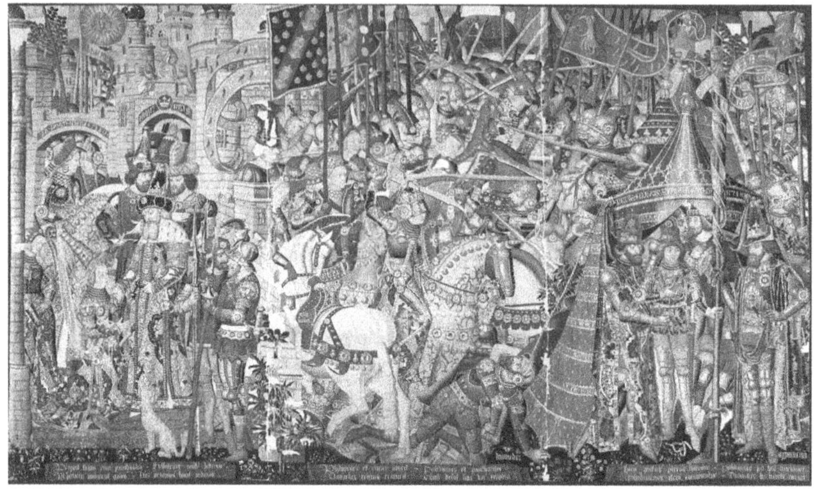

FIGURE 10. *The War of Troy* (1475–90), Tournai, Belgium. Victoria and Albert Museum, London. V&A Images, London / Art Resource, New York.

also means, I think, that these pieces are "packed closely together."[37] Again, Shakespeare is playing with a literal description of the figures: without the illusion of depth, and the accompanying sense of space between them, the represented men appear collaged against each other or packed into a rush-hour subway car.[38] The adjective "compact" also evokes the rhetorical principle of brevity[39]—the counter-principle to the verbal abundance or *copia* that ekphrasis usually represents.

While setting up his reader to think that this ekphrasis will celebrate the completion of the image in the viewer's imagination, Shakespeare instead draws the reader's attention to the object's parts and pieces: "A hand, a

37. *OED*, "compact" (adj.), 1b.

38. William V. Dunning explains, "Before the twelfth century, painters placed one object in front of another only by overlapping, or positioning one figure above another. When one flat object overlapped or was positioned above another, the overlapping shape or the lower shape was considered to be in front, but there did not appear to be any space between them. One flat figure, or part of a figure, looked as if it were cut out of a magazine and pasted flat on another flat figure"; *Changing Images of Pictorial Space: A History of Spatial Illusion in Painting* (Syracuse: Syracuse University Press, 1991), 14–15. See also John White, *The Birth and Rebirth of Pictorial Space* (Cambridge, MA: Belknap Press of Harvard University Press, 1987).

39. A 1576 English translation of a letter by Pliny the Elder refers to "a methode in writing and speaking compact in breuitie" in *A Panoplie of Epistles; or, A Looking Glasse for the Vnlearned*, trans. Abraham Fleming (London: [By H. Middleton] for Ralph Newberie, 1576), 255 (cited in *OED*, "compact," 4b).

foot, a face, a leg, a head / Stood for the whole to be imagined." The list refers to, but does not construct, a fantasy of fullness: what it really offers is an inventory of dismembered body parts. The blazon tradition, by which women are praised by a poet's delineating the parts of their bodies, is thus reimagined: Shakespeare describes men—or, more accurately, the material representations of men—in pieces.[40]

Consider, in contrast, Erasmus's treatment of Virgil's ekphrasis of the falling city. In his *De duplici copia verborum ac rerum commentarii duo,* first published in 1512, Erasmus returns twice to this picture of falling Troy to illustrate verbal practices that did not just allude drily to the subject under discussion but tried to conjure the represented scene so fully that it seemed to unfold before the reader's eyes. Near the beginning of book 1, Erasmus says that Virgil could express Troy's total destruction by referring to "the plains where Troy once stood"[41]—a line so concise that, as Macrobius remarked, it "consumed and swallowed up the city without even allowing the ruin [ruinam] to remain" (5.8).[42] However, Virgil could also recreate the scene so copiously as to make his audience not just *see* the ruins but, more than that, *feel* again the horrors of that long-ago day. The contrast here is between ruins that are "swallowed up" and an experience of the ruins as though in the present. Erasmus then pieces together various lines of the *Aeneid* to reconstruct a passage that laments the city's fall:

> Come is the final day, fate's inevitable doom
> Upon Dardanus' city; we Trojans are no more;
> Gone is Ilium, gone the mighty fame of Teucer's sons.
> Jove is become our foe and has bestowed
> All that was ours on Argos.
> Greeks now triumph in all the blazing city.
> O my country, O Ilium the dwelling place of gods!
> O ramparts of Dardanus' race with all your fame in war!
> Who can unfold in words that murderous night?
> Can any weep the tears those toils deserve?[43]

40. On the Petrarchan blazon tradition and its importance to Shakespeare's Lucrece, see Nancy J. Vickers, "'The blazon of sweet beauty's best': Shakespeare's *Lucrece,*" in *Shakespeare and the Question of Theory,* ed. Patricia Parker and Geoffrey Hartman (New York: Methuen, 1985), 95–115; "Diana Described: Scattered Woman and Scattered Rhyme," *Critical Inquiry* 8, no. 2 (Winter 1981): 265–79; and "'This Heraldry in Lucrece' Face,'" *Poetics Today* 6, nos. 1/2 (1985): 171–84.

41. Virgil, *Aeneid* 3.11: "campos ubi Troia fuit."

42. All quotations of Macrobius from *Saturnalia,* vol. 2, ed. Robert A. Kaster (Cambridge, MA: Loeb Classical Library, 2011).

43. The passage is constructed from parts of the *Aeneid* book 2 (2.324–27, 241–42, 361–63),

Although the writer must beware the dangers of empty verbosity, Erasmus warned, he must also not deny himself, or his audience, the attractions of such rich and full expression. The aesthetic pleasure that the text offers lies in allowing readers to reexperience the terrible historical scene as if it were unfolding now.

In a later section of *De copia* called "Description of a Thing" (Descriptio rei), Erasmus returns to Virgil's depiction of the falling city. Harking back to past literary ekphrases (Ovid's ekphrases of Arachne's tapestry, Homer's of Achilles's shield, and Virgil's of Aeneas's shield), Erasmus describes a "method of enrichment" involving *enargeia*, or vividness. Although Erasmus never uses the word *ekphrasis* (a word that had limited use in the Renaissance), his account repeats the key elements of ekphrasis as given in the *progymnasmata* and as then transmitted through Quintilian.[44] Erasmus writes: "We employ this [method] whenever, for the sake of amplifying or decorating our passage, or giving pleasure to our readers, instead of setting out the subject in bare simplicity, we fill in the colours and set it up like a picture to look at, so that we seem to have painted the scene rather than described it, and the reader seems to have seen rather than read."[45] His most elaborate example is the scene of the falling city. It is as though, he says, the reader were witnessing the scene itself:

> If one were to say that a city had been taken by storm, he would of course imply by such an overall statement all the subsidiary events that such a calamity admits. But, to go on in the exact words of Quintilian: "If you make explicit everything included in this one phrase, we shall witness the flames spreading through homes and temples, and the crash of falling buildings, and all the cries blending into one overriding sound; some people fleeing, not knowing where they are going, others locked in a last embrace of their loved ones, the wails of babies and women, and old men cruelly preserved by fate to see this day;

---

a compilation that is itself taken directly from Macrobius, *Saturnalia* book 5. I am quoting from the *Collected Works of Erasmus, Literary and Educational Writings 2, De copia/De ratione studii*, ed. Craig R. Thompson (Toronto: University of Toronto Press, 1978), 298. The translation of *De copia* is by Betty I. Knott.

44. Quintilian, *Institutes of Oratory; or, Education of an Orator*, vol. 2, trans. Rev. John Selby Watson (London: Bell and Daldy, 1871), 8.3.62–63.

45. *Collected Works of Erasmus*, 577. As I have discussed, the first-through-fourth-century-CE *progymnasmata* define ekphrasis as "an expository speech which vividly brings the subject before the eyes." See George A. Kennedy, trans., *Progymnasmata: Greek Textbooks of Prose Composition and Rhetoric* (Atlanta: Society of Biblical Literature, 2003). On the role of such manuals in the sixteenth-century English classroom and their effects on the period's literature, see Lynn Enterline, *Shakespeare's Schoolroom: Rhetoric, Discipline, Emotion* (Philadelphia: University of Pennsylvania Press, 2012).

> then we shall see the inevitable plundering of secular and sacred, the running to and fro of men carrying off loot and looking for more, prisoners in chains, each in the charge of his personal robber, mothers resisting the abduction of their children, and, wherever anything of greater value has come to light, the victors fighting among themselves. Though the one word 'destruction' [eversio] includes all this, this is a case where to state the whole is less effective than to state all the parts."[46]

If a sense of disjointedness is inherent in the scene, and in Erasmus's characteristically piecemeal borrowing from other authors, the emphasis is on the total cumulative effect of the parts.[47] The rapid succession of emotionally heightened moments, following one another without temporal order, creates an effect of disorientation and terror, as if everything were happening simultaneously and the reader's gaze were being pulled about haphazardly by the overwhelmingly catastrophic scene. The reader is being confronted with a scene that both exceeds her capacity to take it in and yet, anticipating later notions of the sublime,[48] is also emphatically unified under one idea ("the one word 'destruction' includes all this"). The many aspects of the scene of the falling city blur into one overriding effect.

46. *Collected Works of Erasmus*, 577–78, quoting Quintilian 8.3.67–69.

47. While drawing on the authority of the ancient texts from which these fragments are extracted, Erasmus characteristically integrates them into a new discourse continuous with and directed toward the world of the present. Marc Fumaroli compares Erasmus's textual fragments in the *Adages* to broken bits of pagan idols that the Christian orator uses to give iridian color to a "supple and living syncretism." The historical specificity of fragments—as things in themselves with their own time-bound meanings—exerts a kind of pressure that the orator overcomes by integrating them into his own discourse. Fumaroli writes, "The philosophical 'solidity' of the [new orator's] discourse, guaranteed by the antiquity of his sources, is no longer incompatible with the fluidity of the world where incarnated humanity finds itself 'embarked.'" (Translation from the French mine.) Thomas M. Greene writes of Erasmus in a similar vein: "Each commentary, each essay, is arranged around a history of its concrete usages and applications, a history in which the modern instance takes its place, or rather a history from which this new usage, with all its congeries of associations, is in the process of emerging." See Fumaroli, *L'âge de l'éloquence: rhétorique et "res literaria" de la Renaissance au seuil de l'époque classique* (Geneva: Librairie Droz, 2002), 97; Greene, *The Vulnerable Text: Essays in Renaissance Literature* (New York: Columbia University Press, 1986), 11; and Margaret Mann Phillips, *The "Adages" of Erasmus: A Study with Translations* (Cambridge: Cambridge University Press, 1964).

48. Kant says that we experience unboundedness at the same time as "we add to this unboundedness the thought of its totality"; *Critique of Judgment*, trans. Werner S. Pluhar (Indianapolis: Hackett, 1987), 98. For Renaissance versions of the sublime, see David L. Sedley's exploration of how in the sixteenth and seventeenth centuries skepticism led to the aesthetic category of the sublime. See especially the first chapter, which explores Montaigne's proto-sublime responses to Roman ruins, in his *Sublimity and Skepticism in Montaigne and Milton* (Ann Arbor: University of Michigan Press, 2005), 18–42.

Shakespeare, in contrast, emphasizes fragmentation. Whereas Erasmus uses the parts of the scene to reconstruct a complete experience ("all the cries blending into one overall sound"), Shakespeare uses the parts to break down the scene into material fragments. Whereas Erasmus describes Trojan people (babies, mothers, prisoners) in his ekphrasis of Troy's fall, Shakespeare points to the body parts (hand, foot, leg) that make his audience imagine these people.[49] In these ways, Shakespeare both builds on and also reacts against the humanist tradition by subtly shifting the emphasis from a fantasy of the past's resurrected wholeness to a more antiquarian sense of the scene's thingly fragmentation.

Shakespeare explicitly engages the oppositional categories of the whole and parts when he focuses on Lucrece's relationship with this picture of Troy in the second part of the ekphrasis:

> To this well-painted *piece* is Lucrece come,
> To find a face where *all* distress is stelled.
> *Many* she sees, where cares have carved *some*,
> But *none* where *all* distress and dolour dwelled;
> Till she despairing Hecuba beheld,
> Staring on Priam's wounds with her old eyes,
> Which bleeding under Pyrrhus' proud foot lies. (1443–49)

The passage repeatedly refers to various degrees of completion or fullness ("none," "some," "many," "all"). Coming to a "well-painted *piece*," what Lucrece seeks is "all": she wants a face "where *all* distress is stelled" and, again, "where *all* distress and dolour dwelled." The problem of representing this "all" recurs at the end of the poem, when Lucrece appears overwhelmed by an experience that exceeds her ability to tell it: she has, she says, "*moe* woes than words" and can't "tell them *all* with one poor tired tongue" (1615, 1617).[50]

A similar tension arises in *Hamlet* between a humanist fantasy of the past's resurrection and an antiquarian emphasis on the fragments of the historical material record. On the one hand, the past quite literally returns to stalk the present. The Ghost comes back from the dead to demand retroactive, heroic action from the living. On the other hand, the grand figures of the past appear as all-too-material fragments. Hamlet, disillusioned, imagines the dust of Alexander the Great made into clay that's used as the lowly plug of a "bung-hole" in a barrel (5.1.194). In this way, as Keilen explores,

49. Meek, *Narrating the Visual*, 76.
50. My italics.

Hamlet "ridicules the piety and nostalgia of humanism's historical vision."[51] By employing this latter, more material approach to history in his description of Troy's fall in *The Rape of Lucrece*, Shakespeare is, in some ways, more like the period's proto-empiricists, its antiquarians and naturalists, than like the earlier Renaissance humanists.[52]

The image of the old Trojan queen Hecuba in the ekphrasis appears at first to fulfill Lucrece's desire for a face that represents *all* suffering, but Shakespeare soon renders problematic this fantasy. Instead of offering a vivified image of extreme female grief—for example, by portraying Hecuba in the act of weeping or tearing at her hair or beating at her breast (all traditional epic displays of female mourning)—Shakespeare portrays Hecuba as though she were a dissected lifeless thing:

> In her the painter had anatomized
> Time's ruin, beauty's wrack, and grim care's reign.
> Her cheeks with chaps and wrinkles were disguised:
> Of what she was no semblance did remain.
> Her blue blood changed to black in every vein,
> Wanting the spring that those shrunk pipes had fed,
> Showed life imprisoned in a body dead. (1450–56)

The word *anatomized* conveyed then, as it does now, dissection. The first use of this word is in a 1541 book on surgery: "Anathomy is called ryght dyuysyon of membres done for certayne knowleges."[53] As a verb, it can mean analyze, but it also refers to this cutting of bodies into parts.[54] This Greek-based meaning is reinforced by the following line's tri-partite fragmented structure and staccato rhythm: "Time's ruin, beauty's wrack, and grim care's reign." The stanza goes on then to describe Hecuba as the parts of a corpse ("a body dead"): "Her cheeks with chaps and wrinkles were disguised" evokes the aged, dried skin on her face, at the same time as the line

51. Keilen, "Exemplary Metals," 282.

52. Stephanie H. Jed uses the history of Lucrece to explore the development of humanism. Focusing on Coluccio Salutati's version of the story (*Declamatio Lucretiae*, c. 1390), Jed analyzes how the problem of what she calls "chaste thinking" applies not only to Lucretia's sexual chastity but also to "the very structures of her story's transmission." She is especially interested in humanist philological attempts to "castigate" the text, or, literally, make it chaste. Jed, *Chaste Thinking: The Rape of Lucretia and the Birth of Humanism* (Bloomington and Indianapolis: Indiana University Press, 1989).

53. *The Questyonary of Cyrurgyens*, Robert Copland's translation of a work by Guy de Chauliac, cited in *OED*, "anatomy," 1.1a.

54. See *The Body in Parts: Fantasies of Corporeality in Early Modern Europe*, ed. David Hillman and Carla Mazzio (New York: Routledge, 1997).

also evokes her skull. *Chaps* are fissures, as well as jawbones (Hamlet refers to Yorick's skull as "quite chapfallen" [5.1.182]), and *cheeks* in the Middle Ages could similarly refer to jaws.[55] Hecuba's blood is also accounted for: wanting its "spring," it seems no longer to be regenerating and has turned black. The poet seems here almost like a kind of mortician. No longer is he like the mythical doctor Aesculapius, to whom Poliziano referred in order to express the humanists' attempts to resurrect the broken corpus of literature by rejoining its broken parts.

Shakespeare's imagery, which evokes a dissected, lifeless body, goes even further. This is a poem that often associates women's bodies with buildings and falling cities.[56] In an extended series of metaphors, Lucrece's rape is compared to the siege and capture of a city. Her breasts are "turrets" (441) that Tarquin's hand scales; later, her breast is an ivory wall, and Tarquin's hand a ram that batters it. He feels "her heart (poor citizen) distressed, / Wounding itself to death, rise up and fall, / Beating her bulk, that his hand shakes withal. / This moves in him more rage and lesser pity / To make the breach and enter this sweet city" (465–69). After the rape, Lucrece describes herself as "robbed and ransacked" (838).[57]

In keeping with this extended metaphor, the description of Hecuba in the ekphrasis also evokes a broken physical ruin. In his commentary on the line "Time's ruin, beauty's wrack, and grim care's reign" (1451), Burrow glosses *ruin* as "destructive influence," but the power of the stanza depends on our also hearing the more concrete sense of the word: the condition of a structure, especially a building, that has collapsed,[58] or the material that remains after a structure has fallen (*ruin* comes from Latin *ruere,* to fall). Compare Richard Stanyhurst's 1582 translation of the very scene describing Troy's fall in the *Aeneid* book 2: "The old towne fals to ruin" (2.32).[59] It is this more concrete sense of ruin that the poem earlier evoked in Lucrece's

55. The *OED,* "cheek," la, cites Chaucer's *Monk's Tale* 48, "And hadde no wepne but an Asses cheke."

56. For a study of the association of anxieties about the female body and fears of invasion in Elizabethan England in *The Rape of Lucrece, Titus Andronicus,* and *Cymbeline,* see Linda Woodbridge, "Palisading the Elizabethan Body Politic," *Texas Studies in Literature and Language* 33, no. 3, History, Culture, and Self (Fall 1991): 327–54.

57. Lucrece's association with Roman ruins is also suggested by Henry VIII's printer Thomas Berthelet, whose device depicted "Lucrecia Romana" at the moment of her suicide standing proleptically before ruined Roman arches and columns. See Anne Lake Prescott's "Du Bellay and Shakespeare's Sonnets," in *The Oxford Handbook of Shakespeare's Poetry,* ed. Jonathan F. S. Post (Oxford: Oxford University Press, 2013), 134–50.

58. *OED,* "ruin," 1a.

59. Ibid.

complaint to Time, where she lamented that time's glory was "To ruinate proud buildings with thy hours, / And smear with dust their glitt'ring golden towers; / To fill with worm-holes stately monuments, / To feed oblivion with decay of things" (944–47). The fact that this lament uses verbs without time—that is, in the infinitive—constructs a lament about time that is itself timeless, emerging from a perspective on the oblivion of the world that is as ahistorical as the *ubi-sunt* lament that I explored in the Petrarch chapter. But this poem, unlike medieval laments, portrays ruins that do not disappear so quickly into an eschatological perspective; rather, they appear as dilapidated historical things with their own concrete materiality (with dust and worm-holes). Taking the words *ruin* and *wrack* in their concrete sense, the figure of Hecuba starts to evoke what Francis Bacon will describe as one of the "antiquities [which] are history defaced."[60]

Hecuba's association with a run-down monument gains a unique valence through the reference to her "veins." The word evokes not only blood vessels but also, especially in the context of a description of the wondrously verisimilar qualities of an artwork, markings in marble. Shakespeare may be thinking of the 1590 printed edition of *The Countesse of Pembrokes Arcadia*, where Sir Philip Sidney plays on the connection between the "veins" in the stone and in the body:[61]

> A naked *Venus* of white marble, wherein the graver had used such cunning, that the naturall blew veines of the marble were framed in fitte places, to set foorth the beautifull veines of her bodie. At her brest shee had her babe *Aeneas*, who seemed (hauing begun to sucke) to leave that, to looke upon her fayre eyes, which smiled at the babes follie, the meane while the breast running.[62]

Ekphrasis often promises this fullness of representation. Sidney's conceit is that this sculpted fountain is so perfect that the veins the sculptor found in the marble show the veins in the body he was portraying. Shakespeare torques this tradition: while Sidney's Venus embodies youth and fecundity, with her smiling eyes and breast overflowing with liquid, Shakespeare's Hecuba is an image of age and desiccation, "wanting the spring that those shrunk pipes had fed." Shakespeare's metaphor of the shrunken pipes retains the memory of a ruined fountain or aqueduct, which, like the fragments of ancient Roman fountains at that time being recovered, lacked

60. *The Works of Francis Bacon*, vol. 4, ed. James Spedding (London: Longman, 1860), 303.

61. The first *OED* citation of "veins" in stone is from the mid-seventeenth century; see "vein," 5a.

62. *The Prose Works of Sir Philip Sidney*, vol. 1, ed. Albert Feuillerat (Cambridge: Cambridge University Press, 1912), 17–18.

flowing water. The desire that underlies many ekphrases to bring the past to life again turns back on itself in Shakespeare's ekphrasis and registers the fragmented, material nature of the remains it wants to resurrect. In a recent essay on *The Rape of Lucrece,* Belsey explores how, in this ekphrasis of Shakespeare's, visual and verbal motifs come together in a common "longing" for presence.[63] What's at stake in this ekphrasis, she argues, is not just the verbal versus the visual, as in traditional accounts of *paragone,* but the ultimate inability of representation itself to achieve full presence. My contribution is to explore how such a longing for presence reflects changing ideas about materiality and history in the Renaissance, and how these changing ideas came into tension with aesthetic experience.

The imagery of ruins recalls imagery earlier in the poem. In an ekphrasis describing Lucrece, Shakespeare compared her to a tomb or monument. This ekphrasis occurs at the moment when Tarquin first enters Lucrece's chamber to rape her:

> Her lily hand her rosy cheek lies under,
> Coz'ning the pillow of a lawful kiss,
> Who therefore angry seems to part in sunder,
> Swelling on either side to want his bliss,
> Between whose hills her head entombed is;
> Where, like a virtuous monument, she lies,
> To be admired of lewd unhallowed eyes.
> . . .
> Her hair, like golden threads, played with her breath:
> O modest wantons, wanton modesty!
> Showing life's triumph in the map of death,
> And death's dim looks in life's mortality.
> Each in her sleep themselves so beautify
> As if between them twain there were no strife,
> But that life lived in death, and death in life. (386–92, 400–06)

The unsettling effect of these stanzas derives from Shakespeare's use of traditional descriptions of verisimilar art to describe a living person—so that he seems, oddly, to be praising a living woman as being so lifelike. The trope that Shakespeare uses of the hair that plays in the air ("Her hair, like golden threads, played with her breath") reverses the normal relationship between animate and inanimate objects, so that it is the inanimate

63. Belsey, "Invocation of the Visual Image," 196.

that acts on the animate. Praise of hair's movement recurs throughout the tradition of ekphrastic descriptions of art objects,[64] and Pliny groups the ability to represent hair and veins as two major advances toward verisimilar statuary.[65]

But the reference to the "virtuous monument" (391) on a pillow, which has "entombed" (390) Lucrece's head, narrows the reader's focus from art in general to tomb effigies of wives in particular. Women in medieval and Renaissance churches were often shown sleeping on a pillow beside their husbands, as Burrow notes.[66] If Shakespeare's "virtuous monument" suggests memorial statuary, Shakespeare's promise in the dedication of *Venus and Adonis* to produce "some graver labour" (commonly understood as a reference to the more serious epic ambitions of his ensuing *Lucrece*) becomes a kind of pun on this sepulchral sense of "graver." This association is underscored by the allusions to death in the second stanza quoted above, as well as to her "alabaster skin" (419) since alabaster was commonly used for tomb statues.[67] It is as though Lucrece has already become a ruin of the past, anticipating "her future role as a monument,"[68] a theme that I will explore further in the coda.

The colorfulness of Shakespeare's image of Lucrece (lily hand, rosy cheek, green coverlet, eyes like marigolds) contrasts with the colorlessness of Hecuba. Given that medieval tomb effigies were frequently painted, it is as though this first statue-like image (of Lucrece) is unruined; the later one (of Hecuba), ruined. In the first condition, the monument is associated with color, wholeness, and living nature; in the second, it is colorless, broken, and dry. Just as the animistic tapestry in the first room of Spenser's House of Busirane is succeeded by the dusty artifacts in the second room, the imagery of sepulchral monuments in Shakespeare's *The Rape of Lucrece* is followed by imagery of ruins as the poem proceeds. Before

64. For example, Callistratus's *Descriptions* twice mentions this trope: in "On the Statue of Orpheus" (7.430) and in "On the Statue of a Youth" (11.435). Aretino also uses it in his description of Titian's now-lost painting of the Annunciation.

65. Pliny, *Naturalis historia* 34.19.59. The image of Lucrece's head on the pillow also draws on Ovid's description in the *Metamorphoses* of Pygmalion's lifelike statue, which he lays on his bed, with its head on a soft down pillow (10.269).

66. Burrow, *The Complete Sonnets and Poems*, 265. A particularly famous example of such a monument is the effigy of Eleanor of Lancaster (d. 1372) in the Chichester Cathedral, Sussex, made famous by Philip Larkin's poem "An Arundel Tomb."

67. Ibid., 266.

68. Judith Dundas, *Pencils Rhetorique: Renaissance Poets and the Art of Painting* (Newark: University of Delaware Press, 1993), 73.

the rape, the imagery of monuments was associated with life (the monument was a metaphor for Lucrece); after the rape, the monument has become de-animated, desiccated, and dead (evoked through the description of the ruin-like Hecuba). Similarly, the metaphor that Shakespeare uses to describe Tarquin's soul changes from a "fair temple" (719) before the rape to "weak ruins" (720) after the rape—a shift from a structure filled by the divine[69] to a historicized and secularized object that has been emptied out. It is as if the poem is meant to inhabit an older, more medieval mindset in the beginning, where the funereal imagery is made to seem paradoxically alive ("As if between them twain [life and death] there were no strife, / But that life lived in death, and death in life" [405–6]).[70] Then, by the end, the poem encounters its own imagery in a different condition, not as lifelike monuments but as ruins.

SILENT THINGS, THINGS THAT TALK: EPITAPHS AND THE RETURN OF SUBJECTIVITY

I would like to suggest that Shakespeare associates the objective world of broken ruins that emerges in *The Rape of Lucrece* with a larger loss of the innate expressivity of things. Especially in the beginning of the poem, the things of the world have the power to speak directly. It is as though the world were a language that could express itself fully without the mediation of words. Lucrece herself is, in some ways, a thing and speaks as such. In the space of four lines at the beginning of the poem, she is referred to as "treasure" (16), "wealth" (17), "possession" (18), and "fortune" (19). Lucrece's beauty, the narrator says, can "persuade / The eyes of men without an orator" (29–30). The white and red of her skin are objectifications of her virtue and beauty,[71]

69. Burrow glosses the reference, "Know ye not that ye are the Temple of God . . . ?" (1 Corinthians 3:16).

70. Both C. S. Lewis and Douglas Bush remark on the "medieval" quality of Shakespeare's rhetorical techniques in this poem, especially his frequent use of proverbs. C. S. Lewis, *English Literature in the Sixteenth Century, Excluding Drama* (Oxford: Oxford University Press, 1954), 500; Bush, *Mythology and the Renaissance Tradition in English Poetry* (Minneapolis: University of Minnesota Press, 1932), 154. For the medieval versions of Lucrece and their importance to Shakespeare, see Andrew Galloway, "Chaucer's *Legend of Lucrece* and the Critique of Ideology in Fourteenth-Century England," *ELH* 60, no. 4 (Winter 1993): 813–32; Richard Hillman, "Gower's Lucrece: A New Old Source for *The Rape of Lucrece*," *Chaucer Review* 24, no. 3 (Winter 1990): 263–70; Wolfgang P. Müller, "Lucretia and the Medieval Canonists," *Bulletin of Medieval Canon Law* 19 (1989): 13–32.

71. A related treatment of emotions as hypostatized and externalized forces can be found in the twelfth century. Chrétien de Troyes describes Reason and Love acting on Lancelot in a manner that Lewis describes as "the subjectivism of an objective age." Chrétien de Troyes, *The Com-*

each of which struggles to be uppermost in her cheeks (52–77).[72] Hearing her husband praised, Lucrece strikes a pose that could be emblazoned in stained glass, for she is an emblem illustrating universalized, timeless emotions that are directly connected to divine sources of meaning: "Her joy with heaved-up hand she doth express, / And wordless so greets heaven for his success" (111–12). The frequent use of adages, emphasized by printers' marks in the first published edition (quotation marks direct the reader's attention to quotable sayings), asserts generalized truths that Lucrece illustrates. This account of the world as language approximates what Walter Benjamin, in his early writing, describes in theological terms that derive from Jewish mysticism as "unfallen language"—with the adjustment that what is prelapsarian in Benjamin's account is pseudo-medieval in Shakespeare's poem.[73] John Donne discusses a related idea in his *Essayes in Divinity*.[74]

In contrast, as the poem progresses, a gap arises between things and what they mean. Things no longer speak directly. When Lucrece sees in the picture representing Troy's fall the representation of Sinon, the Greek who tricked the Trojans into accepting the Trojan horse, she at first cannot believe that such an innocent-seeming face could have been capable of such deception: "Such signs of truth in his plain face she spied / That she concludes the picture was belied" (1532–33). Yet recalling her own deception by Tarquin, she concludes that only such an innocent-seeming face could have been capable of such lies. As she makes this realization about the distance between appearances and meaning, her language becomes convoluted: "'It

plete Romances of Chrétien de Troyes, trans. David Staines (Bloomington: Indiana University Press, 1990); C. S. Lewis, *The Allegory of Love: A Study in Medieval Tradition* (Oxford: Oxford University Press, 1936), 30.

72. Elizabeth D. Harvey contrasts the descriptions of color associated with Lucrece and Tarquin (who, shortly after the description of the color in Lucrece's cheeks, "colored" his intentions): "Tarquin and Lucrece exemplify the divergent, even contradictory history of color's meanings, for Lucrece embodies color's apparent capacity to express the body's inner secrecy, its hidden truths, whereas Tarquin figures color's capacity to disguise, to present a deceitful cover or corruption of correspondence between inner and outer" (317). See her "Flesh Colors and Shakespeare's Sonnets," in *A Companion to Shakespeare's Sonnets*, ed. Michael Schoenfeldt (Malden, MA: Blackwell, 2007), 314–28.

73. Benjamin's semi-mystical ideas about language are explored most overtly in his early essays "On Language as Such and on the Language of Man" (1916) and "The Task of the Translator" (1921), in *Selected Writings*, vol. 1, *1913–1926*, ed. Marcus Bullock and Michael W. Jennings (Cambridge, MA: Belknap Press of Harvard University Press, 1996), 62–74, 253–63. See also S. Brent Plate, *Walter Benjamin, Religion, and Aesthetics: Rethinking Religion through the Arts* (New York: Routledge, 2005), 65.

74. John Donne, *Essays in Divinity*, ed. Evelyn M. Simpson (Oxford: Oxford University Press, 1952), 23.

cannot be', quoth she, 'that so much guile—'/ She would have said 'can lurk in such a look,' / But Tarquin's shape came in her mind the while, / And from her tongue 'can lurk' from 'cannot' took" (1534–37). A distance has emerged between the "outward" (1545) and the "inward" (1546), a distance that places a new pressure on verbal language. An interpretive gap opens.

One exception to this pattern of increasingly alienated signification is Lucrece's interaction with the maid immediately after the rape, an interaction that returns to a form of connection that is outside language. Without knowing the cause of Lucrece's grief, the maid responds instinctively as though sharing in her mistress's pain:

> But as the earth doth weep, the sun being set,
> Each flower moistened like a melting eye;
> Even so the maid with swelling drops gan wet
> Her circled eyne enforced by sympathy
> Of those fair suns set in her mistress' sky,
> Who in a salt-waved ocean quench their light,
> Which makes the maid weep like the dewy night.
>
> A pretty while these pretty creatures stand,
> Like ivory conduits coral cisterns filling.
> One justly weeps; the other takes in hand
> No cause but company of her drops' spilling. (1226–36)

The first stanza is all one sentence, its unbroken continuity expressive of the fluidity of the images. References to the maid and Lucrece are structured chiastically, as though the two women were blending into one another as drops of water that touch. In Shakespeare's extended metaphor, the flowers express the earth's sadness in the same way that the maid expresses the grief of her mistress, that is, in a manner outside the logic of cause and effect. There is "no cause," Shakespeare says, but that of proximity, "company of her drops' spilling." The imagery is first of natural things, possibly associating this nonverbal and nonrational sympathy with a more primitive state, and then of a kind of fountain, like the rediscovered ancient fountains or aqueducts, but this time in an unruined state full of flowing water ("like ivory conduits coral cisterns filling").

However, if the extra-linguistic communication succeeds in this case, Shakespeare contrasts the positive interaction with the maid against the negative interaction with the messenger in the very next scene. Again, the interaction is nonverbal, but this time communication goes awry. While the groom blushes from a sense of humble dutifulness, Lucrece misreads what the sudden redness in his cheeks signifies (1352–58). When not inscribed in language, the meaning of the image has become unstable. Lucrece thinks the cause of the groom's blush is his knowledge of the rape, whereas the blush really indicates only his bashfulness. Their physical relatedness (the mutual blush) becomes the source of misunderstanding and separation.

The theme of rape allows Shakespeare to explore the connection between brutality and silence. As Lynn Enterline has discussed, rape is an act that poetic tradition renders as unspeakable.[75] In Ovid's highly influential account of Philomel's rape in the *Metamorphoses*, to which Shakespeare frequently refers, not only does the rapist cut out Philomel's tongue, rendering her unable to tell what she has undergone, but even her sister Procne is rendered silent by knowledge of the crime: "Grief restrained her mouth; words sought in language that were bitter enough were lacking" (6.583–85).[76] At the moment of Lucrece's rape, Tarquin muzzles her with her own bedsheets. She is silent because her mouth is bound, but also because of the tomb-like qualities of the imagery: Tarquin "*Entombs* her outcry in her lips' sweet fold" (679). The sexual implications of "her lips' sweet fold" conflates the rape with the act of silencing her, and the reference to the tomb associates this silence with the material, historical record that recurs throughout the poem. Shakespeare seems to have been thinking of a similar constellation of issues when he crafted the mutilated figure of Lavinia in *Titus Andronicus*, published the same year as *The Rape of Lucrece*. Without tongue or hands, "lopped and hewed" (2.3.17), the raped Lavinia resembles an ancient sculpture or some broken unearthed fragment.[77] After comparing her to a fountain, Marcus remarks on her devastating inability to express her pain: "Sorrow concealed, like an oven stopped, / Doth burn the heart to cinders where it is" (2.3.36–7).[78] Again, rape and silence are closely equated, and these are linked with ruin-like materiality.

75. Lynn Enterline, *The Rhetoric of the Body from Ovid to Shakespeare* (Cambridge: Cambridge University Press, 2000), 152–97.

76. "Dolor ora repressit, / verbaque quaerenti satis indignantia linguae / defuerunt." See Mark Amsler, "Rape and Silence: Ovid's Mythography and Medieval Readers," in *Representing Rape in Medieval and Early Modern Literature*, ed. Elizabeth Robertson and Christine M. Rose (New York: Palgrave, 2001), 86.

77. Shakespeare's interest in ruins in *Titus Andronicus* is also suggested by the Second Goth's anachronistic reference to "a ruinous monastery" (5.1.21). See Prescott, "Du Bellay and Shakespeare's Sonnets." On Marcus's description as a subversion of traditions of Petrarchan blazon, see Heather James, *Shakespeare's Troy: Drama, Politics, and the Translation of Empire* (Cambridge: Cambridge University Press, 1997), 64ff.

78. William Shakespeare, *Titus Andronicus*, ed. Jonathan Bate, Arden Shakespeare, 3rd ser. (London: Thomson Learning, 2004).

In Shakespeare's version of the Lucrece story, the raped woman talks much more than she does in most previous authors' versions; traditionally, she says few words before killing herself. However, what Shakespeare's Lucrece articulates is the painful burden of having suffered more than her verbal abilities can convey: "For more it is than I can well express, / And that deep torture may be called a hell / When more is felt than one hath power to tell" (1286–88). Lucrece stands, I am suggesting, not just for the verbal insufficiency often experienced by people who have undergone extreme forms of violence but, at least in key moments, for the *voicelessness of the material historical record itself,* which can come nowhere near to expressing fully the suffering of which it becomes the evidence.

One way that Shakespeare tries to give voice to the historical record is by including lines suggestive of epitaphs—the form by which a tomb is traditionally made to speak. This epitaphic form is one of utmost brevity, a kind of anti-*copia* that demonstrates, as Joshua Scodel puts it, "the poet's 'much in little' power."[79] Of increasing interest to antiquarians, especially near the end of the 1590s (when the Society of Antiquaries produced the "first sustained evaluations of epitaphic writing"[80]), epitaphs were being collected by prominent Elizabethan antiquarians. Scott L. Newstok associates the interest in epitaphs with the period's increasing "emphasis on verification of historical facts."[81] Even fictional epitaphs, created apart from any real tombstones, conveyed what Newstok calls a "*sheen of facticity.*"[82]

Epitaphic poetry is built on the basic form "Here lies. . . ." The prominent antiquarian William Camden, who treats epitaphs in the final section of his 1605 *Remains Concerning Britain,* quotes approximately three dozen examples that employ some variation of this form in English, Latin, or French. "*Hic situs est, Hospes* [Here lies, stranger], as speaking to the reader," is the ancient Latin scaffolding on which, he explains, later epitaphs were built. "So we & other Christians began them [epitaphs] with *Hic deponitur*

79. Joshua Scodel, *The English Poetic Epitaph: Commemoration and Conflict from Jonson to Wordsworth* (Ithaca: Cornell University Press, 1991), 59.

80. Newstok, *Quoting Death in Early Modern England,* 2. See also Kevin Sharpe, *Sir Robert Cotton, 1586–1631: History and Politics in Early Modern England* (Oxford: Oxford University Press, 1979), 20ff.

81. Newstok, *Quoting Death in Early Modern England,* 92.

82. Ibid., 93. Especially interesting is the increased awareness of epitaphs' evidential qualities among early modern English writers. Newstok explains the "antiquarian turn": while Raphael Holinshed somewhat casually uses various texts "that maie serue in good stead of an epitaph" in his accounts of Henry V, VII, and VIII, his successors Abraham Fleming and John Stow show greater hesitation in using material that was not actually found on tombstones (82–108).

[Here is put], *Hic jacet* [Here lies], *Hic requiescit* [Here rests], . . . in French *Icy gist* [Here is entombed]."[83] Such epitaphs could take either a third- or first-person form, as in E. K.'s humorous gloss of Spenser's "Maye": "Ho, Ho, who lies here? / I the good Erle of Devonshere."[84] The fact that this here-lies form not infrequently served as the structure for jokes suggests that the phrase had become as formulaic as a limerick.[85]

The most overt reference to epitaphs in *The Rape of Lucrece* is in the ekphrasis of the picture showing Troy's fall, in lines that start with a Petrarch-like play on the *ubi-sunt* lament and end with an echo of the epitaphic form "here lies":

> Lo, here weeps Hecuba, here Priam dies,
> Here manly Hector faints, here Troilus sounds,
> Here friend by friend in bloody channel lies. (1485–87)

It is as though the poem itself becomes a kind of tomb in which once-living people have been interred. The word *here* begins about ten stanzas scattered throughout the larger poem. For example, after Lucrece delivers her famous pronouncement for posterity ("No dame hereafter living / By my excuse shall claim excuse's giving"), Shakespeare writes: "*Here*, with a sigh as if her heart would break, / She throws forth Tarquin's name" (1714–17). In this instant, Lucrece becomes frozen as a picture for posterity. Most interestingly, Shakespeare echoes this epitaphic form in his next stanza—with the addition of the emphatic "even" for the first and only time in the poem—to depict the many-times-represented moment when Lucrece stabs herself: "*Even here* she sheathed in her harmless breast / A harmful knife" (1723–24). Shakespeare multilayers meaning in this moment: her stabbing herself initiates a new political regime and reminds the reader of the last lines of the *Aeneid*, when Virgil uses the verb *condere* to describe Aeneas stabbing Turnus in the breast (12.950). This word means variously at other key moments in the epic not only *stab* but also *bury*, *hide*, and *found* (as in, found an empire: "So vast was the effort to found [condere] the Roman

83. William Camden, *Remains Concerning Britain*, ed. R. D. Dunn (Toronto: University of Toronto Press, 1984), 320.

84. Cited in Scodel, *The English Poetic Epitaph*, 104. See *The Yale Edition of the Shorter Poems of Edmund Spenser*, ed. William A. Oram, Einar Bjorvand, Ronald Bond, Thomas H. Cain, Alexander Dunlop, and Richard Schell (New Haven: Yale University Press, 1989), 101.

85. Camden offers several pages of examples of humorous epitaphs in this form: for example, "Here lyeth John Cruker a maker of Bellowes, / His craftes-master and King of good-fellowes; / Yet when he came to the hower of his death, / He that made Bellowes, could not make breath" (355); and "Here is Elderton lyeng in dust, / Or lyeng Elderton, chose which you lust" (355).

people"[86]). The establishment of the Republic, like the establishment of empire, emerges from an act of violence that buries the past in silence, in tombs and graves.[87]

Epitaphs, in providing a voice for the dead person or even for the tomb itself, are unique for the way that they speak from the position of an object (the tomb) and from the position of the interred dead subject's nonbeing. After her rape, Lucrece, as though already dead, mourns the loss of her former self. She speaks as if she has already become an exemplary object lesson of history. Describing herself as "bereft" (835) of her honor, Lucrece says:

> My honey lost, and I, a drone-like bee,
> Have no perfection of my summer left. (836–37)

These lines, which have the music of lament, offer in a highly compact form a meditation on the experience of self-loss. However, instead of conveying the coldness of stone, her lines are touched by an unexpected intimacy, conveying the living warmth of nature—of, more specifically, bees in summertime. Lucrece's word, *perfection*, evokes completion, consummation, quintessence. *Perfection* is in these lines the only Latinate word, surrounded by Saxon words like *drone*, *bee*, *summer*, and *honey*. The perfection that Lucrece has lost conflates subtly with the loss of the English language's Latin past, as though her personal loss were connected to language's loss. This is "fallen language" in Benjamin's terms. Yet the Saxon words produce their own unique poetry. While Lucrece mourns that she is devoid of her former perfection, the Saxon words gently suggest that the world is humming and buzzing all around a lament that is already becoming empty. As Bradin Cormack shows about the "microformal" operation of Latinity in the sonnets, Shakespeare's attention to etymological history focuses on "the domain of experience," on the secular sphere of human words, where "forms are real" not because they are pregiven as real through reference to a metaphysical realm of the absolute but, rather, "because they become real" through the workings of the poetry.[88]

86. 1.33: "Tantae molis erat Romanam condere gentem." See Sharon L. James, "Establishing Rome with the Sword: *Condere* in the *Aeneid*," *American Journal of Philology* 116, no. 4. (Winter 1995): 623–37.

87. For an account of *The Rape of Lucrece* as a critique of history-writing, see Heather Dubrow, "The Rape of Clio: Attitudes to History in Shakespeare's *Lucrece*," *English Literary Renaissance* 16, no. 3 (Autumn 1986): 425–41.

88. Bradin Cormack, "Tender Distance: Latinity and Desire in Shakespeare's Sonnets," in *A Companion to Shakespeare's Sonnets*, ed. Michael Schoenfeldt (Malden, MA: Blackwell, 2007), 242–60.

Related experiments in epitaphic poetics are found scattered in Shakespeare's larger oeuvre, like the following line in *Twelfth Night* where Olivia unveils her face for the first time for the disguised Viola:

> Look you, sir, such a one I was this present. (1.5.237–8)[89]

Olivia is referring to the disclosure of a painting, as the Arden edition notes (after all, she explicitly says, "We will draw the curtain and show you the picture"). But so far as I know, scholars have not remarked that the line's strongly melancholic undertone and effect of eerie self-detachment also derive from Shakespeare's use of the *memento mori* trope, the basic form of which is expressed in the beginning of one 1593 epitaph:

> Come nere my friends, behould and see
> Suche as I am, suche shall you bee . . . [90]

Olivia plays on the first-person epitaph's impossible juxtaposition of past ("was") and present ("this present"). While the standard epitaph links the condition of a living stranger with the remains of a dead person (you will be like me, i.e., dead), Olivia, like Lucrece, uses the epitaphic form to link her living consciousness (as the speaking voice) with her object-like, externalized physical being (her body's appearance). In so doing, thingliness becomes a mental state. As though portraying the language's loss of the concrete particular, the line begins with an emphatic series of references to the singular being (Olivia) present in the moment—*such*, *a*, *one*, *I*. But by the end of the line, the embodied person, Olivia, has faded into the abstract realm of generalities and categories that language creates. She has become an *example* of a singular person that once was. Olivia's line follows the epitaphic form so precisely as to mimic the traditional address to the anonymous stranger.[91] Shakespeare's "Look you, sir . . ." parallels the 1593 epitaph's "Come nere my friends. . . ." What is most important for my purposes is the surprising idea that, in adopting the epitaphic form, objects can begin to address subjects.

Returning to *The Rape of Lucrece* and its ekphrasis of the picture showing

89. William Shakespeare, *Twelfth Night*, ed. J. M. Lothian and T. W. Craik, Arden Shakespeare, 2nd ser. (London: Methuen, 1975).

90. The epitaph is John Trustlowe's in Ravenshaw, quoted in Scodel, *The English Poetic Epitaph*, 30. Scodel explains that while the *memento mori* trope declined with the rise of Protestantism, it was still sometimes used in the sixteenth and seventeenth centuries.

91. The *memento mori* epitaphic trope derives from classical examples, first developing in a situation where people were buried along the roadside. Ibid., 33.

the fall of Troy, I find a heightened encounter with a peculiar new form of silence: that of historical material ruins. In the end, what is most striking about the depiction of Troy's fall is that both Lucrece and the ruined Hecuba are painfully unable to express the experience of having suffered brutality. This is the pain that lies buried in the material historical object:

> On this sad shadow Lucrece spends her eyes,
> And shapes her sorrow to the beldam's woes,
> Who nothing wants to answer her but cries,
> And bitter words to ban her cruel foes.
> The painter was no god to lend her those;
> And therefore Lucrece swears he did her wrong,
> To give her so much grief and not a tongue. (1457–63)

Just as Lucrece cannot fully express her suffering ("more is felt than one hath power to tell" [1288]), Hecuba cannot express her experience (the painter gave her "so much grief and not a tongue"). What Lucrece identifies with is precisely the silence and fragmentation that the objectness of Hecuba's ruin-like image embodies.

That is, Lucrece relates to Hecuba not despite Hecuba's brokenness and objectness but precisely because of them. In Shakespeare's ekphrasis, the objective historical artifact (the ruin of Hecuba) becomes an image of the subjective experience of the subject (Lucrece)—the expression of her devastation. But it is also as if the *object* itself desires an outlet, the release into language of the experience that has been buried in it.

One of the major aims of objectivity is to locate knowledge of the object in a realm outside the imagination (and, more generally, outside the subject). But here in the intersubjective world of Shakespeare's poem, the fragmented object turns to look at the subject and, in the beseeching quality of its silence, beckons her to speak for it.

CONCLUSION: FRAGMENTED OBJECTS, FRAGMENTED SUBJECTS

The fragment may be the very image—if not the cliché—of modernity: broken, alienated, dismembered, the ruins of the past evoke a lost world, where once upon a time everything was whole and integrated. Linda Nochlin calls fragments the "metaphor of modernity."[92] She locates the emergence of this

92. Linda Nochlin, *The Body in Pieces: The Fragment as a Metaphor of Modernity* (New York: Thames & Hudson, 1994).

modernity in the French Revolution, when, she says, the fragment was first celebrated. The foot broken off a statue of Louis XIV seems to speak of the breaking down of the old oppressive systems of monarchial power—just as the aristocrats' guillotined heads do. For the Renaissance humanists I have been considering, the lost world where everything was whole and unified was the ancient one; modernity was characterized by a greater sense of fragmentation.

Adorno, too, talks about fragments. For him, the fragment is an aesthetic category that evokes a quality of disintegration in modern art. All major modern artworks, whether they are missing arms or legs or not, express fragmentation, he says, because something in them resists harmony. The parts of the artwork are jagged, push against each other, refuse subordination to the whole. The fragments, in resisting any stagnant unity, embody the artwork's spirit of dialectical self-interrogation. Although he claims that the aesthetic "compulsion to disintegration" started with Beethoven, he illustrates his point by referring to Shakespeare, specifically to Prospero in *The Tempest,* who resists the assuaging quality of seamless illusion by "set[ting] aside the magic wand."[93] Shakespeare also lurks behind a passage of Marx that Nochlin quotes to illustrate a larger sense of modern social fragmentation: "All that is solid melts into air."[94] This line, like Adorno's, alludes to Prospero, specifically to the moment, which I referred to in the opening paragraph of this book, when Shakespeare's sorcerer interrupts the wedding masque that he has conjured to say that all is "melted into air, into thin air" (4.1.150).

These allusions to Shakespeare are not random. Long before Beethoven or Marx, Shakespeare and other Renaissance poets were calling into question the seamlessness of their own poetic and dramatic works, which are animated in no small way by a constant process of self-interrogation. Through its internal complexity such work both embodies and calls into question the spirit of its time, creating and disrupting illusion. In this way, no poetry is more unified, and no poetry is more fragmented.

In *The Rape of Lucrece,* Shakespeare takes up the image of the material fragment. In so doing, he helps bring us full circle. As we first saw inti-

93. Theodor W. Adorno, *Aesthetic Theory,* ed. Gretel Adorno and Rolf Tiedemann, trans. Robert Hullot-Kentor (Minneapolis: University of Minnesota Press, 1997), 45. See Ian Balfour, "'The Whole Is the Untrue': On the Necessity of the Fragment (after Adorno)," in *The Fragment: An Incomplete History,* ed. William Tronzo (Los Angeles: Getty Research Institute, 2009), 83–91.

94. Nochlin, *The Body in Pieces,* 24; Karl Marx and Friedrich Engels, *The Communist Manifesto,* ed. David McLellan (Oxford: Oxford University Press, 1992), 6. See also Marshall Berman, *All That Is Solid Melts into Air: The Experience of Modernity* (New York: Simon & Schuster, 1982).

mated in the chapter on Petrarch, the fragment is suggestive of a newly empiricist approach to history, which attempts to circumscribe the influence of imagination and subjectivity by turning to the things of the world for evidence. But Shakespeare's use of the fragment also points us toward an Adornian self-interrogation of this very same historical practice. In Shakespeare's poem we find Lucrece recognizing herself in the silent fragments she encounters, thereby reanimating these fragments with the very subjectivity of which they, at the same time, mark the loss. Thus, Shakespeare presciently explores problems of objectivity that were just emerging in the late sixteenth century but that have continued to shape the world we live in today. The result is a poem that manages to reflect and critique our current mentality. How can a late sixteenth-century poem accomplish such a seemingly impossible feat? Here's one way: by proving, in the end, more complex than we are.

CHAPTER SIX

Coda: Make Me Not Object

After Virgil's refugees from the Trojan War are shipwrecked on the shores of Carthage, they set out to explore the territory. In a grove, Aeneas comes upon a temple of Juno on the walls of which, amazingly, he encounters paintings of the war he has just lived through. "Behold, there is Priam!" Aeneas exclaims with tears in his eyes (1.461).[1] It is as though the terrible experiences that he has had to hold tightly locked within himself have been suddenly externalized and now stand before him objectively as things.

Transfixed, he studies the sequence of images, recognizing one figure after another—indeed, eventually recognizing himself. The moment when he sees himself is astonishing, not unlike the moment I analyzed at the beginning of this book in Petrarch's *Africa* where the Carthaginian envoys recognized their own things on display in the Temple of Jupiter. In this Virgilian ekphrasis, which Petrarch undoubtedly had in mind, it is as though the present has already become the past—as if Aeneas were already able to witness the historical construction of himself, encountering in these paintings who he *will have become* (in the future perfect tense) once he has been rendered into a thing of history. In his case, the moment is one of almost fantastical fulfillment. "Here are the tears of things," he famously says, "and mortal matters touch the mind" (1.462, sunt lacrimae rerum et mentem mortalia tangunt). These things, whether understood as the events depicted or as the paintings, now have the capacity to move people in a man-

1. "En Priamus!" All citations of the *Aeneid* from Virgil, *Eclogues. Georgics. Aeneid 1–6*, trans. H. R. Fairclough, rev. G. P. Goold (Cambridge, MA.: Loeb Classical Library, 1999). Translations mine.

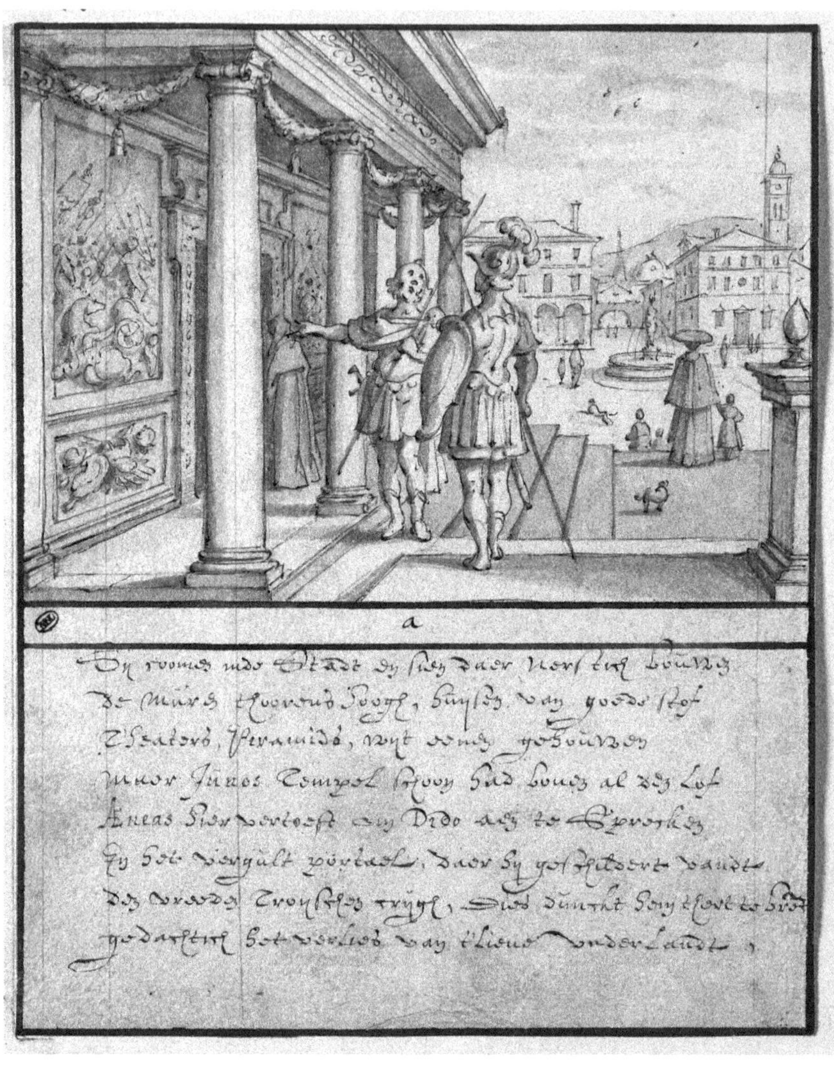

FIGURE 11. Sebastian Vrancx, *Aeneas and his companion before the Temple of Juno* (late sixteenth or early seventeenth century). Louvre, Paris. Photograph by Martine Beck-Coppola. © RMN-Grand Palais / Art Resource, New York.

ner that he imagines as almost tactile—Aeneas's verb is *tangere*, to touch. The Roman desire to, as Shakespeare's Enobarbus will put it, earn "a place i' th' story" (3.13.47) has been achieved.[2]

The payoff is on one level practical: Aeneas can now expect a sympathetic reception in this distant land. Indeed, when Dido learns who he is, it is clear that his fame has preceded him and guaranteed his welcome: "Are you that Aeneas?" (1.617, tune ille Aeneas), she asks, adopting the classical form of a recognition scene, even though she has never before actually met the Trojan hero.

But on another level, such ekphrases point to the meaning of the aesthetic encounter itself, as I and others have emphasized. The Virgilian scene, taken in this sense, might be understood as literalizing G. W. F. Hegel's idea that art allows us to see ourselves. For Hegel, art derives from human inner spiritual development, which, externalized, allows us to recognize our inner state—as though in a kind of spiritual mirror. "The universal need for art," he writes, "is man's rational need to lift the inner and outer world into his spiritual consciousness as an object in which he recognizes again his own self."[3] In this view, the artist renders concrete those aspects of himself that are least concrete by giving them "an outward reality," and thereby "bringing what is in him into sight and knowledge for himself and others."[4] Subjectivity creates an object-version of itself—and, recognizing itself in this externalized thing, gains knowledge of itself. Through this act, human beings partly overcome the indifference of the external world—by shaping some part of it according to their own innermost demands.

Art, if understood in this way, reflects consciousness back to itself out of what is merely material; in so doing, however, it provides a reflection that shows something dead. The price of concretizing ephemerality, allusiveness, or the inchoate nature of subjectivity in this inanimate medium is that the image of the spirit becomes a kind of death mask. (Philosophy, in contrast, reveals the spirit for Hegel not in the alien medium of the material world but in the medium of thought, where, reflecting on itself, thought can finally realize its own nature.) Indeed, in Latin, *imago* can mean a picture as well as a specter or a death mask.

The photograph shows the first-century-CE so-called *Togatus Barberini*

2. William Shakespeare, *Antony and Cleopatra*, ed. John Wilders, Arden Shakespeare, 3rd ser. (London: Thomson Learning, 1995).

3. *Hegel's Aesthetics: Lectures on Fine Art*, vol. 1, trans. T. M. Knox (Oxford: Oxford University Press, 1975), 31.

4. Ibid., 32.

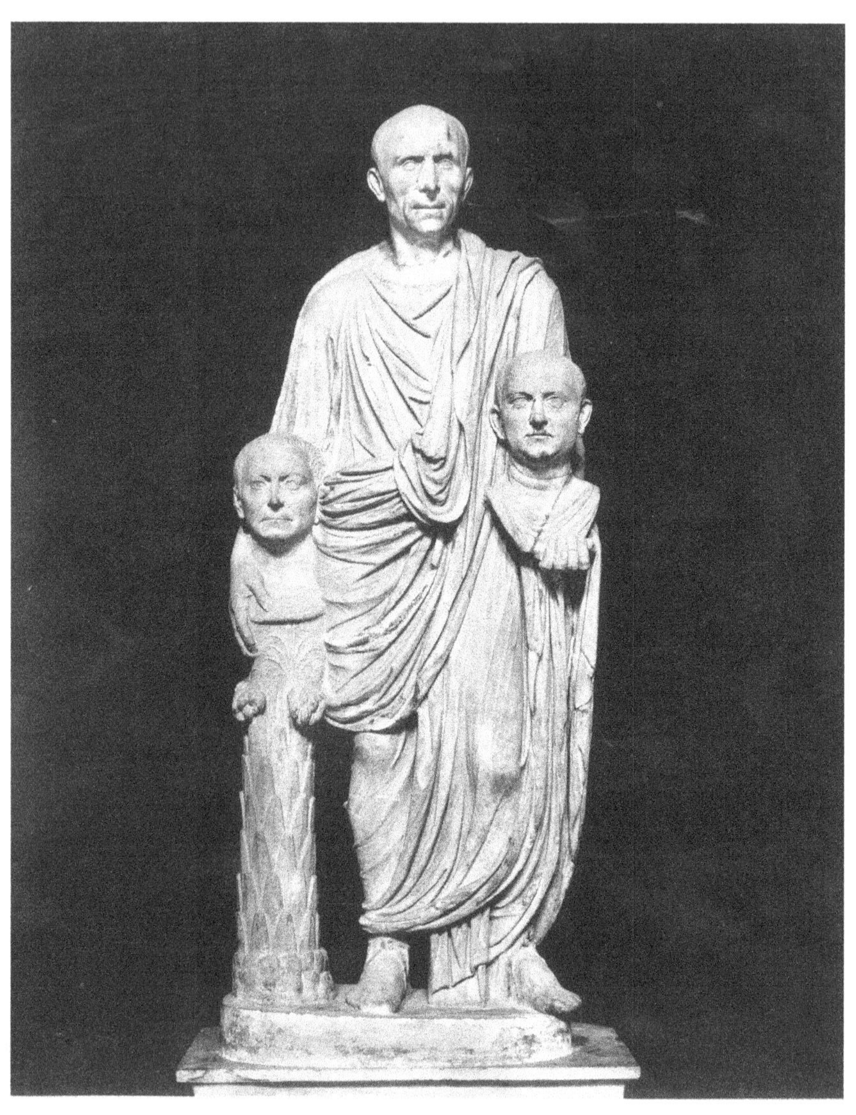

FIGURE 12. Roman patrician with busts of his ancestors (first century CE). Musei Capitolini, Rome. Alinari / Bridgeman Images.

in the Musei Capitolini in Rome. The standing patrician figure, whose identity is unknown, holds the *imagines*, or death masks, of his ancestors. In this sculpture, his head appears no more alive than theirs.[5]

In the twentieth century, Theodor W. Adorno's *Aesthetic Theory* can be understood as a complex critique of this aspect of Hegel's philosophy of art. But we don't have to wait for Adorno to start to discover what is potentially entrapping about this emphasis on art's materiality. Throughout my book, I have been looking at how Renaissance poets used ekphrasis to construct complex aesthetic dynamics that challenge any reductive sense of the artwork's thingliness. From its innermost core, this poetry evokes and also resists its own potential reification. In this brief final chapter, I will dial out from the inner aesthetic dynamics of ekphrasis to consider how Renaissance characters sometimes directly give voice to this desire *not* to be a thing.

Along these lines, I'll pay particular attention to female characters. Throughout the literary tradition, female characters have had their doubts about their future construction as objects of history. Like the conquered Carthaginian men in Petrarch's epic, female characters have often found themselves being rendered into things—and thereby, I would like to suggest, evoke the larger problem for aesthetics that is implicit in this transformation of subjective experience into a static thing.

The tension of the encounter of female characters with future constructions of themselves as things of history starts at the very beginning of the European literary tradition. In the *Iliad*, Helen imagines that she and Paris will be "hereafter . . . made into things of song for the men of the future" (6.357–58, ὀπίσσω / ἀνθρώποισι πελώμεθ' ἀοίδιμοι ἐσσομένοισι).[6] She seems to suspect already what sort of thing she will be made into: reviled among the Trojans, she reports that people shrink when they see her (24.775). Yet, if she anticipates being rendered into a vilified object in future songs, she actually appears in Homer's[7] poetry in a manner that is highly ambiguous.

5. For a dialectical reflection on the relation of statues to their own status as objects, see Kenneth Gross, *The Dream of the Moving Statue* (Ithaca: Cornell University Press, 1992), especially the final chapter, "The Thing Itself (Which Does Not Move)," 167–99. See also the possibility raised by Bill Brown that "art gives [access] to reification, to the dynamics of thingification itself, as to the thingness disclosed by those dynamics," *Other Things* (Chicago: University of Chicago Press, 2015), 173.

6. Greek from perseus.tufts.edu. I'm quoting from Richmond Lattimore, trans., *The Iliad of Homer* (Chicago: University of Chicago Press, 1951).

7. For convenience, I write "Homer" to refer to the many poets who, as current scholars generally agree, developed the *Iliad* and the *Odyssey*.

Partly this is because, for all her world-reputed beauty, he never describes her clearly. In the *Odyssey*, for example, we learn that she speaks to the Achaians hidden in the horse with the voice of each man's wife (4.279). In this scene, she seems to serve as a kind of screen on which the warriors can project their fantasies. Yet her elusiveness is also an effect of her being one of the most peculiarly self-reflective characters in the *Iliad*. The air of uncertainty that hovers around Helen results partly from her self-doubt. She is one of the only characters who reflect on themselves and try to come to terms with their experiences. In one scene, the radically unfixed quality of her mental life takes the form of painful self-reflection:

> And I wish bitter death had been what I wanted, when I came hither
> Following your son, forsaking my chamber, my kinsmen,
> My grown child, and the loveliness of girls my own age.
> It did not happen that way: and now I am worn with weeping.
> This now I will tell you in answer to the question you asked me.
> That man is Atreus' son Agamemnon, widely powerful,
> At the same time a good king and a strong spearfighter,
> Once my kinsman, dog-faced one that I am. *Did this ever happen?*
> [εἴ ποτ' ἔην γε] (3.173–80)[8]

The final, disquieting phrase deserves more attention than it has received: εἴ ποτ' ἔην γε, which literally means "if ever was."[9] It recurs six times in Homer's corpus: three times in the *Odyssey* and three times in the *Iliad*. Lattimore translates the phrase differently every time it appears.[10] The poet's narrating voice never says it; only the characters do. In the *Odyssey*, each of Odysseus's three principal relations (Penelope, Telemachos, and Laertes) say this phrase in reference to Odysseus, as if they were beginning to doubt

8. I have slightly altered Lattimore's translation. In the last line, he writes "slut" for κυνώπιδος; I prefer the more literal phrase "dog-faced one."

9. Laura M. Slatkin has kindly pointed out in an email that the verb (ἔην) can be understood as third person singular or, more radically still, first person singular.

10. In the *Iliad*, 3.180, 11.762, 24.426; in the *Odyssey*, 15.268, 19.315, 24.289. The phrase is ambiguous. While Gottfried Hermann understands it, as I basically do, as suggesting a conditional construction that implies a feeling that everything might not be any more real than a dream, Walter Leaf argues that the phrase carries no such implication. Rather, for Leaf, it is a rhetorical way of calling attention to a concomitant circumstance—the phrase is less like "if ever was," he says, and more like "don't forget that he was." He quotes Georg Curtius, who suggests that we translate the phrase as something like "*surely* once he was" (which Leaf thinks goes a bit too far). See Homer, *The Iliad*, vol. 1, *Books I–XII*, ed. Walter Leaf (Amsterdam: Adolf M. Hakkert, 1960), 132–33. See also G. S. Kirk, *The Iliad: A Commentary*, vol. 1, *Books 1–4* (Cambridge: Cambridge University Press, 1985), 290–91.

their memory of him. And in a manner not so dissimilar, Priam says the phrase in the *Iliad* after his son Hektor has died, and Nestor says it in reference to the greatness of his own youthful self. And here Helen uses it to express a quality of disbelief, or at least an experience of tension between her subjective feeling and the objective knowledge of events. As painful as her self-castigating thoughts may be, these thoughts represent a dynamic form of self-reflection, whereby she tries to reconcile herself to the reality of what has in fact happened.

Perhaps it is no coincidence that Helen is one of the few mortals in the *Iliad* who is shown crafting an art object, a red robe. It represents the battles of the Trojan War, as we learn in the epic's first ekphrasis of an artwork:

> . . . she was weaving a great web,
> a red folding robe, and working into it the numerous struggles
> of Trojans, breakers of horses, and bronze-armoured Achaians,
> struggles that they endured for her sake at the hands of the war god. (3.125–28)

These "numerous struggles" are, of course, the very battles of which Homer's own epic is made. In this sense, the ekphrasis seems to be an image of the *Iliad* in miniature. Understood in this way, Helen would be none other than Homer's own surrogate. She is the one who attempts to construct an image of the war, in this way, too, trying to come to terms with events as they develop. The robe is described as in process and unfinished, recalling of course Penelope's tapestry in the *Odyssey*, which she weaves during the day and unweaves again at night. These artworks, forestalling closure, may reflect a process of reevaluation as events change and consciousness unfolds.[11] If so, they may present an idea of art that is different from the more reified kind, an idea that is perhaps more like Homer's own poem. Adorno will refer to Penelope's act of weaving and unweaving as a metaphor for the dynamic existence of a fully complex art object, which, in constantly reevaluating its own assertions, resists any reified or didactic understanding of its message.[12]

In the Renaissance, questions about the meaning of historical objects

11. Laura M. Slatkin explores how the *Odyssey* plays with the tension of being its own ultimate but also endlessly unfinished, open-ended return song. See her "Homer's *Odyssey*," in *A Companion to Ancient Epic*, ed. John Miles Foley (Malden, MA, and Oxford: Blackwell, 2009), 315–29.

12. Theodor W. Adorno, *Aesthetic Theory*, ed. Gretel Adorno and Rolf Tiedemann, trans. Robert Hullot-Kentor (Minneapolis: University of Minnesota Press, 1997), 186. This dynamic sense of an artwork's life is also central to Gross's account of statues in his *Dream of the Moving Statue*, where he writes about the moment that an artwork falls silent—not only because it "drops out of dialogue with the world, with history," but also because it "drops out of dialogue with itself" (198).

take on new energy in response to the rise of empiricism, as I have been exploring throughout this book, and occasionally give rise to literary characters who are shown reflecting on their own imminent reifications as objects of a future history. I have already touched on the example of Shakespeare's Lucrece. Her concern with her future reputation exists in Shakespeare's earliest sources: in the ancient historian Livy's rendition of the story, she famously says just before killing herself, "Let no unchaste woman live by the example of Lucrece" (Nec ulla deinde inpudica Lucretiae exemplo vivet).[13] She does not want anyone in the future to justify an unchaste life by claiming her example. But Shakespeare greatly emphasizes this concern with future history—so much so that, at times, it almost seems as if she already knows that her story will be told and retold, and that paintings, sculptures, and engravings will portray her image. In one scene, she expresses the feeling that the story of her fall will be imprinted on her physical body:

> Make me not object to the tell-tale day;
> The light will show charactered in my brow
> The story of sweet chastity's decay,
> The impious breach of holy wedlock vow.
> Yea, the illiterate that know not how
> To cipher what is writ in learned books
> Will quote my loathsome trespass in my looks. (806–12)[14]

Soon, it almost seems as if she is not only imaginatively reading the story that she will become; she is competing for authorship of it.[15] In a sense, her suicide is a decision to try to become "mistress of my fate" (1069). As popular as is the image of her about to be raped, more popular perhaps is the one where she is about to plunge a dagger in her own chest, that is, the one that she constructs, in however disturbing a fashion.

Throughout his corpus, Shakespeare emphasizes the Romans' tendency to imagine themselves proleptically as future constructions of history. About *Antony and Cleopatra*, W. B. Worthen and Alan Stewart emphasize that the play tests the claims of Cleopatra's theatrical performance versus Octavius Caesar's anticipation of written history: "Caesar's characterization of An-

13. Livy, *History of Rome*, books 1–2, trans. B. O. Foster (Cambridge, MA: Loeb Classical Library, 1919), 1.58.10–11.

14. William Shakespeare, *The Complete Sonnets and Poems*, ed. Colin Burrow (Oxford: Oxford University Press, 2002).

15. On the theme of Lucrece as author, see Amy Greenstadt, "'Read it in me': The Author's Will in *Lucrece*," *Shakespeare Quarterly* 57, no. 1 (Spring 2006): 45–70.

tony consistently privileges the absent 'character' of history over the present 'character' of performance."[16] On one level, this competition concerns the power of historical texts over the power of drama, but Worthen's language also evokes absence over presence—where the absent is understood as the future construction of a moment after it has been rendered into a historiographical text. As Stewart emphasizes, the play frequently shows Octavius trying to control his future legacy. When, for example, the news arrives that Antony has killed himself, Octavius responds by offering his letters, the documentary evidence that will prove that he had always treated Antony well.[17] In contrast to the future-directed focus of the Romans, the Egyptians in this play assert an engagement with the present that is emphatically multivalent, undetermined, and open to conflicting interpretations. Cleopatra exemplifies this "infinite variety" (2.2.246) of life in the present. No one can quite manage to get a hold on who she is. In sharp contrast to figures like Brutus and Cassius, who, with the blood of Caesar still sticky on their hands, already look forward to the day when "this our lofty scene" (*Julius Caesar* 3.1.112) will be reenacted in performances, Cleopatra relishes no such image of a future performance of herself. Instead, she tells her waiting woman:

> Nay, 'tis most certain, Iras. Saucy lictors
> Will catch at us like strumpets, and scald rhymers
> Ballad us out o'tune. The quick comedians
> Extemporally will stage us and present
> Our Alexandrian revels; Antony
> Shall be brought drunken forth; and I shall see
> Some squeaking Cleopatra boy my greatness
> I' th' posture of a whore. (5.2.213–20)

The image of a drunken Antony recalls a famous ekphrasis of him when, in order to cast aspersion on him, Cicero described him vomiting in an assembly before the people.[18] This image was then used as a school text, incorporated into English grammar schools through its use by Quintilian

16. W. B. Worthen, "The Weight of Antony: Staging 'Character' in *Antony and Cleopatra*," *Studies in English Literature, 1500–1900* 26, no. 2 (Spring 1986), 299, quoted in Alan Stewart, "Lives and Letters in *Antony and Cleopatra*," *Shakespeare Studies* 35 (2007): 100.

17. "Go with me to my tent, where you shall see / How hardly I was drawn into this war, / How calm and gentle I proceeded still / In all my writings" (5.1.73–76), quoted in Stewart, "Lives and Letters in *Antony and Cleopatra*," 77.

18. See Cicero's *Philippics* and Plutarch's *Life of Antony*.

(*Institutio* 8.4.8) and Erasmus (*De copia*, method 9). Cleopatra's wonderful use of *boy* as a verb, which suggests the self-alienation involved by being juxtaposed against "*my* greatness," produces a peculiar meta-aesthetic "pop" since, of course, a boy actor would be speaking this very line. On one level, the moment where we are watching this scene is the very moment Cleopatra is imagining: some boy is *boying* her greatness. Yet, to the extent that Shakespeare's play is able to push against this imagined pipsqueak performance, we're actually made to feel the greatness of the reality that such a performance would flout. The only way we can feel this greatness is through Shakespeare's art, insofar as his play is better than the performance she imagines, insofar as we can experience Shakespeare's Cleopatra as capacious, multivalent, playful, and suggestive of endless interpretations.

Interestingly, the only defense that Cleopatra can imagine is to make herself into a deadly kind of marble image—but one of which she is at least the author, and through which she can assert her regal status. Resolving on death, she promises to give up change: "My resolution's placed, and I have nothing / Of woman in me. Now from head to foot / I am marble-constant. Now the fleeting moon / No planet is of mine" (5.2.237–40). In this "marble-constant" suicide, she becomes ironically almost Roman.

In contrast, one female character resists being equated with an eternalized marble figure of herself, in this case a statue that already exists. The Duchess of Malfi, in John Webster's 1613–14 play of that name, solicits the love of her steward Antonio, by trying to differentiate herself from the image that, as a widow, she has been made to represent:

> Make not your heart so dead a piece of flesh
> To fear more than to love me. Sir, be confident—
> What is't distracts you? This is flesh and blood, sir:
> 'Tis not the figure cut in alabaster
> Kneels at my husband's tomb. Awake, awake, man! (1.2.361–65)[19]

Against social convention, she protests that she is not a statuary monument but rather a living person—not made of stone, but rather of "flesh and blood." Transfixed and awed by her, the steward, too, seems stone-like. The Duchess, adopting the role of a kind of female Pygmalion, seeks to transform, then, not only herself but also him from their stony states. It is into the present moment that she attempts to release both herself and him,

19. John Webster, *The Duchess of Malfi*, ed. Leah S. Marcus (London: Arden Shakespeare, 2009).

so that they can claim their erotically embodied and playful existences in the here and now.[20]

So far in this coda, I have looked at women who want to resist their reification as future images of history. A similar dynamic plays out in relation to other disempowered characters. Earlier in the book, for example, I looked at defeated men, the Carthaginian envoys of Petrarch's *Africa,* who found themselves similarly entrapped as reified things. To this list of characters could be added a couple of compelling fools, Don Quixote and Sancho Panza. Near the end of book 2 of *El ingenioso hidalgo don Quijote de la Mancha,* they come upon an inn where the walls are hung with painted tapestries showing classical epic heroines. In one case, the image of Helen seems to be the very kind that she had been fearing—one that makes her into an object of ridicule. She is shown "laughing, slyly and cunningly," as she is being abducted "not . . . very unwillingly."[21] Reflecting on such images, Sancho says that he bets that a history of their own adventures will soon be painted on the walls of taverns, inns, and barbershops. "But I'd like it done by the hands of a painter better than the one who did these," Sancho says. Agreeing, Don Quixote laments that the writer who's been producing the unauthorized sequel to their adventures is just as bad: he seems to write simply "whatever came out" (lo que saliere).[22]

Yet where does that criticism leave Cervantes's own book? Recall the kind of reified history, "carved in bronze, sculpted in marble, and painted on tablets as a remembrance in the future," that Don Quixote initially dreamed of his adventures inspiring. "Who can doubt," he asked himself as he rode out on his first adventure, "that in times to come, when the true history of my famous deeds comes to light, the wise man who compiles them, when he begins to recount my first sally so early in the day, will write in this manner: 'No sooner had rubicund Apollo spread over the face of the wide and spacious earth the golden strands of his beauteous hair, no sooner had diminutive and bright-hued birds with dulcet tongues . . . ,'" and so on, through a matted nest of periphrastic, curlicued, and emphatically artificial lines.[23] If that is the kind of writing that Don Quixote likes, then what he doesn't like may not be so bad. After all, Cervantes's book is not such an

20. On statuary imagery, and the complex and often contradictory desires to be stone and to be freed from stone, see Gross, *The Dream of the Moving Statue.*

21. Miguel de Cervantes, *Don Quixote,* trans. Edith Grossman (New York: Ecco, 2003), 923. Thanks to James Mandrell and Dian Fox for responding to my questions about Cervantes.

22. Ibid.

23. Ibid., 25.

artifical, cliché-ridden text, any more than it is the result merely of "whatever came out." In resisting reified conclusions, it is a book that becomes something more dynamic and hard to pin down, perhaps something more like life itself, experienced subjectively and objectively—dialectically—as it unfolds.

In the case of *Don Quixote*, as well as of the other texts I have been examining, our experience of the characters' subjectivity emerges in no small way through the characters' anxious contemplations of themselves as the reified things of a future history—things, we are made to see, that are inadequate to the changeability and complexity of a living person. And what things wouldn't be so inadequate? Well, perhaps the multivalent, self-reflective texts that our authors have actually written, the final meaning of which cannot be pinned down. Perhaps Adorno is right that subjectivity wants an object version of itself, but it also wants to resist the object's rigidity. Tom Huhn explains Adorno's idea: "The task of subjectivity is not of course to become complete, for that would signal but another version of static rigidification. The task is rather for subjectivity to go on with itself, to become more of what it already is."[24]

In the end (by which I mean of course merely the end of my book), perhaps we might consider the female voices as the voices of the poems themselves. If these female characters do not want to be understood as reified things of a future history, perhaps neither do these old, dog-eared, underlined, scrawled-on books of Renaissance poetry, which now lie piled here before me on my desk. To the extent that Renaissance literary texts continue to reveal themselves in the light of their readers' further interpretation and intersubjective involvement, such books are, in this spirit, things that aren't things.

24. Tom Huhn, "Introduction: Thoughts beside Themselves," in *The Cambridge Companion to Adorno*, ed. Tom Huhn (Cambridge: Cambridge University Press, 2004), 8.

Bibliography

Achilles Tatius. *Leucippe and Clitophon*. Trans. Tim Whitmarsh, with an introduction by Helen Morales. Oxford: Oxford University Press, 2001.

Adorno, Theodor W. *Aesthetic Theory*. Ed. Gretel Adorno and Rolf Tiedemann. Trans. Robert Hullot-Kentor. Minneapolis: University of Minnesota Press, 1997.

———. "Bach Defended against His Devotees." In *Prisms*, trans. Samuel Weber and Shierry Weber, 133–46. Cambridge, MA: MIT Press, 1981.

———. *Frankfurter Adorno Blätter VIII*. Ed. Rolf Tiedemann. Munich: Edition Text + Kritik, 2003.

———. *Hegel: Three Studies*. Trans. Shierry Weber Nicholsen. Cambridge, MA: MIT Press, 1993.

———. *Lectures on Negative Dialectics*. Ed. Rolf Tiedemann. Trans. Rodney Livingstone. Malden, MA: Polity Press, 2008.

———. *Minima Moralia: Reflections from Damaged Life*. Trans. E. F. N. Jephcott. London: Verso, 2005.

———. *Negative Dialectics*. Trans. E. B. Ashton. New York: Continuum, 1973.

———. *Notes to Literature*. Ed. Rolf Tiedemann. Trans. Shierry Weber Nicholsen. 2 vols. New York: Columbia University Press, 1991–92.

Adorno, Theodor W., et al. *The Positivist Dispute in German Sociology*. Trans. Glyn Adey and David Frisby. London: Heinemann, 1976.

Aït-Touati, Frédérique. *Fictions of the Cosmos: Science and Literature in the Seventeenth Century*, trans. Susan Emanuel. Chicago: University of Chicago Press, 2011.

Alpers, Paul J. *The Poetry of "The Faerie Queene."* Princeton: Princeton University Press, 1967.

Alpers, Svetlana. *The Art of Describing: Dutch Art in the Seventeenth Century*. Chicago: University of Chicago Press, 1983.

Altman, Joel B. *The Tudor Play of Mind: Rhetorical Inquiry and the Development of Elizabethan Drama*. Berkeley: University of California Press, 1978.

Ames-Lewis, Francis. *The Intellectual Life of the Early Renaissance Artist*. New Haven: Yale University Press, 2000.

Ammianus Marcellinus. *The History*. Trans. J. C. Rolfe. Cambridge, MA: Loeb Classical Library, 1950.

Amsler, Mark. "Rape and Silence: Ovid's Mythography and Medieval Readers." In *Representing Rape in Medieval and Early Modern Literature*, ed. Elizabeth Robertson and Christine M. Rose, 61–96. New York: Palgrave, 2001.

Apted, M. R., and W. Norman Robertson. "Four 'Drollities' from the Painted Ceiling Formerly at Prestongrange, East Lothian." *Proceedings of the Society of Antiquaries of Scotland* 106 (1974–75): 158–60.

Apuleius. *The. xi. Bookes of the Golden Asse, conteininge the Metamorphosie of Lucius Apuleius, enterlaced with sondrie pleasaunt and delectable Tales, with an excellent Narration of the Mariage of Cupide and Psiches, set out in the. iiij. v. and vj Bookes*. Trans. William Adlington. London: Henry Wykes, 1566. Early English Books Online, http://eebo.chadwyck.com.

Aristotle. *On Poetics*. Trans. Seth Benardete and Michael Davis. South Bend, IN: St. Augustine's Press, 2002.

———. *Rhetoric*. Trans. W. Rhys Roberts. Mineola, NY: Dover Publications, 2004.

Aston, Margaret. "English Ruins and English History: The Dissolution and the Sense of the Past." *Journal of the Warburg and Courtauld Institutes* 36 (1973): 231–55.

Athenaeus. *The Deipnosophists*, vol. 1–7. Trans. Charles Burton Gulick. London: W. Heinemann; New York: Putnam, 1927–41.

Audsley, William James, and George Ashdown Audsley. *Popular Dictionary of Architecture and the Allied Arts*, vol. 2. New York: G. P. Putnam's Sons, 1881.

Auerbach, Erich. *Dante: Poet of the Secular World*. Trans. Ralph Manheim. New York: New York Review Books, 2007.

———. *Mimesis: The Representation of Reality in Western Literature*. Trans. Willard R. Trask. Princeton: Princeton University Press, 1953.

———. *Scenes from the Drama of European Literature*. Minneapolis: University of Minnesota Press, 1984.

Augustine. *Confessions*. Trans. R. S. Pine-Coffin. London: Penguin, 1961.

———. *City of God*. Trans. Henry Bettenson. London: Penguin, 1984.

Bacon, Francis. *The Advancement of Learning*. Ed. William Aldis Wright. Oxford: Clarendon Press, 1869.

———. *The New Organon*. Ed. Lisa Jardine and Michael Silverthorne. Cambridge: Cambridge University Press, 2000.

———. *The Works of Francis Bacon*, vol. 4. Ed. James Spedding. London: Longman, 1860.

Balfour, Ian. "'The Whole Is the Untrue': On the Necessity of the Fragment (after Adorno)." In *The Fragment: An Incomplete History*, ed. William Tronzo (Los Angeles: Getty Research Institute, 2009), 83–91.

Barkan, Leonard. *The Gods Made Flesh: Metamorphosis and the Pursuit of Paganism*. New Haven: Yale University Press, 1986.

———. *Mute Poetry, Speaking Pictures*. Princeton: Princeton University Press, 2013.

———. *Unearthing the Past: Archaeology and Aesthetics in the Making of Renaissance Culture*. New Haven: Yale University Press, 1999.

Barocchi, Paola, ed. *Scritti d'arte del cinquecento*, vol. 1. Milan; Naples: R. Ricciardi, 1971.

Bartsch, Shadi. *Decoding the Ancient Novel: The Reader and the Role of Description in Heliodorus and Achilles Tatius*. Princeton: Princeton University Press, 1989.

Baudelaire, Charles. *"The Painter of Modern Life" and Other Essays*. Trans. Jonathan Mayne. London and New York: Phaidon Press, 1995.

Baxandall, Michael. *Giotto and the Orators: Humanist Observers of Painting in Italy and the Discovery of Pictorial Composition, 1350–1450*. Oxford: Oxford University Press, 1971.

Bearden, Elizabeth B. *The Emblematics of the Self: Ekphrasis and Identity in Renaissance Imitations of Greek Romance*. Toronto: University of Toronto Press, 2012.

Belsey, Catherine. "Invocation of the Visual Image: Ekphrasis in *Lucrece* and Beyond." *Shakespeare Quarterly* 63, no. 2 (Summer 2012): 175–98.

Benjamin, Walter. *The Origin of German Tragic Drama*. Trans. John Osborne. New York: Verso, 1998.

———. *Selected Writings*, vol. 1, *1913–1926*. Ed. Marcus Bullock and Michael W. Jennings. Cambridge, MA: Belknap Press of Harvard University Press, 1996.

Bennett, Jane. "The Force of Things: Steps toward an Ecology of Matter." *Political Theory* 32, no. 3 (June 2004): 347–72.

Berger, Harry, Jr. "Busirane and the War between the Sexes: An Interpretation of *The Faerie Queene* III.xi–xii." *English Literary Renaissance* 1, no. 2 (Spring 1971): 99–121.

Berman, Marshall. *All That Is Solid Melts into Air: The Experience of Modernity*. New York: Simon & Schuster, 1982.

Bernardo, Aldo S. *Petrarch, Scipio and the "Africa": The Birth of Humanism's Dream*. Baltimore: Johns Hopkins Press, 1962.

Berry, Christopher J. *The Idea of Luxury: A Conceptual and Historical Investigation*. Cambridge: Cambridge University Press, 1994.

Bertran de Born. *The Poems of the Troubadour Bertran de Born*. Ed. William D. Paden Jr., Tilde Sankovitch, and Patricia H. Stäblein. Berkeley: University of California Press, 1986.

Bewes, Timothy. *Reification; or, The Anxiety of Late Capitalism*. London: Verso, 2002.

Blanchard, Marc Eli. *Description, Sign, Self, Desire: Critical Theory in the Wake of Semiotics*. The Hague: Mouton, 1980.

Blumenberg, Hans. *Shipwreck with Spectator: Paradigm of a Metaphor for Existence*. Trans. Steven Rendall. Cambridge, MA: MIT Press, 1997.

———. *Work on Myth*. Trans. Robert M. Wallace. Cambridge, MA: MIT Press, 1985.

Boethius. *Theological Tractates*. Trans. H. F. Stewart, E. K. Rand, and S. J. Tester. *The Consolation of Philosophy*. Trans. H. F. Stewart. Cambridge, MA: Loeb Classical Library, 1973.

Bowie, Andrew. *Aesthetics and Subjectivity: From Kant to Nietzsche*. Manchester: Manchester University Press, 2003.

Bowra, C. M. *From Virgil to Milton*. London: Macmillan, 1962.

Boyle, Robert. *Certain Physiological Essays and Other Tracts: Written at Distant Times, and on Several Occasions*. London: Printed for Henry Herringman, 1669.

Braden, Gordon. *The Classics and English Renaissance Poetry: Three Case Studies*. New Haven: Yale University Press, 1978.

Braider, Christopher. *Refiguring the Real: Picture and Modernity in Word and Image, 1400–1700*. Princeton: Princeton University Press, 1993.

Brown, Bill. *Other Things*. Chicago: University of Chicago Press, 2015.

Brown, Georgia E. "Breaking the Canon: Marlowe's Challenge to the Literary Status Quo in *Hero and Leander*." In *Marlowe, History, and Sexuality: New Critical Essays on Christopher Marlowe*, ed. Paul Whitfield White, 59–76. New York: AMS Press, 1998. 59–75.

———. "Gender and Voice in *Hero and Leander*." In *Constructing Christopher Marlowe*, ed. J. A. Downie and J. T. Parnell, 148–63. Cambridge: Cambridge University Press, 2000.

———. "Marlowe's Poems and Classicism." In *The Cambridge Companion to Christopher Marlowe*, ed. Patrick Cheney, 106–26. Cambridge: Cambridge University Press, 2004.

———. *Redefining Elizabethan Literature*. Cambridge: Cambridge University Press, 2004.

Brown, Peter. *Power and Persuasion in Late Antiquity: Towards a Christian Empire*. Madison: University of Wisconsin Press, 1992.

Bühler, Curt F. "Aldus Manutius and His First Edition of the Greek Musaeus." In *Scritti sopra Aldo Manuzio*, ed. Roberto Ridolfi. Florence: L. S. Olschki, 1955.

Burke, Peter. *The Renaissance Sense of the Past*. New York: St. Martin's Press, 1969.

Burnyeat, Myles, and Michael Frede, eds. *The Original Sceptics: A Controversy*. Indianapolis: Hackett, 1998.

Bush, Douglas. *Mythology and the Renaissance Tradition in English Poetry*. Minneapolis: University of Minnesota Press, 1932.

Callimachus and Musaeus. (Callimachus) *Aetia, Iambi, Hecale, and Other Fragments*; (Musaeus) *Hero and Leander*. Trans. C. A. Trypanis, Thomas Gelzer, and Cedric Whitman. Cambridge, MA: Loeb Classical Library, 1975.

Camden, William. *Britannia*. Trans. Philemon Holland (1607). Hypertext critical edition ed. Dana F. Sutton at http://www.philological.bham.ac.uk/cambrit/.

———. *Remains Concerning Britain*. Ed. R. D. Dunn. Toronto: University of Toronto Press, 1984.

Campbell, Mary Baine. *Wonder and Science: Imagining Worlds in Early Modern Europe*. Ithaca: Cornell University Press, 1999.

Campbell, Thomas P. *Henry VIII and the Art of Majesty: Tapestries at the Tudor Court*. New Haven: Yale University Press, 2007.

———. *Tapestry in the Renaissance: Art and Magnificence*. New Haven: Yale University Press, 2002.

Candlin, Fiona, and Raiford Guins, eds. *The Object Reader*. London and New York: Routledge, 2009.

Carruthers, Mary. *The Craft of Thought: Meditation, Rhetoric, and the Making of Images, 400–1200*. Cambridge: Cambridge University Press, 1998.

Cassirer, Ernst. *The Individual and the Cosmos in Renaissance Philosophy*. Trans. Mario Domandi. Chicago: University of Chicago Press, 2010.

Caylus, Anne Claude de. *Recueil d'antiquités*. Paris, 1752–67.

Cervantes, Miguel de. *Don Quixote*. Trans. Edith Grossman. New York: Ecco, 2003.

Chastel, André. "Sens et non-sens à la Renaissance. La question des chimères." *Archivio di filosofia* (1980): 183–89.

Cheney, Donald. "Spenser's Hermaphrodite and the 1590 *Faerie Queene*." *PMLA* 87, no. 2 (March 1972): 192–200.

Cheney, Patrick, ed. *The Cambridge Companion to Christopher Marlowe*. Cambridge: Cambridge University Press, 2004.

———. *Marlowe's Counterfeit Profession: Ovid, Spenser, Counter-Nationhood*. Toronto: University of Toronto Press, 1997.

Choay, Françoise. *The Invention of the Historic Monument*. Trans. Lauren M. O'Connell. Cambridge: Cambridge University Press, 2001.

Chrétien de Troyes. *The Complete Romances of Chrétien de Troyes*. Trans. David Staines. Bloomington: Indiana University Press, 1990.

Cicero. *Orations: Pro archia. Post reditum in senatu. Post reditum ad quirites. De domo sua. De haruspicum responsis. Pro Plancio*. Trans. N. H. Watts. Cambridge, MA: Loeb Classical Library, 1923.

Clark, Donald Lemen. "The Rise and Fall of Progymnasmata in Sixteenth and Seventeenth Century Grammar Schools." *Speech Monographs* 19, no. 4 (Nov. 1952): 259–63.

Colvin, Sidney. "The Sack of Troy in Shakespeare's 'Lucrece' and in Some Fifteenth-Century Drawings and Tapestries." In *A Book of Homage to Shakespeare*, ed. Israel Gollancz, 88–99. Oxford: Humphrey Milford, Oxford University Press, 1916.

Comanini, Gregorio. *The Figino; or, On the Purpose of Painting: Art Theory in the Late Renaissance*. Ed. and trans. Ann Doyle-Anderson and Giancarlo Maiorino. Toronto: University of Toronto Press, 2001.

Cormack, Bradin. "Tender Distance: Latinity and Desire in Shakespeare's Sonnets." In *A Companion to Shakespeare's Sonnets*, ed. Michael Schoenfeldt, 242–60. Malden, MA: Blackwell, 2007.

Croce, Benedetto. *History: Its Theory and Practice*. Trans. Douglas Ainslie. New York: Harcourt, Brace, 1921.

Croft-Murray, Edward. *Decorative Painting in England, 1537–1837*, vol. 1. London: Country Life, 1962.

Cunningham, Valentine. "Why Ekphrasis?" *Classical Philology* 102, no. 1 (Jan. 2007): 57–71.

Dacos, Nicole. *La découverte de la Domus Aurea et la formation des grotesques à la Renaissance*. London: Warburg Institute; Leiden: E. J. Brill, 1969.

———. *The Loggia of Raphael: A Vatican Art Treasure*. Trans. Josephine Bacon. New York: Abbeville Press, 2008.

Dante Alighieri. *The Divine Comedy: Purgatorio*. Trans. John D. Sinclair. New York: Oxford University Press, 1939.

Daston, Lorraine, and Peter Galison. "The Image of Objectivity." *Representations* 40, Special Issue: Seeing Science (Autumn 1992): 81–128.

———. *Objectivity*. New York: Zone Books, 2007.

Dear, Peter. *Revolutionizing the Sciences: European Knowledge and Its Ambitions, 1500–1700*. Princeton: Princeton University Press, 2009.

De Grazia, Margreta. "Anachronism." In *Cultural Reformations: Medieval and Renaissance in Literary History*, ed. Brian Cummings and James Simpson, 13–32. Oxford: Oxford University Press, 2010.

De Grazia, Margreta, Maureen Quilligan, and Peter Stallybrass, eds. *Subject and Object in Renaissance Culture*. Cambridge: Cambridge University Press, 1996.

Dionisotti, A. C. "On Fragments in Classical Scholarship." In *Collecting Fragments/Fragmente sammeln*, ed. Glenn W. Most, 1–33. Göttingen: Vandenhoeck & Ruprecht, 1997.

Di Sciacca, Claudia. *Finding the Right Words: Isidore's "Synonyma" in Anglo-Saxon England*. Toronto: University of Toronto Press, 2008.

Dobb, Maurice. *Studies in the Development of Capitalism*. London: George Routledge & Sons, 1946.

Dolven, Jeff. *Scenes of Instruction in Renaissance Romance*. Chicago: University of Chicago Press, 2007.

Doni, Anton Francesco. *Disegno*. Venice, 1549.

Donkin, R. A. *Beyond Price: Pearls and Pearl-Fishing: Origins to the Age of Discoveries*. Philadelphia: American Philosophical Society, 1998.

Donne, John. *Essays in Divinity*. Ed. Evelyn M. Simpson. Oxford: Oxford University Press, 1952.

Dotti, Ugo. *Vita di Petrarca*. Rome: Laterza, 1987.

DuBois, Page. *History, Rhetorical Description and the Epic: From Homer to Spenser*. Cambridge: D. S. Brewer, 1982.

Dubrow, Heather. *Deixis in the Early Modern English Lyric: Unsettling Spatial Anchors like "Here," "This," "Come."* Houndmills, Basingstoke, Hampshire, and New York: Palgrave Macmillan, 2015.

———. "The Rape of Clio: Attitudes to History in Shakespeare's *Lucrece*." *English Literary Renaissance* 6, no. 3 (Autumn 1986): 425–41.

Dundas, Judith. *Pencils Rhetorique: Renaissance Poets and the Art of Painting*. Newark: University of Delaware Press, 1993.

Dunning, William V. *Changing Images of Pictorial Space: A History of Spatial Illusion in Painting*. Syracuse: Syracuse University Press, 1991.

Edwards, Catharine. *Writing Rome: Textual Approaches to the City*. Cambridge: Cambridge University Press, 1996.

Elias, Norbert. "The Kitsch Style and the Age of Kitsch." In *The Norbert Elias Reader*, ed. Johan Goudsblom and Stephen Mennell, 26–35. Oxford: Blackwell, 1998.

Elsner, Jaś. *Art and the Roman Viewer: The Transformation of Art from the Pagan World to Christianity*. Cambridge: Cambridge University Press, 1995.

———. *Roman Eyes: Visuality and Subjectivity in Art and Text*. Princeton: Princeton University Press, 2007.

Enterline, Lynn. "Elizabethan Minor Epic." In *The Oxford History of Classical Reception in English Literature*, vol. 2, *1558–1660*, ed. Patrick Cheney and Philip Hardie, 253–72. Oxford: Oxford University Press, 2015.

———. *The Rhetoric of the Body from Ovid to Shakespeare*. Cambridge: Cambridge University Press, 2000.

———. *Shakespeare's Schoolroom: Rhetoric, Discipline, Emotion*. Philadelphia: University of Pennsylvania Press, 2012.

Erasmus. *Collected Works of Erasmus: Literary and Educational Writings 2, De copia/De ratione studii*. Ed. Craig R. Thompson. Toronto: University of Toronto Press, 1978.

Erasmus, H. J. *The Origins of Rome in Historiography from Petrarch to Perizonius*. Assen: Van Gorcum, 1962.

Evans, Joan. *A History of the Society of Antiquaries*. Oxford: Oxford University Press by Charles Batey for the Society of Antiquaries, 1956.

Evett, David. "Mammon's Grotto: Sixteenth-Century Visual Grotesquerie and Some Features of Spenser's *Faerie Queene*." *English Literary Renaissance* 12, no. 2 (Spring 1982): 180–209.

Fanon, Frantz. *Black Skin, White Masks*. Trans. Richard Philcox. New York: Grove Press, 2008.

Feldherr, Andrew, ed. *The Cambridge Companion to the Roman Historians*. Cambridge: Cambridge University Press, 2009.

Fenzi, Enrico. *Pétrarque*. Trans. Gérard Marino. Paris: Les Belles Lettres, 2015.

Ferguson, Arthur B. *Clio Unbound: Perception of the Social and Cultural Past in Renaissance England*. Durham: Duke University Press, 1979.

Ferguson, Margaret W. *Trials of Desire: Renaissance Defenses of Poetry*. New Haven: Yale University Press, 1983.

Findlen, Paula. "The Museum: Its Classical Etymology and Renaissance Genealogy." In *Museum Studies: An Anthology of Contexts*, ed. Bettina Messias Carbonell, 23–45. Malden, MA: Blackwell, 2012.

———. *Possessing Nature: Museums, Collecting, and Scientific Culture in Early Modern Italy*. Berkeley: University of California Press, 1994.

Finkelstein, Andrea. *Harmony and Balance: An Intellectual History of Seventeenth-Century English Economic Thought*. Ann Arbor: University of Michigan Press, 2000.

Fleming, Abraham. *A Panoplie of Epistles; or, A Looking Glasse for the Vnlearned*. London: [By H. Middleton] for Ralph Newberie, 1576.

Fletcher, Angus. *The Prophetic Moment: An Essay on Spenser*. Chicago: University of Chicago Press, 1971.

———. *Time, Space, and Motion in the Age of Shakespeare*. Cambridge, MA: Harvard University Press, 2007.

Foster, Roger. *Adorno: The Recovery of Experience*. Albany: State University of New York Press, 2007.

Fowler, Alastair. *Renaissance Realism: Narrative Images in Literature and Art*. Oxford: Oxford University Press, 2003.

Fried, Michael. "Art and Objecthood." In Fried, *Art and Objecthood: Essays and Reviews*, 148–72. Chicago: University of Chicago Press, 1998.

Friedman, Lionel J. "The Ubi Sunt, the Regrets, and Effictio." *Modern Language Notes* 72, no. 7 (Nov. 1957): 499–505.

Froben, Johann. *Aesopi Phrygis vita et fabellae*. Basle, 1518. Available online at http://www.archive.org/stream/aesopiphrygisvit00home#page/34/mode/2up.

Fumaroli, Marc. *L'âge de l'éloquence: rhétorique et "res literaria" de la Renaissance au seuil de l'époque classique*. Geneva: Librairie Droz, 2002.

Galloway, Andrew. "Chaucer's *Legend of Lucrece* and the Critique of Ideology in Fourteenth-Century England." *ELH* 60, no. 4 (Winter 1993): 813–32.

Gent, Lucy. *Picture and Poetry, 1560–1620: Relations between Literature and the Visual Arts in the English Renaissance*. Leamington Spa: James Hall Publishing, 1981.

Giamatti, A. Bartlett. *The Earthly Paradise and the Renaissance Epic*. New York: W. W. Norton, 1989.

Gibbon, Edward. *The History of the Decline and Fall of the Roman Empire*, vols. 1–3. Ed. David Womersley. London: Penguin, 1994.

———. *Memoirs of My Life*. Ed. Betty Radice. London: Penguin, 1984.

Giglioni, Guido. "Mastering the Appetites of Matter: Francis Bacon's *Sylva Sylvarum*." In *The Body as Object and Instrument of Knowledge: Embodied Empiricism in Early Modern Science*, ed. Charles T. Wolfe and Ofer Gal, 149–67. Dordrecht, Netherlands, and New York: Springer, 2010.

Gilbert, Neal W. "A Letter of Giovanni Dondi dall'Orologio to Fra' Guglielmo Centueri: A

Fourteenth-Century Episode in the Quarrel of the Ancients and Moderns." *Viator* 8 (1977): 299–346.

Gill, Roma. Review of *The Poems of Christopher Marlowe*, ed. Millar MacLure. *Review of English Studies* 21, no. 83 (Aug. 1970): 346–48.

Gilman, Ernest B. *Iconoclasm and Poetry in the English Reformation: Down Went Dagon*. Chicago: University of Chicago Press, 1986.

Gilson, Étienne. *Les idées et les lettres*. Paris: J. Vrin, 1932.

Goldhill, Simon. *Foucault's Virginity: Ancient Erotic Fiction and the History of Sexuality*. Cambridge: Cambridge University Press, 1995.

Goldhill, Simon, and Robin Osborne, eds. *Art and Text in Ancient Greek Culture*. Cambridge: Cambridge University Press, 1994.

Golding, Arthur. *Ovid's "Metamorphoses."* Ed. Madeleine Forey. Baltimore: Johns Hopkins University Press, 2001.

Gombrich, E. H. *Art and Illusion: A Study in the Psychology of Pictorial Representation*. Princeton: Princeton University Press, 1960.

Grady, Hugh. *Shakespeare and Impure Aesthetics*. Cambridge: Cambridge University Press, 2009.

———. *Shakespeare's Universal Wolf: Studies in Early Modern Reification*. Oxford: Oxford University Press, 1996.

Grafton, Anthony. "The Ancient City Restored: Archaeology, Ecclesiastical History, and Egyptology." In *Rome Reborn: The Vatican Library and Renaissance Culture*, ed. Anthony Grafton, 87–123. Washington, DC: Library of Congress, 1993.

———. "*Fragmenta Historicorum Graecorum*: Fragments of Some Lost Enterprises." In *Collecting Fragments/Fragmente sammeln*, ed. Glenn W. Most, 124–43. Göttingen: Vandenhoeck & Ruprecht, 1997.

———. *Joseph Scaliger: A Study in the History of Classical Scholarship*. 2 vols. Oxford: Clarendon Press, 1983–93.

———. "The New Science and the Traditions of Humanism." In *The Cambridge Companion to Renaissance Humanism*, ed. Jill Kraye, 203–23. Cambridge: Cambridge University Press, 1996.

———. "Renaissance Readers and Ancient Texts: Comments on Some Commentaries." *Renaissance Quarterly* 38, no. 4 (Winter 1985): 615–49.

———. *What Was History? The Art of History in Early Modern Europe*. Cambridge: Cambridge University Press, 2007.

Grafton, Anthony, with April Shelford and Nancy Siraisi. *New Worlds, Ancient Texts: The Power of Tradition and the Shock of Discovery*. Cambridge, MA: Harvard University Press, 1992.

Greenblatt, Stephen. *Marvelous Possessions: The Wonder of the New World*. Chicago: University of Chicago Press, 1991.

———. *Renaissance Self-Fashioning: From More to Shakespeare*. Chicago: University of Chicago Press, 1980.

Greene, Thomas M. *The Descent from Heaven: A Study in Epic Continuity*. New Haven: Yale University Press, 1963.

———. *The Light in Troy: Imitation and Discovery in Renaissance Poetry*. New Haven: Yale University Press, 1982.

———. *Poésie et magie*. Paris: Julliard, 1991.

———. *The Vulnerable Text: Essays in Renaissance Literature*. New York: Columbia University Press, 1986.

Greenstadt, Amy. "'Read it in me'": The Author's Will in *Lucrece*." *Shakespeare Quarterly* 57, no. 1 (Spring 2006): 45–70.

Gregerson, Linda. *The Reformation of the Subject: Spenser, Milton, and the English Protestant Epic*. Cambridge: Cambridge University Press, 1995.

Grogan, Jane. *Exemplary Spenser: Visual and Poetic Pedagogy in "The Faerie Queene."* Burlington, VT: Ashgate, 2009.

Gross, Kenneth. *The Dream of the Moving Statue*. Ithaca: Cornell University Press, 1992.

———. *Spenserian Poetics: Idolatry, Iconoclasm, and Magic*. Ithaca: Cornell University Press, 1985.

Haber, Judith. "'True-loves Blood': Narrative and Desire in *Hero and Leander*." *English Literary Renaissance* 28, no. 3 (Autumn 1998): 372–86.

Hadas, Moses, trans. *Three Greek Romances*. Indianapolis: Bobbs-Merrill, 1964.

Hadfield, Andrew. *Shakespeare and Republicanism*. Cambridge: Cambridge University Press, 2005.

Hagstrum, Jean H. *The Sister Arts: The Tradition of Literary Pictorialism and English Poetry from Dryden to Gray*. Chicago: University of Chicago Press, 1958.

Hall, Edward. *The Triumphant Reigne of Kyng Henry the VIII*. London: T. C. & E. C. Jack, 1904.

Hall, Kim F. *Things of Darkness: Economies of Race and Gender in Early Modern England*. Ithaca: Cornell University Press, 1995.

Halliwell, Stephen. *The Aesthetics of Mimesis: Ancient Texts and Modern Problems*. Princeton: Princeton University Press, 2002.

Hampton, Timothy. *Writing from History: The Rhetoric of Exemplarity in Renaissance Literature*. Ithaca: Cornell University Press, 1990.

Hankins, James. "Petrarch and the Canon of Neo-Latin Literature," 2004, available online at http://nrs.harvard.edu/urn-3:HUL.InstRepos:3342975.

Harris, Jonathan Gil. *Untimely Matter in the Time of Shakespeare*. Philadelphia: University of Pennsylvania Press, 2009.

Harris, Jonathan Gil, and Natasha Korda, eds. *Staged Properties in Early Modern English Drama*. Cambridge: Cambridge University Press, 2002.

Harte, N. B. "State Control of Dress and Social Change in Pre-Industrial England." In *Trade, Government and Economy in Pre-Industrial England: Essays Presented to F. J. Fisher*, ed. D. C. Coleman and A. H. John, 132–65. London: Weidenfeld & Nicolson, 1976.

Harvey, Elizabeth D. "Flesh Colors and Shakespeare's Sonnets." In *A Companion to Shakespeare's Sonnets*, ed. Michael Schoenfeldt, 314–28. Malden, MA: Blackwell, 2007.

Haskell, Francis. *History and Its Images: Art and the Interpretation of the Past*. New Haven: Yale University Press, 1993.

Hawkes, David. "Against Materialism in Literary Theory." In *The Return of Theory in Early Modern English Studies: Tarrying with the Subjunctive*, ed. Paul Cefalu and Bryan Reynolds, 237–57. London: Palgrave Macmillan, 2011.

———. "Materialism and Reification in Renaissance Studies" (review article). *Journal for Early Modern Cultural Studies* 4, no. 2 (Fall/Winter 2004): 114–29.

Heffernan, James A. W. *Museum of Words: The Poetics of Ekphrasis from Homer to Ashbery*. Chicago: University of Chicago Press, 1993.

Hegel, G. W. F. *Aesthetics: Lectures on Fine Art*, vol. 1. Trans. T. M. Knox. Oxford: Oxford University Press, 1975.

———. *Phenomenology of Spirit*. Trans. A. V. Miller. Oxford: Oxford University Press, 1977.

Helfer, Rebeca. *Spenser's Ruins and the Art of Recollection*. Toronto: University of Toronto Press, 2012.

Herbermann, Charles G., Edward A. Pace, Condé B. Pallen, Thomas J. Shahan, and John J. Wynne, eds. *The Catholic Encyclopedia*. New York: Robert Appleton, 1909.

Herman, Peter C. *Squitter-wits and Muse-haters: Sidney, Spenser, Milton and Renaissance Antipoetic Sentiment*. Detroit: Wayne State University Press, 1996.

Hillman, David, and Carla Mazzio. *The Body in Parts: Fantasies of Corporeality in Early Modern Europe*. New York: Routledge, 1997.

Hillman, Richard. "Gower's Lucrece: A New Old Source for *The Rape of Lucrece*." *Chaucer Review* 24, no. 3 (Winter 1990): 263–70.

Hofmann, Heinz. "The *Expositi* of Lorenzo Gambara di Brescia: A Sixteenth-Century Adaptation in Latin Hexameters of Longus' *Daphnis and Chloe.*" In *Fictional Traces: Receptions of the Ancient Novel*, vol. 1, ed. Marília P. Futre Pinheiro and Stephen J. Harrison, 107–26. Groningen: Barkhuis Publishing and Groningen University Library, 2011.

Hollander, John. *The Gazer's Spirit: Poems Speaking to Silent Works of Art*. Chicago: University of Chicago Press, 1995.

Homer. *The Iliad*. Ed. Walter Leaf. 2 vols. Amsterdam: Adolf M. Hakkert, 1960.

———. *The Iliad of Homer*. Trans. Richmond Lattimore. Chicago: University of Chicago Press, 1951.

———. *The Odyssey of Homer*, books 1–12. Ed. Thomas W. Allen. Oxford: Oxford University Press, 1917.

Horace. *Satires. Epistles. Ars poetica*. Trans. H. Rushton Fairclough. Cambridge, MA: Loeb Classical Library, 1929.

Horkheimer, Max, and Theodor W. Adorno. *Dialectic of Enlightenment: Philosophical Fragments*. Ed. Gunzelin Schmid Noerr. Trans. Edmund Jephcott. Stanford: Stanford University Press, 2002.

Horowitz, Gregg M. "Art History and Autonomy." In *The Semblance of Subjectivity: Essays in Adorno's Aesthetic Theory*, ed. Tom Huhn and Lambert Zuidervaart, 259–86. Cambridge, MA: MIT Press, 1997.

Howard, Donald R. *The Idea of the Canterbury Tales*. Berkeley: University of California Press, 1976.

Huhn, Tom. "Introduction: Thoughts beside Themselves." In *The Cambridge Companion to Adorno*, ed. Tom Huhn, 1–18. Cambridge: Cambridge University Press, 2004.

Huizinga, Johan. *The Autumn of the Middle Ages*. Trans. Rodney J. Payton and Ulrich Mammitzsch. Chicago: University of Chicago Press, 1996.

Hullot-Kentor, Robert. *Things Beyond Resemblance: Collected Essays on Theodor W. Adorno*. New York: Columbia University Press, 2006.

Hulse, Clark. *Metamorphic Verse: The Elizabethan Minor Epic*. Princeton: Princeton University Press, 1981.

———. *The Rule of Art: Literature and Painting in the Renaissance*. Chicago: University of Chicago Press, 1990.

Hutson, Lorna. *Circumstantial Shakespeare*. Oxford: Oxford University Press, 2015.

———. *The Invention of Suspicion: Law and Mimesis in Shakespeare and Renaissance Drama*. Oxford: Oxford University Press, 2007.

Jacks, Philip. *The Antiquarian and the Myth of Antiquity: The Origins of Rome in Renaissance Thought*. Cambridge: Cambridge University Press, 1993.

James, Heather. "The Poet's Toys: Christopher Marlowe and the Liberties of Erotic Elegy." *Modern Language Quarterly* 67, no. 1 (March 2006): 103–27.

———. *Shakespeare's Troy: Drama, Politics, and the Translation of Empire*. Cambridge: Cambridge University Press, 1997.

James, Sharon L. "Establishing Rome with the Sword: *Condere* in the *Aeneid*." *American Journal of Philology* 116, no. 4 (Winter 1995): 623–37.

Jardine, Lisa. *Worldly Goods: A New History of the Renaissance*. New York and London: W. W. Norton, 1996.

Jarvis, Simon. "Adorno, Marx, Materialism." In *The Cambridge Companion to Adorno*, ed. Tom Huhn, 79–100. Cambridge: Cambridge University Press, 2004.

Jay, Martin. *Marxism and Totality: The Adventures of a Concept from Lukács to Habermas*. Berkeley: University of California Press, 1984.

———. *Songs of Experience: Modern American and European Variations on a Universal Theme*. Berkeley and Los Angeles: University of California Press, 2005.

Jeanneret, Michel. *A Feast of Words: Banquets and Table Talk in the Renaissance*. Trans. Jeremy Whiteley and Emma Hughes. Cambridge: Polity Press, 1991.

Jed, Stephanie H. *Chaste Thinking: The Rape of Lucretia and the Birth of Humanism*. Bloomington and Indianapolis: Indiana University Press, 1989.

Joyce, Hetty. "Grasping at Shadows: Ancient Paintings in Renaissance and Baroque Rome." *Art Bulletin* 74, no. 2 (June 1992): 219–46.

Kahn, Coppélia. *Roman Shakespeare: Warriors, Wounds and Women*. London and New York: Routledge, 1997.

Kahn, Victoria. *The Future of Illusion: Political Theology and Early Modern Texts*. Chicago: University of Chicago Press, 2014.

Kahn, Victoria, and Lorna Hutson, eds. *Rhetoric and Law in Early Modern Europe*. New Haven: Yale University Press, 2001.

Kant, Immanuel. *Critique of Judgment*. Trans. Werner S. Pluhar. Indianapolis: Hackett, 1987.

Kaske, Carol V. *Spenser and Biblical Poetics*. Ithaca: Cornell University Press, 1999.

Kaster, Robert A. *Guardians of Language: The Grammarian and Society in Late Antiquity*. Berkeley: University of California Press, 1988.

Keach, William. *Elizabethan Erotic Narratives: Irony and Pathos in the Ovidian Poetry of Shakespeare, Marlowe, and Their Contemporaries*. New Brunswick: Rutgers University Press, 1977.

Keilen, Sean. "Exemplary Metals: Classical Numismatics and the Commerce of Humanism." *Word & Image* 18, no. 3 (July–Sept. 2002): 282–94.

Kelley, Donald R. *Faces of History: Historical Inquiry from Herodotus to Herder*. New Haven: Yale University Press, 1998.

Kelly, Gavin. "Ammianus Marcellinus: Tacitus' Heir and Gibbon's Guide." In *The Cambridge Companion to the Roman Historians*, ed. Andrew Feldherr, 348–61. Cambridge: Cambridge University Press, 2009.

Kennedy, George A., trans. *Progymnasmata: Greek Textbooks of Prose Composition and Rhetoric*. Atlanta: Society of Biblical Literature, 2003.

King, John N. *Spenser's Poetry and the Reformation Tradition*. Princeton: Princeton University Press, 1990.

Kirk, G. S. *The Iliad: A Commentary*, vol. 1, *Books 1–4*. Cambridge: Cambridge University Press, 1985.

Kirkham, Victoria, and Armando Maggi, eds. *Petrarch: A Critical Guide to the Complete Works*. Chicago: University of Chicago Press, 2009.

Knapp, James A. *Image Ethics in Shakespeare and Spenser*. New York: Palgrave Macmillan, 2011.

Krautheimer, Richard, and Trude Krautheimer-Hess. *Lorenzo Ghiberti*. Princeton: Princeton University Press, 1956.

Krieger, Murray. *Ekphrasis: The Illusion of the Natural Sign*. Baltimore: Johns Hopkins University Press, 1992.

Kris, Ernst, and Otto Kurz. *Legend, Myth, and Magic in the Image of the Artist: A Historical Experiment*. New Haven: Yale University Press, 1979.

Land, Norman E. *The Viewer as Poet: The Renaissance Response to Art*. University Park: Pennsylvania State University Press, 1994.

Lee, Rensselaer W. *Ut Pictura Poesis: The Humanistic Theory of Painting*. New York: W. W. Norton, 1967.

Lenker, Lagretta Tallent. *Fathers and Daughters in Shakespeare and Shaw*. Westport, CT: Greenwood Press, 2001.

Lessing, Gotthold Ephraim. *Laocoön: An Essay on the Limits of Painting and Poetry*. Trans. Edward Allen McCormick. Baltimore: Johns Hopkins University Press, 1984.

Levao, Ronald. "Francis Bacon and the Mobility of Science." *Representations* 40, Special Issue: Seeing Science (Autumn 1992): 1–32.

———. *Renaissance Minds and Their Fictions: Cusanus, Sidney, Shakespeare*. Berkeley: University of California Press, 1985.

Levin, Harry. *The Myth of the Golden Age in the Renaissance*. Bloomington: Indiana University Press, 1969.

Levine, Joseph M. *The Autonomy of History: Truth and Method from Erasmus to Gibbon*. Chicago: University of Chicago Press, 1999.

———. *Humanism and History: Origins of Modern English Historiography*. Ithaca: Cornell University Press, 1987.

Levy, F. J. *Tudor Historical Thought*. San Marino, CA: Huntington Library, 1967.

Lewis, C. S. *The Allegory of Love: A Study in Medieval Tradition*. Oxford: Oxford University Press, 1936.

———. *English Literature in the Sixteenth Century, Excluding Drama*. Oxford: Clarendon Press, 1954.

Livy. *History of Rome*, books 1–2. Trans. B. O. Foster. Cambridge, MA: Loeb Classical Library, 1919.

Longus. *Les amovrs pastorals de Daphnis et de Chloé, escriptes premierement en grec par Longus, & pius traduictes en François*. Paris pour Vincent Sertenas, demeurant en le rue neuue nostre Dame, à l'enseigne sainct lehan l'Euangeliste: et en sa boutique au Palais, en la gallerie par ou on va à la chancellerie, 1559.

———. *Daphnis and Chloe. Excellently describing the weight of affection, the simplicitie of loue, the purport of honest meaning, the resolution of men, and disposition of Fate, finished in a Pastorall, and interlaced with the praises of a most peerlesse Princesse . . . and therefore termed by the name of The Shepheards Holidaie. By Angell Daye*. London: Robert Waldegrave, 1587.

Looney, Dennis. *Compromising the Classics: Romance Epic Narrative in the Italian Renaissance*. Detroit: Wayne State University Press, 1996.

L'Orange, H. P. *Art Forms and Civic Life in the Late Roman Empire*. Princeton: Princeton University Press, 1965.

Löwith, Karl. *Meaning in History*. Chicago: University of Chicago Press, 1949.

Lucan. *The Civil War*. Trans. J. D. Duff. Cambridge, MA: Loeb Classical Library, 1928.

Lynch, William T. "A Society of Baconians?: The Collective Development of Bacon's Method in the Royal Society of London." In *Francis Bacon and the Refiguring of Early Modern Thought: Essays to Commemorate "The Advancement of Learning" (1605–2005)*, ed. Julie Robin Solomon and Catherine Gimelli Martin, 173–202. Burlington, VT: Ashgate, 2005.

MacCormack, Sabine G. *Art and Ceremony in Late Antiquity*. Berkeley: University of California Press, 1981.

Mack, Peter. *Elizabethan Rhetoric: Theory and Practice*. Cambridge: Cambridge University Press, 2002.

MacMullen, Ramsay. "Some Pictures in Ammianus Marcellinus." *Art Bulletin* 46, no. 4 (Dec. 1964): 435–56.

Macrobius. *Saturnalia*, vol. 2. Ed. Robert A. Kaster. Cambridge, MA: Loeb Classical Library, 2011.

Marchesi, Simone. "Petrarch's Philological Epic (*Africa*)." In *Petrarch: A Critical Guide to the Complete Works*, ed. Victoria Kirkham and Armando Maggi, 113–30. Chicago: University of Chicago Press, 2009.

Marlowe, Christopher. *The Collected Poems of Christopher Marlowe*. Ed. Patrick Cheney and Brian J. Striar. Oxford: Oxford University Press, 2006.

———. *The Complete Plays*. Ed. Frank Romany and Robert Lindsey. London: Penguin, 2003.

———. *The Complete Poems and Translations*. Ed. Stephen Orgel. New York: Penguin, 2007.

———. *Hero and Leander*. Ed. Louis L. Martz. New York: Johnson Reprint, 1972.

———. *Marlowe's Poems*. Ed. L. C. Martin. New York: Dial Press, 1931.

———. *The Poems of Christopher Marlowe*. Ed. Millar MacLure. London: Methuen, 1968.

Martindale, Andrew. *"The Triumphs of Caesar" by Andrea Mantegna in the Collection of Her Majesty the Queen at Hampton Court*. London: Harvey Miller, 1979.

Marx, Karl, and Friedrich Engels. *The Communist Manifesto*. Ed. David McLellan. Oxford: Oxford University Press, 1992.

Maus, Katharine Eisaman. *Inwardness and Theatre in the English Renaissance*. Chicago: University of Chicago Press, 1995.

Mazzocco, Angelo. "Petrarca, Poggio, and Biondo: Humanism's Foremost Interpreters of Roman Ruins." In *Francis Petrarch, Six Centuries Later: A Symposium*, ed. Aldo Scaglione, 353–63. Chapel Hill: Department of Romance Languages, University of North Carolina, 1975.

Mazzotta, Giuseppe. *The Worlds of Petrarch*. Durham: Duke University Press, 1993.

Meek, Richard. *Narrating the Visual in Shakespeare*. Burlington, VT: Ashgate, 2009.

Miller, Anthony. *Roman Triumphs and Early Modern English Culture*. Houndmills, Basingstoke, Hampshire, and New York: Palgrave, 2001.

Miller, David Lee. *The Poem's Two Bodies: The Poetics of the 1590 "Faerie Queene."* Princeton: Princeton University Press, 1988.

Miller, Peter N. "Description Terminable and Interminable: Looking at the Past, Nature, and Peoples in Peiresc's Archive." In *Historia: Empiricism and Erudition in Early Modern Europe*, ed. Gianna Pomata and Nancy G. Siraisi, 355–97. Cambridge, MA: MIT Press, 2005.

———, ed. *Momigliano and Antiquarianism: Foundations of the Modern Cultural Sciences*. Toronto: University of Toronto Press, 2007.

———. *Peiresc's Europe: Learning and Virtue in the Seventeenth Century*. New Haven: Yale University Press, 2000.

Milton, John. *Paradise Lost*. Ed. William Kerrigan, John Rumrich, and Stephen M. Fallon. New York: Random House, 2007.

Mitchell, W. J. T. *Picture Theory: Essays on Verbal and Visual Representation*. Chicago: University of Chicago Press, 1994.

Momigliano, Arnaldo. "Ancient History and the Antiquarian." *Journal of the Warburg and Courtauld Institutes* 13, nos. 3/4, (1950): 285–315.

———. *The Classical Foundations of Modern Historiography*. Berkeley: University of California Press, 1990.

———. "The Lonely Historian Ammianus Marcellinus." In Momigliano, *Essays in Ancient and Modern Historiography*, 127–40. Chicago: University of Chicago Press, 2012.

Montaigne, Michel de. *Essais, Livres I–III*. Paris: Garnier-Flammarion, 1969.

Moretti, Franco. *Distant Reading*. London: Verso, 2013.

Moshenska, Joe. "Why Can't Spenserians Stop Talking about Hegel? A Response to Gordon Teskey." *Spenser Review* 44.1.2 (Spring–Summer 2014).

Most, Glenn W. "On Fragments." In *The Fragment: An Incomplete History*, ed. William Tronzo, 9–20. Los Angeles: Getty Research Institute, 2009.

Muir, Tom. "Specters of Spenser: Translating the *Antiquitez*." *Spenser Studies* 25 (2010): 327–61.

Müller, Wolfgang P. "Lucretia and the Medieval Canonists." *Bulletin of Medieval Canon Law* 19 (1989): 13–32.

Murrin, Michael. *The Allegorical Epic: Essays in Its Rise and Decline*. Chicago: University of Chicago Press, 1980.

Nagel, Thomas. *The View from Nowhere*. Oxford: Oxford University Press, 1986.

Nelson, William. *Fact or Fiction: The Dilemma of the Renaissance Storyteller*. Cambridge, MA: Harvard University Press, 1973.

Newby, Zahra. "Absorption and Erudition in Philostratus' *Imagines*." In *Philostratus*, ed. Ewen Bowie and Jaś Elsner, 322–42. Cambridge: Cambridge University Press, 2009.

Newman, Jane O. "'And Let Mild Women to Him Lose Their Mildness': Philomela, Female Violence, and Shakespeare's *The Rape of Lucrece*." *Shakespeare Quarterly* 45, no. 3 (Autumn 1994): 304–26.

Newman, John Kevin. *The Classical Epic Tradition*. Madison: University of Wisconsin Press, 1986.

Newstok, Scott L. *Quoting Death in Early Modern England: The Poetics of Epitaphs beyond the Tomb*. Houndmills, Basingstoke, Hampshire, and New York: Palgrave Macmillan, 2009.

Nietzsche, Friedrich. *On the Advantage and Disadvantage of History for Life*. Trans. Peter Preuss. Indianapolis: Hackett, 1980.

Nochlin, Linda. *The Body in Pieces: The Fragment as a Metaphor of Modernity*. New York: Thames & Hudson, 1994.

Nohrnberg, James. *The Analogy of "The Faerie Queene."* Princeton: Princeton University Press, 1976.

Norton, Glyn P., ed. *The Cambridge History of Literary Criticism*, vol. 3, *The Renaissance*. Cambridge: Cambridge University Press, 1999.

O'Connell, Caryn. "Bacon's Hints: The *Sylva Sylvarum*'s Intimate Science." *Studies in Philology* 113, no. 3 (Summer 2016): 634–67.

Ogilvie, Brian W. *The Science of Describing: Natural History in Renaissance Europe*. Chicago: University of Chicago Press, 2006.

Oliver, Revilo P. "Salutati's Criticism of Petrarch." *Italica* 16, no. 2 (June 1939): 49–57.

Östenberg, Ida. *Staging the World: Spoils, Captives, and Representations in the Roman Triumphal Procession*. Oxford: Oxford University Press, 2009.

Otto, Bishop of Freising. *The Two Cities: A Chronicle of Universal History to the Year 1146 A.D.* Trans. Charles Christopher Mierow. New York: Columbia University Press, 2002.

Ovid. *Metamorphoses*, books 1–5. Trans. Frank Justus Miller. Rev. G. P. Goold. Cambridge, MA: Loeb Classical Library, 1977.

Pattison, Mark. *Isaac Casaubon, 1559–1614*. London: Longmans, Green, 1875.

Peacham, Henry. *The Art of Drawing*. London, 1606.

———. *Prince Henry Revived*. London, 1615.

Perseus Digital Library Project. Ed. Gregory R. Crane. http://www.perseus.tufts.edu.

Petrarch. *Petrarch's "Africa."* Trans. Thomas G. Bergin and Alice S. Wilson. New Haven: Yale University Press, 1977.

———. *L'Afrique: 1338–1374*. Trans. Rebecca Lenoir. Grenoble: Éditions Jérôme Millon, 2002.

———. *Invectives*. Trans. David Marsh. Cambridge, MA: I Tatti Renaissance Library, Harvard University Press, 2003.

———. *Letters on Familiar Matters, Rerum familiarum libri*, vol. 3, *Books XVII–XXIV.* Trans. Aldo S. Bernardo. New York: Italica Press, 2005.

———. *Lettres familières, IV–VII. Refum familiarum, IV–VII*. Ed. and trans. Ugo Dotti, Christophe Carraud, Frank La Brasca, and André Longpré. Paris: Les Belles Lettres, 2002.

———. *Letters of Old Age, Rerum senilium libri*. Trans. Aldo S. Bernardo, Saul Levin, and Reta A. Bernardo. 2 vols. Baltimore: Johns Hopkins University Press, 1992.

———. *Petrarch's Lyric Poems: The "Rime sparse" and Other Lyrics*. Trans. Robert M. Durling. Cambridge, MA: Harvard University Press, 1976.

———. *Remedies for Fortune Fair and Foul*. Trans. Conrad H. Rawski. Bloomington: Indiana University Press, 1991.

Phillips, Margaret Mann. *The "Adages" of Erasmus: A Study with Translations*. Cambridge: Cambridge University Press, 1964.

Philostratus the Elder. *Imagines* (with Philostratus the Younger, *Imagines* and Callistratus, *Descriptions*). Trans. Arthur Fairbanks. Cambridge, MA: Loeb Classical Library, 1931.

Picciotto, Joanna. "Reforming the Garden: The Experimentalist Eden and *Paradise Lost*." *ELH* 72, no. 1 (Spring 2005): 23–78.

Pico della Mirandola, Giovanni. "Oration on the Dignity of Man." Trans. Elizabeth Livermore Forbes. In *The Renaissance Philosophy of Man*, ed. Ernst Cassirer et al., 223–54. Chicago: University of Chicago Press, 1948.

Plate, S. Brent. *Walter Benjamin, Religion, and Aesthetics: Rethinking Religion through the Arts*. New York: Routledge, 2005.

Pliny the Elder. *Natural History*. Trans. H. Rackham. Cambridge, MA: Loeb Classical Library, 1938–63.

Pocock, J. G. A. *The Machiavellian Moment: Florentine Political Thought and the Atlantic Republican Tradition*. Princeton: Princeton University Press, 1975.

Poliziano, Angelo. *The "Stanze" of Angelo Poliziano*. Trans. David Quint. University Park: Pennsylvania State University Press, 1993.

Pollitt, J. J. *The Art of Rome, c. 753 B.C.–337 A.D.: Sources and Documents*. Englewood Cliffs, NJ: Prentice-Hall, 1966.

Polybius. *Histories*, vol. 1. Trans. Evelyn S. Shuckburgh. London and New York: Macmillan, 1889.

Pomata, Gianna. "Observation Rising: Birth of an Epistemic Genre, 1500–1650." In *Histories of Scientific Observation*, ed. Lorraine Daston and Elizabeth Lunbeck, 45–80. Chicago: University of Chicago Press, 2011.

Pomata, Gianna, and Nancy G. Siraisi, eds. *Historia: Empiricism and Erudition in Early Modern Europe*. Cambridge, MA: MIT Press, 2005.

Poovey, Mary. *A History of the Modern Fact: Problems of Knowledge in the Sciences of Wealth and Society*. Chicago: University of Chicago Press, 1998.

Prescott, Anne Lake. "Du Bellay and Shakespeare's Sonnets." In *The Oxford Handbook of Shakespeare's Poetry*, ed. Jonathan F. S. Post, 134–50. Oxford: Oxford University Press, 2013.

———. "The Stuart Masque and Pantagruel's Dreams." *ELH* 51, no. 3 (Autumn 1984): 407–30.

Puttenham, George. *The Art of English Poesy: A Critical Edition*. Ed. Frank Whigham and Wayne A. Rebhorn. Ithaca: Cornell University Press, 2007.

Quint, David. *Epic and Empire: Politics and Generic Form from Virgil to Milton*. Princeton: Princeton University Press, 1993.

———. "Humanism and Modernity: A Reconsideration of Bruni's *Dialogues*." *Renaissance Quarterly* 38, no. 3 (Autumn 1985): 423–45.

Quintilian. *Institutes of Oratory; or, Education of an Orator*. Trans. Rev. John Selby Watson. 2 vols. London: Bell & Daldy, 1871–73.

Rabelais, François. *Gargantua*. Paris: Éditions du Seuil, 1973.

———. *Gargantua et Pantagruel. Les oevvres de M. François Rabelais, docteur en medecine: contenans la vie, faicts, & dicts heroïques de Gargantua & de son filz Pantagruel: auec la prognostication Pantagrueline*. France, 1556.

———. *La plaisante, et ioyeuse histoyre du grand geant Gargantua/prochainement reueue & beaucoup augmentée par l'au[t]heur mesme*. Valence: Chéz Claude La Ville, 1547 [s.l., s.n., c. 1600].

Reeves, Eileen. *Painting the Heavens: Art and Science in the Age of Galileo*. Princeton: Princeton University Press, 1997.

Riggs, David. *The World of Christopher Marlowe*. New York: Henry Holt, 2004.

Roche, Thomas P., Jr. *The Kindly Flame: A Study of the Third and Fourth Books of Spenser's "Faerie Queene."* Princeton: Princeton University Press, 1964.

Rose, Gillian. *The Melancholy Science: An Introduction to the Thought of Theodor W. Adorno*. London: Macmillan, 1978.

Roskill, Mark W. *Dolce's "Aretino" and Venetian Art Theory of the Cinquecento*. Toronto: University of Toronto Press in association with the Renaissance Society of America, 2000.

Rossi, Andreola. "Remapping the Past: Caesar's Tale of Troy (Lucan *BC* 9.964–99)." *Phoenix* 55, nos. 3/4 (Autumn/Winter 2001): 313–26.

Rossky, William. "Imagination in the English Renaissance: Psychology and Poetic." *Studies in the Renaissance* 5 (1958): 49–73.

Scodel, Joshua. *The English Poetic Epitaph: Commemoration and Conflict from Jonson to Wordsworth*. Ithaca: Cornell University Press, 1991.

———. *Excess and Mean in Early Modern English Literature*. Princeton: Princeton University Press, 2002.

Sedley, David L. *Sublimity and Skepticism in Montaigne and Milton*. Ann Arbor: University of Michigan Press, 2005.

Semler, L. E. "Breaking the Ice to Invention: Henry Peacham's *The Art of Drawing* (1606)." *Sixteenth Century Journal* 35, no. 3 (Fall 2004): 735–50.

Shakespeare, William. *Antony and Cleopatra*. Ed. John Wilders. Arden Shakespeare, 3rd ser. London: Thomson Learning, 1995.

———. *The Complete Sonnets and Poems*. Ed. Colin Burrow. Oxford: Oxford University Press, 2002.

———. *Hamlet*. Ed. Ann Thompson and Neil Taylor. Arden Shakespeare, 3rd ser. London: Thomson Learning, 2006.

———. *Titus Andronicus*. Ed. Jonathan Bate. Arden Shakespeare, 3rd ser. London: Thomson Learning, 2004.

———. *Twelfth Night*. Ed. J. M. Lothian and T. W. Craik. Arden Shakespeare, 2nd ser. London: Methuen, 1975.

Shapin, Steven. *Never Pure: Historical Studies of Science as if It Was Produced by People with Bodies, Situated in Time, Space, Culture, and Society, and Struggling for Credibility and Authority*. Baltimore: Johns Hopkins University Press, 2010.

Shapiro, Barbara J. *A Culture of Fact: England, 1550–1720*. Ithaca: Cornell University Press, 2000.

Shapiro, Lisa. "Instrumental or Immersed Experience: Pleasure, Pain and Object Perception in Locke." In *The Body as Object and Instrument of Knowledge: Embodied Empiricism in Early Modern Science*, ed. Charles T. Wolfe and Ofer Gal, 265–85. Dordrecht, Netherlands, and New York: Springer, 2010.

Sharpe, Kevin. *Sir Robert Cotton, 1586–1631: History and Politics in Early Modern England*. Oxford: Oxford University Press, 1979.

Showalter, Elaine. *Sexual Anarchy: Gender and Culture at the Fin de Siècle*. New York: Viking, 1990.

Sidney, Philip. *An Apology for Poetry (or The Defence of Poesy)*. Ed. Geoffrey Shepherd. Revised and expanded for 3rd ed. by R. W. Maslen. Manchester: Manchester University Press, 2002.

———. *The Prose Works of Sir Philip Sidney*, vol. 1. Ed. Albert Feuillerat. Cambridge: Cambridge University Press, 1912.

Silberman, Lauren. *Transforming Desire: Erotic Knowledge in Books III and IV of "The Faerie Queene."* Berkeley: University of California Press, 1995.

Simeoni, Gabriele. *Les illustres obseruations antiques*. Lyon: Ian De Tournes, 1558.

Simpson, James. "Subjects of Triumph and Literary History: Dido and Petrarch in Petrarch's *Africa* and *Trionfi*." *Journal of Medieval and Early Modern Studies* 35, no. 3 (Fall 2005): 489–508.

Siraisi, Nancy G. "*Historiae*, Natural History, Roman Antiquity, and Some Roman Physicians." In *Historia: Empiricism and Erudition in Early Modern Europe*, ed. Gianna Pomata and Nancy G. Siraisi, 325–54. Cambridge, MA: MIT Press, 2005.

Slatkin, Laura M. "Homer's *Odyssey*." In *A Companion to Ancient Epic*, ed. John Miles Foley, 315–29. Malden, MA, and Oxford: Blackwell, 2009.

Smalley, Beryl. *The Study of the Bible in the Middle Ages*. Notre Dame: University of Notre Dame Press, 1964.

Solomon, Julie Robin. *Objectivity in the Making: Francis Bacon and the Politics of Inquiry*. Baltimore and London: Johns Hopkins University Press, 1998.

Spenser, Edmund. *The Faerie Queene*. Ed. A. C. Hamilton, Hiroshi Yamashita, Toshiyuki Suzuki, and Shohachi Fukuda. Harlow, UK: Longman, Pearson Education, 2007.

———. *A View of the State of Ireland: From the First Printed Edition (1633)*. Ed. Andrew Hadfield and Willy Maley. Oxford: Blackwell, 1997.

———. *The Yale Edition of the Shorter Poems of Edmund Spenser*. Ed. William A. Oram, Einar Bjorvand, Ronald Bond, Thomas H. Cain, Alexander Dunlop, and Richard Schell. New Haven: Yale University Press, 1989.

Springer, Lawrence A. "The Cult and Temple of Jupiter Feretrius." *Classical Journal* 50, no. 1 (Oct. 1954): 27–32.

Spitzer, Leo. "Geistesgeschichte vs. History of Ideas as Applied to Hitlerism." *Journal of the History of Ideas* 5, no. 2 (April 1944): 191–203.

———. *Linguistics and Literary History: Essays in Stylistics*. Princeton: Princeton University Press, 1948.

Stalnaker, Joanna. *The Unfinished Enlightenment: Description in the Age of the Encyclopedia*. Ithaca: Cornell University Press, 2010.

Steinberg, Leo. *The Sexuality of Christ in Renaissance Art and in Modern Oblivion*. Chicago: University of Chicago Press, 1996.

Stewart, Alan. "Lives and Letters in *Antony and Cleopatra*." *Shakespeare Studies* 35 (2007): 77–104.

Stubbes, Philip. *The Anatomie of Abuses*. London: Richard Jones, 1583. Early English Books Online, http://eebo.chadwyck.com.

Summers, Claude J. "*Hero and Leander*: The Arbitrariness of Desire." In *Constructing Christopher Marlowe*, ed. J. A. Downie and J. T. Parnell, 133–47. Cambridge: Cambridge University Press, 2000.

Summers, David. *The Judgment of Sense: Renaissance Naturalism and the Rise of Aesthetics*. Cambridge: Cambridge University Press, 1987.

———. *Michelangelo and the Language of Art*. Princeton: Princeton University Press, 1981.

Summit, Jennifer. "Topography as Historiography: Petrarch, Chaucer, and the Making of Medieval Rome." *Journal of Medieval and Early Modern Studies* 30, no. 2 (Spring 2000): 211–46.

Swain, Simon. *Hellenism and Empire: Language, Classicism, and Power in the Greek World, AD 50–250*. Oxford: Clarendon Press, 1996.

Teskey, Gordon. "Thinking Moments in *The Faerie Queene*." *Spenser Studies* 22 (2007): 103–24.

Thomas, Keith. *Religion and the Decline of Magic: Studies in Popular Beliefs in Sixteenth- and Seventeenth-Century England*. New York: Charles Scribner's Sons, 1971.

Thompson, David, and Alan F. Nagel, eds. and trans. *The Three Crowns of Florence: Humanist Assessments of Dante, Petrarca and Boccaccio*. New York: Harper & Row, 1972.

Tilg, Stefan. "On the Origins of the Modern Term 'Epyllion': Some Revisions to a Chapter in the History of Classical Scholarship." In *Brill's Companion to Greek and Latin Epyllion and Its Reception*, ed. Manuel Baumbach and Silvio Bär, 29–54. Leiden: Brill, 2012.

Tormo y Monzó, Elías. *Os desenhos das antigualhas que vio Francisco d'Ollanda, pintor portugués, 1539–1540*. Madrid: Ministerio de Asuntos Exteriores, 1940.

Tuell, Anne K. "The Original End of *Faerie Queene*, Book III." *Modern Language Notes* 36, no. 5 (May 1921): 309–11.

Tuve, Rosemond. *Elizabethan and Metaphysical Imagery: Renaissance Poetic and Twentieth-Century Critics*. Chicago: University of Chicago Press, 1947.

Twain, Mark. *The Innocents Abroad; or, The New Pilgrims' Progress; Being Some Account of the Steamship Quaker City's Pleasure Excursion to Europe and the Holy Land; With Descriptions of Countries, Nations, Incidents and Adventures, as They Appeared to the Author*. Hartford, CT: American Publishing, 1869.

Valerius Maximus. *Memorable Doings and Sayings*. Trans. D. R. Shackleton Bailey. Cambridge, MA: Loeb Classical Library, 2000.

Van Es, Bart. *Spenser's Forms of History*. Oxford: Oxford University Press, 2002.

Vasari, Giorgio. *Lives of the Artists*, vol. 1. Trans. George Bull. London: Penguin, 1965.

Vickers, Nancy J. "'The blazon of sweet beauty's best': Shakespeare's *Lucrece*." In *Shakespeare and the Question of Theory*, ed. Patricia Parker and Geoffrey Hartman, 95–115. New York: Methuen, 1985.

———. "Diana Described: Scattered Woman and Scattered Rhyme." *Critical Inquiry* 8, no. 2 (Winter 1981): 265–79.

———. "'This Heraldry in Lucrece' Face.'" *Poetics Today* 6, nos. 1/2 (1985): 171–84.

Vine, Angus. *In Defiance of Time: Antiquarian Writing in Early Modern England*. Oxford: Oxford University Press, 2010.

Virgil. *Aeneid 7–12. Appendix Vergiliana*. Trans. H. R. Fairclough. Rev. G. P. Goold. Cambridge, MA: Loeb Classical Library, 2000.

———. *Eclogues. Georgics. Aeneid 1–6*. Trans. H. R. Fairclough. Rev. G. P. Goold. Cambridge, MA: Loeb Classical Library, 1999–

Vives, Juan Luis. *De anima et vita*. Ed. Mario Sancipriano. Torino: Bottega d'Erasmo, 1959.

Warburg, Aby. *The Renewal of Pagan Antiquity: Contributions to the Cultural History of the European Renaissance*. Trans. David Britt. Los Angeles: Getty Research Institute for the History of Art and the Humanities, 1999.

Weaver, William P. *Untutored Lines: The Making of the English Epyllion*. Edinburgh: Edinburgh University Press, 2012.

Webb, Ruth. *Ekphrasis, Imagination and Persuasion in Ancient Rhetorical Theory and Practice*. Farnham, England, and Burlington, VT: Ashgate, 2009.

———. "Picturing the Past: Uses of Ekphrasis in the *Deipnosophistae* and Other Works of the Second Sophistic." In *Athenaeus and His World: Reading Greek Culture in the Roman Empire*, ed. David Braund and John Wilkins, 218–26. Exeter: University of Exeter Press, 2000.

Webster, Graham. *The Roman Imperial Army of the First and Second Centuries A.D.* Norman: University of Oklahoma Press, 1998.

Webster, John. *The Duchess of Malfi*. Ed. Leah S. Marcus. London: Arden Shakespeare, 2009.

Weil, Simone. "The *Iliad* or The Poem of Force." In *Simone Weil: An Anthology*, ed. Siân Miles. New York: Grove Press, 1986.

Weiss, Roberto. *The Renaissance Discovery of Classical Antiquity*. Oxford: Blackwell, 1969.

Wells-Cole, Anthony. *Art and Decoration in Elizabethan and Jacobean England: The Influence of Continental Prints, 1558–1625*. New Haven and London: Yale University Press, 1997.

White, John. *The Birth and Rebirth of Pictorial Space*. Cambridge, MA: Belknap Press of Harvard University Press, 1987.

Whitmarsh, Tim, ed. *The Cambridge Companion to the Greek and Roman Novel*. Cambridge: Cambridge University Press, 2008.

Wilkins, Ernest H. "Petrarch's Coronation Oration." *PMLA* 68, no. 5 (Dec. 1953): 1241–50.

Wofford, Susanne Lindgren. "Britomart's Petrarchan Lament: Allegory and Narrative in *The Faerie Queene* III, iv." *Comparative Literature* 39, no. 1 (Winter 1987): 28–57.

Wolff, Samuel Lee. *The Greek Romances in Elizabethan Prose Fiction*. New York: Columbia University Press, 1912.

Woodbridge, Linda. "Palisading the Elizabethan Body Politic." *Texas Studies in Literature and Language* 33, no. 3, History, Culture, and Self (Fall 1991): 327–54.

Worthen, W. B. "The Weight of Antony: Staging 'Character' in *Antony and Cleopatra*." *Studies in English Literature, 1500–1900* 26, no. 2 (Spring 1986): 295–308.

Wright, C. E. "The Elizabethan Society of Antiquaries and the Formation of the Cottonian Library." In *The English Library before 1700*, ed. Francis Wormald and C. E. Wright, 176–212. London: Athlone Press, 1958.

Wroth, Lawrence C. *The Voyages of Giovanni da Verrazzano, 1524–1528*. New Haven: Yale University Press for the Pierpont Morgan Library, 1970.

Zak, Gur. *Petrarch's Humanism and the Care of the Self*. Cambridge: Cambridge University Press, 2010.

Zeitlin, Froma I. "Figure: Ekphrasis." *Greece & Rome* 60, no. 1 (April 2013): 17–31.

———. "The Poetics of *Eros*: Nature, Art, and Imitation in Longus' *Daphnis and Chloe*." In *Before Sexuality: The Construction of Erotic Experience in the Ancient Greek World*, ed. David M. Halperin, John J. Winkler, and Froma I. Zeitlin, 417–64. Princeton: Princeton University Press, 1990.

Index

Page numbers in italics refer to figures.

www.ingramcontent.com/pod-product-compliance
Lightning Source LLC
LaVergne TN
LVHW052340100826
845147LV00021B/1126